The Visual Basic® Style Guide

ISBN 0-13-088361-1

90000

9 780130 883612

PRENTICE HALL PTR MICROSOFT® TECHNOLOGIES SERIES

NETWORKING

- Microsoft Technology: Networking, Concepts, Tools
  Woodard, Gattuccio, Brain

- NT Network Programming Toolkit
  Murphy

- Building COM Applications with Internet Explorer
  Loveman

- Understanding DCOM
  Rubin, Brain

- Web Database Development for Windows Platforms
  Gutierrez

PROGRAMMING

- The COM and COM+ Programming Primer
  Gordon

- Window's 2000 Web Applications Developer's Guide
  Yager

- The Visual Basic Object and Component Handbook
  Vogel

- Developing Solutions with Office 2000
  Componenets and VBA
  Aitken

- Windows Shell Programming
  Seely

- The Visual Basic Style Guide
  Patrick

- Introduction to Windows 98 Programming
  Murray, Pappas

- Developing Professional Applications for
  Windows 98 and NT Using MFC, Third Edition
  Brain, Lovette

- Win 32 System Services: The Heart of
  Windows 98 and Windows NT, Third Edition
  Brain

- Multithreaded Programming with Win32
  Pham, Garg

- Visual Basic 6: Design, Specification, and Objects
  Hollis

- ADO Programming in Visual Basic 6
  Holzner

- Visual Basic 6: Error Coding and Layering
  Gill

- Visual C++ Templates
  Murray, Pappas

- Introduction to MFC Programming with Visual C++
  Jones

- MFC Programming in C++ with the
  Standard Template Libraries
  Murray, Pappas

- COM-CORBA Interoperability
  Geraghty, Joyce, Moriarty, Noone

- Distributed COM Application Development Using
  Visual Basic 6.0
  Maloney

- Distributed COM Application Development Using
  Visual C++ 6.0
  Maloney

- Understanding and Programming COM+:
  A Practical Guide to Windows 2000 DNA
  Oberg

- ASP/MTS/ADSI Web Security
  Harrison

- Microsoft Site Server 3.0 Commerce Edition
  Libertone, Scoppa

- Building Microsoft SQL Server 7 Web Sites
  Byrne

ADMINISTRATION

- Windows 2000 Hardware and Disk Management
  Simmons

- Creating Active Directory Infrastuctures
  Simmons

- Windows 2000 Registry
  Sanna

- Configuring Windows 2000 Server
  Simmons

- Tuning and Sizing NT Server
  Aubley

- Windows NT Cluster Server Guidebook
  Libertone

- Windows NT 4.0 Server Security Guide
  Goncalves

- Windows NT Security
  McInerney

- Supporting Windows NT and 2000
  Workstation and Server
  Mohr

- Zero Administration Kit for Windows
  McInerney

- Designing Enterprise Solutions
  with Microsoft Technologies
  Kemp, Kemp, Goncalves

PRENTICE HALL PTR MICROSOFT® TECHNOLOGIES SERIES

Tim Patrick

The Visual Basic Style Guide

Prentice Hall PTR, Upper Saddle River, NJ 07458
www.phptr.com

Library of Congress Cataloging-in-Publication Data

Patrick, Tim,
    The visual basic style guide / Tim Patrick.
      p. cm. -- (Prentice Hall PTR Microsoft technologies series)
    ISBN 0-13-088361-1
    1. Microsoft Visual BASIC. 2. BASIC (Computer program language) I. Title. II.
    Series
    QA76.73.B3 P2545 2000
    005.26'8--dc21   00-039196

Editorial/Production Supervision: *Benchmark Productions, Inc.*
Project Coordinator: *Anne Trowbridge*
Acquisitions Editor: *Mike Meehan*
Marketing Manager: *Bryan Gambrel*
Manufacturing Buyer: *Maura Goldstaub*
Cover Design: *Anthony Gemmellaro*
Cover Design Direction: *Jerry Votta*
Series Design: *Gail Cocker-Bogusz*

Prentice Hall books are widely used by corporations and government agencies for training, marketing, and resale.

The publisher offers discounts on this book when ordered in bulk quantities. For more information, contact Corporate Sales Department, Phone: 800-382-3419; fax: 201-236-7141; email: corpsales@prenhall.com or write Corporate Sales Department, Prentice Hall PTR, One Lake Street, Upper Saddle River, NJ 07458.

Printed in the United States of America

10 9 8 7 6 5 4 3 2 1

ISBN 0-13-088361-1

Prentice-Hall International (UK) Limited, *London*
Prentice-Hall of Australia Pty. Limited, *Sydney*
Prentice-Hall Canada Inc., *Toronto*
Prentice-Hall Hispanoamericana, S.A., *Mexico*
Prentice-Hall of India Private Limited, *New Delhi*
Prentice-Hall of Japan, Inc., *Tokyo*
Pearson Education Asia Pte. Ltd.
Editora Prentice-Hall do Brasil, Ltda., *Rio de Janeiro*

To Spencer Patrick, my beloved son.

CONTENTS

I still remember the first computer program I wrote. I composed it while standing in front of a *TRS-80* at a Radio Shack store in Missoula, Montana. Then a 12-year-old, I had just seen my first "real" computer a few weeks earlier in my classroom. Our teacher taught us everything that he knew about the computer over one or two days, and I was fascinated. Cautiously I approached the sleek gray terminal with its glowing phosphor screen. With excitement welling up inside of me, I set my mind on the task at hand, reached out for the keyboard, and programmed my first software application.

```
10 FOR I = 1 TO 1000
20    PRINT I, I + 1
30 NEXT I
40 END
```

It may seem infantile, especially when you consider what you can do with the same amount of code in some more modern languages. But for a seventh grader with his first chance to write a real program, it was grand. It opened a whole new world for me. I can still recall the feeling I had as I stood there, watching the columns of numbers racing down the screen. That same feeling comes back to me every time I write a working program.

Over the years I have learned to write programs longer than four lines. I took the standard academic and business path through PASCAL, 8086 assembly language, LISP, C, and C++, but today I spend most of my programming career with a variant of the language that my fingers first typed: *Microsoft Visual Basic*. And why not? Visual Basic allows me to write complex applications for Microsoft Windows in a fraction of the time that it would take me to write the same programs in C or C++, with or without class libraries such as MFC and OWL. Visual Basic makes the creation of Windows applications literally child's play. However, along with the ease of Windows programming has come the ease of writing bad programs.

In the early days of computers, the skill of programming was limited to a few geeks who spent their lives cooped up in a stadium-sized computer room with a brain the size of a four-function calculator (the computer's brain, not the geeks'). These progenitors of modern software engineers spent hours choosing just the right punch cards to calculate π to 10 decimal places. The most powerful computers of the time were expensive, slow, and short on memory. It was in the programmer's (and his employer's) best interest to write well-crafted, concise, and error-free code the first time. Style was not an issue; if it worked, it was good enough.

Today the computing horizon is quite different. Once there were a few ENIAC-shaped mud huts; now Pentium-class high-rises dot the landscape. The latest machines are orders of magnitude faster than anything imaged by Charles Babbage, and they are priced within the budget of most technology-crazed consumers. The modern business climate requires that the average person understand how to operate a computer. With the advent of (relatively) easy-to-use programming languages such as BASIC, some employers are asking their business experts to translate that business knowledge into working computer applications.

Consider the case of Joe, an accountant for a small manufacturing company. Joe has worked for years literally "keeping the books." One day, Joe's supervisor, knowing that Joe is the resident expert on accounting practices, presents him with an IBM PC and a copy of *dBase II*. Daunted at first, Joe digs in to the database, and after months of feverish activity, shows off his new accounting package.

No one is more surprised than Joe to find that the program actually does accounting. Still, he knows that it is not quite right, and it is always a few dollars and cents off at the end of the month. Over the next few years Joe works hard at fixing and improving the program, as well as writing numerous reports demanded by various departments. Finally the day comes for Joe to retire, and Sue, his assistant, is given the keys to the *dBase* program. Along with those keys Sue receives a "good luck" from Joe, but scant information about how the program works.

You already know the rest of the story. The program is in a hideous state of disrepair, but since Sue is as much a novice as Joe was, she is at a loss as to how to fix the application. If this story was unique we would simply sigh and say, "Oh poor Sue." But this situation happens on a daily basis across the computer world. Instead of pity for Sue, we often have to console ourselves.

Obscure programming practices are not limited to untrained business users. Programming students are often tempted with languages that invite them to write strange source code. One of the first languages I used in school was a flavor of BASIC found on the PDP 11/70 hosted operating system RSTS/E. This version of BASIC did not require whitespace to be placed between most language constructs. Therefore, it was possible to write the same four-line program shown earlier using a single, compressed statement.

```
FORI=1TO1000\PRINTI,I+1\NEXTI\END
```

It even allowed this reversed syntax.

```
PRINTI,I+1FORI=1TO1000
```

Imagine entire applications written in this compressed format! Because the interpreter focused on the extraction of known keywords from any statement, it allowed the programmer to write very unsightly code that did not run any faster than the equivalent code with whitespace included. Consider the following program.

```
10A$(I)=" "FORI=1TO9\B$="-+-+-"\C$="|"\X=1\R$=""\T=0
20GOSUB500
25IFX=1THENPRINT"YOUR TURN:";ELSEPRINT"TRY AGAIN:";
30INPUTQ$\P=INT(Q$)\X=2\IFA$(P)<>" "THENGOTO20
40X=1\A$(P)="X"\T=T+1
50GOSUB1000\IFR$="X"THENPRINT"YOU WIN!"\GOTO10
60IFT=9THENPRINT"DRAW"\GOTO10
70M=INT(RND(9))\IFA$(M)<>" "THENGOTO70\A$(M)="O"
80GOSUB1000\IFR$="O"THENGOSUB500\PRINT"I WIN!"\GOTO10
90GOTO20
500PRINT"BOARD  LEGEND"\FORC1=1TO3
510PRINTA$(((C1-1)*3)+1);C$;A$(((C1-1)*3)+2);
515PRINTC$;A$(((C1-1)*3)+3);
520PRINT"   ";((C1-1)*3)+1;C$;
525PRINT((C1-1)*3)+2;C$;((C1-1)*3)+1
530IFC1<3THENPRINTB$
540NEXTC1\RETURN
1000RESTORE\R$=""\FORC1=1TO8\READT1\READT2\READT3
1010Q$=A$(T1)+A$(T2)+A$(T3)
1015IFQ$="XXX"THENR$="X"\IFQ$="OOO"THENR$="O"
1020NEXTC1\RETURN
1030DATA1,2,3,4,5,6,7,8,9,1,4,7,2,5,8,3,6,9,1,5,9,3,5,7
```

I am sure that you will soon figure out the purpose of this application. (See the answer at the end of this Preface just to be sure.) Can you picture an entire business application written in this style? Can you picture yourself being asked to fix such an application?

Visual Basic is a little more strict in the area of statement formatting, but it is still possible to write programs that are both internally (code) and externally (user interface) displeasing. When I was taking programming classes in school, I thought it was clever to write obfuscated code in this manner.[1] This feeling ended when, in my first programming job, I was asked to fix someone else's muddled application. From that point on I was committed to writing clear, concise, and readable code that was pleasing for both the programmer and for the user. This book is a guide to help you travel this same path. In this text you will find a clear differentiation between *unprofessional* programs—

---

[1] There is an annual contest where examples of obfuscated code written in C are submitted and judged for their obscurity. See the Web site at http://reality.sgi.com/csp/ioccc/ for examples of how not to write programs!

those that are aesthetically and logically annoying to both the user and other programmers that may review the code—and *professional* programs.

Who Is This Book For?

This book is for everyone who cares about Visual Basic applications, and the development process surrounding these applications. Microsoft Visual Basic is very popular, outselling Microsoft's own C/C++ compiler by a factor of five to one.[2] Many of these units are sold to weekend programmers with little or no training in programming practices. You can walk in to any major bookseller and see shelf after shelf of books with names like *Learn Visual Basic in Your Sleep* and *Visual Basic in 21 Minutes*. These books are great for learning the usage and syntax of Visual Basic, but they often fall short when it comes to training the eager developer how to program *well*. *The Visual Basic Style Guide* is written for the Visual Basic programmer who wishes to enhance his or her professional and technical programming methods and style. If you are such a programmer, read on!

Writing professional Visual Basic programs does take effort, lots of effort. Still, effort alone will not bring about the quality that you seek. This book contains lists of guidelines for writing good Visual Basic programs. Yet more than that, it promotes an attitude, an environment of the mind in which healthy Visual Basic programs are formed.

The Visual Basic language now reaches out into other areas of software development. With the advent of Visual Basic for Applications and Visual Basic, Scripting Edition, more and more programmers are relying on Visual Basic for their many software solutions. *The Visual Basic Style Guide* is designed for use with each of the flavors of Visual Basic.

Acknowledgments

As is to be expected with any paperweight-sized manual, many of my friends were involved in the development and production of this book.

I first thank you, my God, without whom the desire to put any words to paper would never have been felt in my heart. You filled me with an interest, a hope, and a desire to write, and then you brought it to pass. For that, and for all of the other miraculous things you have done in my life, I am eternally grateful.

---

[2] A *ComputerWorld* article from the February 17, 1997, issue (volume 31, number 7, page 43) states that 2.5 million copies of Visual Basic have been sold, compared to 500,000 copies of Visual C++. This estimate appeared just before the release of the very popular Visual Basic 5.0.

Bob McGrath, friend extraodinaire, humble in heart, user of proper English, kind to strangers. The suggestions you brought to each and every sentence of the manuscript made it what it is, at least in its good parts. Your concern to see a quality book prompted you to write such elegant phrases on the drafts as "get rid of these vacuous sentences" and "what??? explain or rewrite." For all this and more, I truly thank you.

Ben Johnson, cohort in Visual Basic escapades. Thank you for the encouragement you gave me through your excitement in writing applications of a consistent quality. To be honest, I was a little concerned about the future of Visual Basic programmers until you showed up.

Peter Ladley, a fellow author and friend. Thank you for stretching the limits of my English usage. I look forward to several more exciting Scrabble matches, although I still have not found a dictionary with those words in it.

Thomas Trzyna, professor, dean, and associate provost at Seattle Pacific University, thank you. Before I met you, the majority of my experiences in writing were negative. You opened a door of words through which few wished to walk, and you walked through it with me.

Claire Horne of the Moore Literary Agency, you went the extra mile for the publication of this guide, always buffeting difficult news with encouragement. Thank you for your kind words.

Kit Wray and Kent Brown, both from *Highlights for Children*, thank you for your willingness to take timeless characters and add to them the element of time. I still cannot believe that I was able to work so closely today with such vivid memories from my childhood.

Mike Meehan, Diane Spina, Lisa Iarkowski, and Anne Trowbridge, all from Prentice Hall PTR, thank you for your belief that a few suggestions on programming should actually bear your name.

Dmitri Nerubenko and Greg deZarn-O'Hare, from Benchmark Productions, thank you for applying standards and excellence to this book on standards and excellence.

Maki, my wife, the other part of me, how can I thank you sufficiently without breaking into tears? Your care, your encouragement, and your patience throughout this project have gone well beyond reasonable expectations. Thank you for understanding when I seemed to snuggle up to the keyboard instead of to you. Thank you for homemade hot chocolate after 11:00 at night. Thank you for saying "I do" almost 10 years ago. I love you.

Spencer, my son, my own son, my only son, I thank you too. Thank you for letting me work on this book after we played each night. Thank you for saying, "Daddy, don't work too much." Thank you for making houses out of sofa pillows together. Before you were born, I thought it would be nice to have children. Now that you are here, I know that it is you who I always wanted in my family. I love you.

P.S. The program listed earlier is a tic-tac-toe game.

Structure

Programming is one of those great careers that combine both the structure of logic and the creativity of art. This mixture extends to the development of an application's source code, its user interface, and supporting components such as on-line help and technical documentation. This first section of the book examines these components as a complete system, one in which the whole is incomplete without all of its parts.

Professional Programming as Style

Walk into any dentist's office and you will probably find copies of *Highlights for Children* on various tables and magazine racks. As a child I would nervously bide my time behind the covers of this journal. As you may recall, every issue of *Highlights* has a cartoon series named "Goofus and Gallant." The panels of the strip present contrasting views of the lives of two young boys, Goofus, an incorrigible troublemaker, and Gallant, every mother's favorite child.

Goofus and Gallant are still the same ages they were decades ago, but what if they did grow up? Imagine that they are both in their early thirties and they both happen to be programmers (see Figures 1–1 and 1–2).

Goofus and Gallant truly represent the opposite ends of the selfishness continuum; most people fall somewhere in between these two extremes. Still, these two characters portray two paths that can be followed in many areas of life: the path of reckless selfishness and the path of thoughtful professionalism.

Although you purchased a book on programming style, you are really holding a book on professionalism. Without maintaining a professional demeanor in your programming endeavors, you will not create quality systems. Of course anyone can make something look good, but thoughtfulness and a concern for quality are requirements to make something, such as an application, good on its own. This volume begins the discussion of style with its most important focus: professionalism in programming.

What is professional programming? Is it holding down a job at a software company? Is it having "software engineer" or "programmer/analyst" printed on your business card? While professional programmers often have these things, they alone do not indicate who is truly professional. Professionalism is something that grows and lives inside the heart of the programmer.

3

Figure 1-1

Goofus starts writing code without putting much thought into the user's needs or his company's concerns.

Figure 1-2

Gallant works with the user and his coworkers to design and implement the best software solution.

Good style flows from this wellspring of quality, affecting not only the programmer's applications, but his or her entire work ethic.

Programming in Visual Basic is fun because it is so simple to create a full-fledged Windows application. When the Visual Basic development environment first starts up, you are presented with a blank form that represents a fully functional Windows program (just press F5 to prove it). The programmer's job is to mold that core program into a useful and useable application. However, not all Visual Basic programs are created equal. Some applications exhibit the characteristics of a professional program. These characteristics include, but are not limited to, a consistent user interface, clearly defined usage, user documentation, and freedom from bugs. Other applications lack some or all of these features. There are many reasons why poor Visual Basic programs are written.

- **Lack of planning.** Active development of the application begins without careful consideration of the flow of the program, or the needs of the user.
- **Lack of skill or talent.** One or more of the programmers or managers involved in the Visual Basic project are not adequately prepared to meet the challenge of professional Visual Basic application development.
- **Lack of training.** Although those involved in the project are competent enough to complete the project, proper tools, training, and documentation are either unavailable or overlooked.
- **Lack of management.** A disproportionate share of the burden of project management is placed on the shoulders of the programmer(s) instead of on management.
- **Lack of time.** A predetermined implementation schedule fails to take into account the complexities of application development and deployment.
- **Lack of discipline.** A clear set of rules, guidelines, and constraints, whether formal or informal, are placed neither on the management of the Visual Basic project, nor on the activities of the programmers.
- **Lack of scope.** New components of the project are added on a continual basis without proper analysis of needs or time requirements.

Any one of these symptoms can lead to the eventual downfall of a Visual Basic application. When several (or all) of these deficiencies are combined, failure is almost certain. However, these problems can all be prevented, and the chances of success substantially improve by applying the effective methods described in this book.

Goals of Professional Programming

Very few developers sit down before the keyboard simply to string random Visual Basic statements together. Rather, there is a purpose, a goal in writing a block of code. The primary goals of professional software development have to do with meeting the needs of various individuals and groups.

Meeting the Needs of the User

All applications are developed for one or more users. Sometimes you write a quick program simply for yourself, to fulfill an immediate processing requirement. At other times you are involved in large-scale, year-long development projects that will eventually be deployed to thousands of users. In both cases, your primary goal is to meet the needs of the user of the application. If you fail to provide the software that the user needs, you fail to deliver quality software, no matter how good it looks.

Computer users have a job to do, and your application automates that job process. The ultimate design goal of an application is to have the user forget that he or she is using a computer program, and instead, simply perform the desired problem-solving task. Your program should be a natural extension of the workflow that is already part of the user's business.

Meeting the Needs of Your Employer

Unless you are working for a nonprofit agency, there is a pretty good chance your company exists in order to make a profit. This holds true for both the self-employed and the multi-billion-dollar corporation. Companies remain profitable by meeting the needs of their customers. You help fulfill both aspects of your company's mission by developing professional software applications.

Meeting your company's needs extends to your managers and coworkers as well. When you develop software in a professional manner, you help to advance the interests of all those around you.

Meeting the Programmer's Needs

Looking after your own personal and professional needs will have a beneficial impact on your software development projects. If you are unhappy with your company or colleagues, or dislike programming because you have to reinvent a methodology every time you start a new project, the quality of your work will likely suffer. However, if you receive satisfaction from your work and enjoy the process of programming high-quality Visual Basic applications, that will shine through brightly in your finished products.

Software development allows for a wonderful mix of challenge and predictability. The challenge comes from stretching your skills into new, untried areas. The predictability comes from the standards that enable you to write consistent, high-quality applications. Some of these standards exist in the syntax of Visual Basic itself. Other standards are created from your own experience, or learned from external sources such as this book. When you expand your programming range by tackling technical challenges, and you learn and apply a rigorous programming methodology, the result will be top-notch programs and applications.

A System for Professional Programming

Who would have thought that typing a few thousand lines of code could satisfy the needs of so many people? Yet that happens every time the professional Visual Basic developer delivers a quality product. So how does one ensure this success on a regular basis? How does a programmer work in a professional manner? Quality programming is accomplished by applying a methodology, a standardized way of attacking complex programming tasks. The method described in *The Visual Basic Style Guide* has three components, representing the three main divisions of the book.

Structure

When building a home, once you have the foundation in place, you can move on to the structure of the edifice. The same is true of application development. The structure of a software application includes elements such as the logic of the program, the user interface, and supporting documentation. Also, your own personal style plays a large part in how the structure will form over the lifetime of a development project.

The various aspects of application development structure are covered in the first part of this book, *Structure*. This section begins with this chapter, and continues on through Chapter 5. In these chapters you will encounter numerous guidelines used in the development of all professional software applications.

Chapter 1, *Professional Programming as Style*. The first chapter, which you are now reading, focuses on the goals and activities of professional software application development.

Chapter 2, *Using Declaration*. This chapter is dedicated to the importance of object nomenclature and consistency within the source code. The chapter stresses standards and stability throughout all aspects of an application's source code.

Chapter 3, *Commenting and Style*. Along with the chapter on documentation (Chapter 5), this chapter discusses the importance of documentation within the source code itself. The professional Visual Basic programmer must demand that adequate documentation appear both within the application source code and in other external forms. The second part of this chapter discusses style, the personality that the developer brings to the source code.

Chapter 4, *User Interface Consistency*. The user of any software will always notice problems and inconsistencies within the user interface of an application. This chapter stresses the importance of stable user interfaces, and provides examples of when and how to use various interface components.

Chapter 5, *Documentation*. Besides the software itself, the documentation is the most visible component of any application. Therefore, it needs to be every bit as professional as the source code. This chapter focuses on the need for complete, clear, and high-quality documentation, both for the user community and for the technical staff who develop and maintain the application.

Foundation

The foundation of professional software development appears in the heart of the programmer. The core attitudes that help shape the individual also help to shape the programs written by that individual. If you have a professional attitude, the quality of your attitude will show itself in your applications.

While there are many parts to this foundational attitude, the three elements that affect software development the most are *discipline*, *planning*, and *ethics*. These essential attitudes are discussed in detail in the second part of this book, *Foundation*, encompassing Chapters 6, 7, and 8. These three chapters appear in the middle of this volume to show that they are at the center, at the focus, of the professional way of software development. Much as the planets revolve around the Sun in our solar system, the other activities of professional programming revolve around these three core elements. Without these elements, quality programming is difficult, if not impossible, to attain.

Chapter 6, *Discipline*. Discipline delves into the mind of the Visual Basic programmer, where all quality development begins. After covering the many reasons why discipline is important to the developer, this chapter discusses various methods of instilling discipline.

Chapter 7, *Planning*. This chapter discusses the importance of planning in the daily work of the Visual Basic developer. Much time is spent focusing on the needs of the user, and the reasons for adequate planning.

Chapter 8, *Ethics*. Without ethics, discipline and planning are at the mercy of every whim of the developer, good or bad. This chapter discusses those facets of ethics that pertain to software development, including honesty, quality, humility, and others.

Standards

In the building of any modern structure, there are various standards that must be followed to make sure not only that the structure will last a long time, but that it will maintain its high level of quality and value. These standards are used as consistent guides during the construction process. Software development uses comparable standards. This is apparent to the programmer because the syntax of a programming language requires a certain amount of standardization. These intrinsic standards may be enough to write a working program, but they are insufficient to produce the quality or longevity needed to solve real-world business problems. A full set of application development standards brings consistency and quality to the programming process.

The third and final section of this book, *Standards*, codifies such a set of standards. Guidelines covering all aspects of the Visual Basic language and its components are examined and stated in Chapters 9 through 12. This section is meant to be handled like a well-worn reference book. Read it through once, then reference its parts frequently during application design and development.

Chapter 9, *Declaration Standards*. This chapter provides a complete reference (summarized in Chapter 2) of naming conventions to be used within a Visual Basic application.

Chapter 10, *Keyword Reference*. The largest of the reference chapters, this chapter provides usage and standards information on all of the keywords used in Visual Basic, Visual Basic for Applications, and Visual Basic, Scripting Edition. Each keyword includes recommendations and frequent examples of correct and incorrect usage.

Chapter 11, *Control and User Interface Standards*. This chapter provides guidelines and sample source code for the most popular user interface controls provided with Visual Basic.

Chapter 12, *Database Standards*. Most Visual Basic applications exist to present information to and gather information from a user, all of which is stored in a database. This final chapter of the book lists standards that should be used when communicating with databases.

Summary

Fulfilling the needs of everyone involved in a software development project can sometimes seem unattainable. Yet with the proper methods and standards, you will be adequately prepared to meet, and even surpass, those goals. As you move through the remainder of this book, recall often the three primary aspects of professional software development: foundation, structure, and standards.

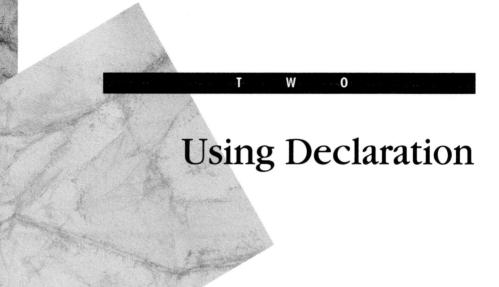

Using Declaration

Intelligent declaration is at the heart of quality application development. As we will soon find out, declaration is so much more than naming standards. It is a system of development that touches every portion of your Visual Basic source code. This chapter is tightly coupled with Chapter 9, *Declaration Standards*, in Part 3 of this book.

What Is Declaration?

Declaration is the means by which data, functionality, and information in a program are identified. Although most programmers think of variables when the word "declaration" is bantered around, declaration covers a wider range of programming tasks, one of which is variable definition.

Declaration has a larger impact on the end user's experience than does style or commenting (which are discussed in Chapter 3, *Commenting and Style*), so an added amount of care needs to be placed on its usage. Although the use or avoidance of a consistent naming system may have no effect on the final compiled product, many other aspects of declaration can dramatically affect the speed, robustness, and correctness of your Visual Basic application.

Not every programming language requires the use of variables for data storage. Consider LISP, one of the more common non-procedural languages. Although variables are available in LISP, you have to neither use them nor declare them to have a working program, even a somewhat complex program. Yet even LISP has some forms of declaration. How much more, then, does Visual Basic have, with its abundance of data and procedure types.

Among the forms of declaration discussed in this chapter are the following.

- Local, module, and global variable names and data types
- Public and private subroutine, function, and property names
- Parameter names and data types, and function return values
- Line labels
- Control names
- Database object references
- Declare statements
- Intrinsic constants and values accessed through type libraries
- User-defined data type tags and elements
- Enumerated data types
- Programmer-defined constants
- Class names and members
- Custom control properties and elements
- Form, module, custom control, property page (etc.) definitions
- Order of major routine components

And you thought we were just going to talk about variables.

Why Declare?

Because of the procedural nature of Visual Basic, there is no way around declaration. Even if you purge your program of Option Explicit and Dim statements, the very presence of variables, routines, and controls implies the use of declaration. So a better question than "Why declare?" is "Why declare correctly?"

Like the use of good style, a coherent system of declaration adds internal stability and organization to your source code. One of the main goals of all professional programming activity is the production of a quality application, and the effective use of declaration gives you a head start, even before you type one line of logic.

While the primary beneficiary of professional coding style is the programmer, good use of declaration also affects the user. The better the use of declaration, the better the experience for both the programmer and the user.

Among the many benefits of professional declaration are the following.

Clarity

The number one reason for using professional declaration in your application source code is clarity. Think back to your eighth grade English class. You worked hard for weeks on your biographical report of George Washington (actually, you procrastinated and wrote it the night before it was due), and no one was more surprised than you when it came back with some corrections on it. One of the corrections was the word "awkward" scribbled in red pen next to several of the sentences. What was wrong with these sentences? They lacked clarity. The information conveyed to the reader was probably accurate, and some of the ideas presented revealed an understanding on your part of the topic of the report. Still, those sentences were rather clumsy. I can still imagine my English teacher writhing in pain as she read my own unpolished works.

Professional declaration brings a level of clarity to your source code that it truly needs. The whole reason for writing an application in the first place is to solve some problem. Including sloppy declarations in your code just piles one problem on another.

Consistency

When declaration is implemented properly, a consistency begins to permeate your application. Visual Basic provides many tools that make it easy to add consistent declarations to your application. Visual Basic 4.0 introduced intrinsic data constants through type library definitions. These predefined constants (like vbRightJustify and vbTab) give consistent meaning to your control property values. Programmer-defined enumerated data types (with the Enum keyword) and standard constants allow you to create your own intrinsic constant sets. Most importantly, declaration includes an overall ordering of source code within each subroutine and function of your application, providing a consistent approach to writing routines.

Expectations Fulfilled

Using professional declaration provides a miniature contract between you, the programmer, and your code. When you create a variable, you expect certain things of that variable. For example, if you declare an integer in your code:

```
Dim nCounter As Integer
```

certain expectations come to mind. You can expect that nCounter will be used to "count" something. You also know that there cannot be more than 65,536 of those things (actually, only 32,767 of those things, since Visual Basic integers are signed). Assigning common names to variables and other elements within your code gives you a level of confidence about how those elements will act in your program.

Increased Recognition

Applying a consistent order and naming structure to your source code provides an increased level of code recognition. This is especially important for those times when you must return to a section of code days (or even years) after it was originally written. When you standardize your code with professional declarations, the amount of time it takes to grasp the workings of a routine is greatly reduced. You know that certain elements of the routine will appear in certain locations, and if they are moved or missing, your brain immediately throws out red flags that alert you to potential problems.

Reduced Memory Usage

The Visual Basic environment makes use of a "project name table" and other development tables that, although roomy, do have upper limits. Inconsistent or wasteful naming conventions can eat away at these limits, reducing the overall availability of memory during development, and possibly giving you a more sluggish response from the Visual Basic development environment.

Visual Confirmation

Consistent declaration provides immediate confirmation of data type conversions when a Visual Basic statement involves data of multiple types. For example:

```
nFinalValue = lOriginalValue * 100
```

should give you an uneasy feeling in your stomach. You can anticipate the declarations of the two variables used in the preceding statement.

```
Dim nFinalValue As Integer
Dim lOriginalValue As Long
```

Now a quick look at the original assignment of nFinalValue makes you worry. A long integer value is multiplied, and then assigned to a short integer. Although the range of values upon which you work may be small, the potential for problems in such code is there, and at the very least, lOriginalValue may be wasting 16 bits if it is only used to store small values.

How to Use Declaration

Earlier in this chapter I listed a variety of Visual Basic source code components that fell under the wide umbrella of declaration. In our how-to discussion of this topic, we can group these elements into four major areas: variable data declaration, constant data declaration, other declarations, and the order of code within a routine.

Variable Data Declaration

It is possible to write a small, useful Visual Basic application without variables, but such cases are rare. The use of variables are core to real-world

Visual Basic applications. Ensuring they are declared correctly bestows on them their due recognition.

USE OPTION EXPLICIT

Use Option Explicit. I repeat, use Option Explicit. Did I mention that you should always use Option Explicit? If you ignore everything else in this chapter, heed this one item: use Option Explicit! These two little words at the beginning of the Declarations section of each module will save you countless hours of debugging. In fact, although I am not a math major, I am sure that the number of bugs introduced by not using Option Explicit increases exponentially with the size of the source code.

Some versions of Microsoft Visual Basic shipped with Option Explicit turned off by default. If you have not yet done so, bring up the Visual Basic *Options* dialog, and select the *Require Variable Declaration* checkbox. If you are developing in Visual Basic, Scripting Edition, be sure to add Option Explicit to the top of each source file.

Option Explicit, as I am sure you already know, requires that all variables and constants be declared with the Dim statement (or the related ReDim, Public, Private, Static, Const, and Enum keywords) before they can be used. This feature prevents you from writing the following faulty code:

```
Public Function AMOrPM(nHour As Integer) As String
    ' ----- A useless, and incorrect, function
    If ((nHour Mod 24) < 12) Then
        AMOrPM = "A"
    Else
        AMOrPN = "P"
    End If
End Function
```

Without Option Explicit, this function compiles, and runs, without any indication of a problem. Yet the routine will never return "P" because "P" is assigned to the incorrect variable. Here is a fun game you and your friends can play. Take a large Visual Basic application that is void of Option Explicit statements and add in Option Explicit to every Declarations section. Then, before compiling the application, have everyone make a guess as to how many compile-time errors will occur that stem from undefined variables and constants. The winner gets to debug the application. Be assured, the fun will go on and on for hours.

NEVER USE DEFTYPE

Visual Basic provides DefInt, DefStr, and several other related functions, all grouped under the name DefType. Never use these statements in your application. The DefType statements allow you to declare variables, functions, and Property Get routines without specifying the As clause. The data type of the variable or return value will be set to the proper data type based on the first letter of the variable name, function name, or Property Get name. By default, all variables and functions in Visual Basic are of the type Variant. The statement

```
DefInt A-C
```

causes all untyped variables, functions, and Property Get statements within the scope of the DefInt statement that start with the letters A, B, or C (case is ignored) to be cast as integers. Using the DefType keywords removes a level of clarity from your source code, and it opens your application up to errors during those times when you inadvertently name a variable with the wrong initial letter. If you insist on using DefType in your code, let it be the following:

```
DefObj A-Z
```

This statement causes all non-typed variables and functions to type themselves as objects. What a fantastic way to add that little touch of mystery to your program.

VBScript uses only the Variant data type. Therefore, the DefType statements are absent.

ALWAYS USE DATA TYPES

This rule has a corollary: Avoid the use of Variants where possible. Avoiding the DefType keyword prevents you from altering the default data type, but you can still create variables that use the default data type. In Visual Basic, the default data type is Variant. Variants are very flexible; they can store strings, numbers, dates, arrays, and almost any other type of data. Its ability to automatically convert between the different data types that it understands makes it the perfect choice as the only data type available in VBScript. Also, Variants are often used to pass values in COM libraries. However, in standard Visual Basic applications, the uses of the Variant data type should be few and far between.

The Variant data type is one feature of Visual Basic that makes it a "weakly typed" language, as opposed to a "strongly typed" language. Strongly typed languages (such as C) force all variables to adhere to the data type under which they are defined. An integer is an integer is an integer. Through the use of "casts" the programmer can migrate information of one data type into a variable of another type. C does include some automatic data type coercion, as in short to long integer data conversion. Yet some of the most up-to-date C and C++ compilers will generate warnings if you attempt to pass a regular (short) integer value to a function that expects a long integer. (Visual Basic does enforce some type coercion restrictions. For example, you cannot assign a text string of a number to a floating point variable without first converting it.)

Although Visual Basic is weakly typed, the professional Visual Basic programmer can write applications that look similar to strongly typed languages. Unfortunately, Visual Basic makes it so easy to write your code without giving a thought to the data type. For example, you know that

```
Dim nValue As Integer
```

will provide you with a nice, 16-bit integer to work with. But how about this declaration?

```
Dim nValue, nCounter As Integer
```

What is the data type of nValue? If you answered "integer," you will need to return to the Visual Basic Programmer's Guide for the correct answer: Variant. Unless you are using Visual Basic, Scripting Edition, always avoid this multiple-declaration syntax. Instead, declare only one variable with each Dim, Static, Public, or Private statement.

All parameters to functions and subroutines need to be typed for data as well, even if the data type of a parameter will be Variant. Always include the As clause at the end of a function declaration.

```
Public Function QueryResults(anResults() As Integer) _
        As Boolean
```

Visual Basic 4.0 introduced data types to constants.

```
Public Const COL_WORKDATE As Long = 1
Public Const MSG_PROBLEM As String = "Problem Encountered"
```

Specifying data types on all variables, parameters, and constants reduces the chance for error from data that was incorrectly coerced from one data type to another. When you allow your variables to default to the Variant data type, you introduce the chance that data will not remain as you expected. For example, consider the following code snippet:

```
Dim bTest As Boolean
Dim nTest As Integer
Dim vntTest As Variant

bTest = True
vntTest = bTest
nTest = bTest
MsgBox nTest & ", " & vntTest
```

Forgetting for the moment that this is useless code, which of the following will appear in the message box when the code executes?

A. -1, -1
B. -1, True
C. The code does not compile

The correct answer is "B." Starting with Visual Basic 4.0, True and False became significantly different from the Visual Basic 3.0 equivalents of -1 and 0. Variants retain the full attributes of their Boolean counterparts, while integers take on only the integral value. In the absence of integer coercion, the Variant produces the string version of the Boolean value, resulting in "True" appearing in the message box.

There are a few places where the use of Variants is valid. If you do not know in advance what data type will be stored in a variable, then Variant is the right choice. ParamArray parameters to functions and subroutines must be Variant. Using the IsMissing function with optional arguments requires that the arguments be of type Variant. Captured database data from random tables and fields is a good use for Variants. When you write in VBScript, you have no choice but to use the Variant data type. Variants are large (22 bytes minimum per variable!) and definitely not type safe, but there are legitimate uses for them. Just be careful.

USE HUNGARIAN NOTATION

Now we come to the part of the chapter you've all been waiting for: naming conventions. Specifically, the Hungarian naming convention discussion that no good Windows programming book can be without. Invented by Charles Simonyi of Microsoft, this naming system permits variables to carry a lot of information in a little space. Each Hungarian variable name is packed with its data type, its scope, and its purpose. Each Hungarian variable name is composed of four components:

```
[scope][tag]basename[qualifier]
```

The *scope* indicates the number of routines in which the variable can be used. The values for the scope are listed in Table 2.1.

Table 2.1	Hungarian Scope Values
Value	**Meaning**
g	A global variable, accessible from all routines within the application.
m	A module-level variable, accessible from the routines within the same module, form, class, property page, custom control, etc., in which the variable is defined.
x	A local variable, defined with the Static keyword.
nothing	If no scope is supplied, the variable is a local variable, limited in scope to the routine in which the variable is defined.

The *tag* section identifies the data type of the variable, including whether the variable is an array variable or not. Table 2.2 gives some examples of the tag values used in Visual Basic applications. See Chapter 9 for a more complete listing of these tags.

Table 2.2	Sample Hungarian Tag Values
Value	**Meaning**
a	Usually only one tag appears within a variable name. *A* is the lone exception. This specification appears before the main tag within the variable, and indicates that the variable is an array variable. For example, anToys is an integer array of toys.
b	Boolean data type. In Visual Basic 3.0, Boolean values were declared as Integer. Visual Basic 4.0 introduced a true Boolean data type.
cbo	ComboBox control, including the drop-down combo, simple combo, and drop-down list styles.
chk	CheckBox control.
dt	Date data type for handling dates or times.
fc	Currency data type.
fd	Double data type.
frm	Form module, both Single Document Interface (SDI) and Multi Document Interface (MDI) styles.
fs	Single data type.
l	Long data type (the tag is the letter *ell*).
lst	ListBox control, both standard and checkbox styles.
n	Integer data type.
rs	DAO and ADO Recordset data types, including table, snapshot, and Dynaset-style Recordsets.
s	String data type. For fixed length strings, append the size of the string to the end of the variable name, as in sBuffer200.
txt	TextBox control, both single-line and multi-line styles.

The *basename* is the traditional variable name that we all know and love. It always begins with a capital letter, and continues in a mixed-case fashion. *Qualifier* is intended to indicate variations of a basename, such as "Next," "Prev," "First," "Last," and so on, but I always combine basename and qualifier into a single logical chunk. When forming your basename-qualifier pair, avoid abbreviations that would confuse another reader. While "dtSlsHistBeg" may seem clear to you, "dtSalesHistoryBegins" will be clear to everyone.

Hungarian-style names are great because you can immediately tell what data type a variable is, and its probable definition location. Some examples will suffice.

- **nCounter**—A local loop counter variable.
- **gsUserName**—A global string variable indicating a user name.
- **madtActivity**—A module-level array of date variables used to track Activity dates.

Control names (both those declared in code and those drawn on a form) use the Hungarian naming convention, but the scope is left off of the drawn versions since form-based controls are module-level in scope by definition.

Another aspect of the Hungarian naming convention is that type-declaration characters become unnecessary. These characters, the most famous of which is "$" for string variables, appear at the end of variables, providing an implicit form of type declaration. You should refrain from using these characters in variable names, although there are other legitimate uses for these characters. For example, you can force integer values to the Long data type by appending them with the "&" type-declaration character.

```
lResult = CLng(nFactor) * 100&
```

The proper use of Hungarian naming also puts an end to that dreadful habit of using one- or two-character variable names. While it is feasible to create a two-character variable name that is still Hungarian in nature, resist the temptation to do so at all costs. Short variable names are void of all descriptive meaning, and they are difficult to locate when scanning the source code visually.

There are a few exceptions to the Hungarian-only rule. Most of them fall under the so-called "grandfather clause" of variable nomenclature rules. The traditional names given to event arguments are off limits for renaming. For example, the standard argument list for the MouseMove event is:

```
Button As Integer, Shift As Integer, X As Single, Y As Single
```

Since these arguments have been used in Visual Basic applications since time immemorial, there is no need to convert them to their Hungarian counterparts, even though this particular argument list contains two frightful one-character variable names. Also, code obtained from the API Text Viewer supplied with Visual Basic, or from other Windows Software Development Kit (SDK) sources, need not be converted.

LIMIT SCOPE WHERE POSSIBLE

The event-driven nature of Visual Basic makes it almost impossible to write a program without global variables. (I have known programmers who get around this by treating hidden form labels as variables, but I wonder how different that really is.) Global and module-level variables are a necessity in Visual Basic, but they should be used with caution. There is nothing inherently wrong with global (a.k.a. Public) variables, but the mere fact that a variable can change value from one end of a routine to another when no logic within the routine acted on the variable should be cause for alarm. Therefore, limit and carefully control the use of your global and module-level variables. When practical, make global variables module-level. Where possible, make module-level variables local.

When you do use global variables, constants, declares, enumerated data types, and user-defined data types, define them all in a single module, named something like "global.bas." This makes them easy to find and track. (Third-party supplied constant files can be left in their own files for easy update when future versions are released.)

REMOVE UNUSED VARIABLES, PROCEDURES, AND OTHER OBJECTS

And once you have removed all of these space-wasters, see if you have two or more routines that perform the same function, and combine them.

Constant Data Declaration

As with variables, there are guidelines for defining and creating constants that will bring additional consistency to your source code.

USE INTRINSIC CONSTANTS

The latest Visual Basic type libraries include a myriad of constants to make your source code more readable. Quick, without looking ahead, what is the result of the following lines of code?

```
Private Sub Form_MouseDown(Button As Integer, _
      Shift As Integer, X As Single, Y As Single)
   Me.ForeColor = &H8000000D
   Me.ScaleMode = 3
   Me.Line (X - 10, Y - 10)-(X + 10, Y + 10), , BF
End Sub
```

Perhaps the following code will be a little more clear.

```
Private Sub Form_MouseDown(Button As Integer, _
      Shift As Integer, X As Single, Y As Single)
   ' ----- Draw a highlighted box around the mouse
   Me.ForeColor = vbHighlight
   Me.ScaleMode = vbPixels
   Me.Line (X - 10, Y - 10)-(X + 10, Y + 10), , BF
End Sub
```

There is not much difference between the two versions of this event, but the second version frees me from looking up in the on-line help the "magic numbers" used on the first two logic lines.

USE ENUMERATED DATA TYPES

Using the Enum statement provides two advantages. First, it logically groups associated user-defined constants together. Second, when you declare a variable as the type of one of your defined Enums, a list of choices appears when you assign a value in code to that variable (when you have Visual Basic's *Auto-List Members* feature enabled). Always identify a group of enumerated constants with a common prefix, as the Visual Basic intrinsic constants have.

```
Public Enum EnumBeverage
    bevSodaPop = 1
    bevMilk = 2
    bevJuice = 3
    bevCoffee = 4
    bevTea = 5
    bevDoubleTallSkinnyLatte = 6
End Enum
```

If you are designing an ActiveX component, you can make an enumerated data type available to the user of the component as intrinsic constants.

USE CONSTANTS

Not every constant fits into an enumeration. For those additional needs, user-defined constants increase the clarity of your source code. Like variables, constants have three levels of scope: global, module, and local. Your own global constants should be placed in a single module, preferably in the same Declarations section where you placed all of the global variables. (Third-party constant files can be maintained separately for easy upgrades later.) Create module-level constants when those values will truly be needed only in a single module. Never use local constant declaration; constants used in a single routine should be placed in the Declarations section of that module. This allows you to update any constants from a single convenient and known location. It also helps other programmers find them quickly and easily.

How many constants should you use? While many programmers fall into the trap of adding too few constants to their applications, it is also possible to overburden the code with dozens, or hundreds, of superfluous constants. In general, you should create a constant whenever a new programmer would wonder why, for instance, the number 5 appears in the middle of an expression.

```
If (nStoreType = 5) Then
```

I tend to use constants primarily for numeric values, but Visual Basic allows you to create constants based on most of the basic built-in data types.

```
Public Const PROGRAM_TITLE As String = "My Calculator"
Public Const START_DATE As Date = "12-Jan-1998"
```

By default, constants are Variants, and we all know what that means. Make frequent use of the As clause when defining constants.

Other Declarations

In addition to variables and constants, there are a few other significant elements found within Visual Basic source code that depend on quality declaration usage.

SUBROUTINES, FUNCTIONS, AND PROPERTIES

Always specify the Private or Public keyword when defining a function, subroutine, or property (Let, Set, Get). Make sure that all arguments, and the return value for functions, use the As clause. Otherwise, you end up with "headless" procedures, those subroutines and functions that are all body and no head.

```
Function ActOnInput(a, b, c)
    ' ----- What are a, b, and c?  What is the return
    '         type or range of values?
    ...
    ...
End Function
```

You do not need to use Hungarian naming standards when identifying procedures. Subroutines do not return a value, so there is nothing on which to base the Hungarian names. Functions follow this logic for consistency. The names should still appear in a mixed-case format.

LINE LABELS

Provide meaningful mixed-case names for line labels referenced by GoTo and GoSub statements. I will avoid the traditional argument about the use or disuse of the GoTo statement. One of the goals of professional Visual Basic programming is to provide clean, easy-to-read source code. Sometimes this will mean using the GoTo statement to avoid endless nesting in conditions and loops. At other times this will require the avoidance of all GoTo and GoSub statements.

When you do use GoTo and GoSub, use a common set of label names for common features. For example, always give your standard error handling section in each routine the same name, something like "ErrorHandler." When you have multiple labels in a single subroutine or function, using common names over and over again leaves no doubt about the use of each section.

DECLARE STATEMENTS

Be as clear about data types in your Declare statements as you are in function and subroutine definitions. In fact, be even clearer: always use the ByRef and ByVal keywords for every argument in a Declare's argument list.

USER-DEFINED DATA TYPE TAGS AND ELEMENTS

Use meaningful mixed-case names for all tags and elements.

```
Public Type CustomerType
    lCustNumber As Long
    sFullName As String
    sPhoneNumber As String
    bGoodCredit As Boolean
End Type
```

If you are using one of the Microsoft-supplied types for use in API calls (such as the often used RECT type), you may need to abandon the higher calling to a standard naming convention in deference to tradition.

DATABASE OBJECT NAMES

If your application design and implementation requires that you create a new database, establish a set of rules and conventions for the naming and data typing of each table, field, and object within your database. I tend to be a little less stringent about my database field naming; although I mix-case all of my object names (which is ignored by databases like Oracle anyway), I do not use Hungarian naming on my field names. The Hungarian prefixes used in Visual Basic do not always correspond one-to-one to database objects. Also, databases are frequently used by multiple sources, including applications written in other languages that either do not employ the Hungarian naming system, or use different prefixes than the ones common to Visual Basic. See Chapter 12, *Database Standards*, for more information about working with databases and database objects.

CUSTOM CONTROL PROPERTIES

When creating custom ActiveX controls, use mixed-case, non-Hungarian names for the publicly exposed property names. This keeps your control in sync with all other controls already on the market. If you are implementing a property that has the same functionality as one of the controls shipped with Visual Basic, use the same property name as the one supplied by Microsoft.

STRING VS. VARIANT BUILT-IN FUNCTIONS

Visual Basic provides String and Variant versions of several built-in functions. To increase processing speed, and to introduce better control of your data, always use the string versions of these functions. For example, always use Left$() instead of Left(). If you are programming in Visual Basic, Scripting Edition, you are required to use the Variant versions.

Order of Code

As with most other activities within the realm of professional Visual Basic programming, applying a consistent order to your procedure code may have no effect on the compiled application; Visual Basic does not care where Dim statements appear in your routine. But good programmers do care, and they faithfully use a predetermined pattern in the structure of each routine. Fortunately, this pattern is very flexible, so that you will not have to contort your code to fit into the pattern.

The pattern I use is divided into 12 sections, many of which are optional depending on the complexity of the routine.

- Heading
- Introductory Comment
- Variable Declaration
- Initialization of Error Handler
- Default Assignment of Function Return
- Initialization
- Body of Logic
- Final Assignment of Function Return
- Exit from Logic
- GoSub Handler(s)
- Error Handler(s)
- Footing

Well, it does not look very much like a Visual Basic procedure. Fortunately, it is only a model into which all routines do fit.

HEADING

This section contains the opening declaration statement for the Sub, Function, or Property.

INTRODUCTORY COMMENT

This is the summary comment that provides an overview of your routine. Chapter 3 discusses this "why" comment in all its glory. This section is required in every routine.

VARIABLE DECLARATION

Add all of your Dim, Static, and ReDim statements in this section, before any other logic statements. Put the Static and ReDim statements last, as some third-party code checkers complain if they appear before Dim statements. (Of course, ReDim statements may also appear within the body of your logic as needed.) Place all Const statements in the Declarations section of the module, not within a routine.

INITIALIZATION OF ERROR HANDLER

If your procedure contains a standard error handler, include the initial On Error statement in this section.

```
On Error GoTo ErrorHandler
```

DEFAULT ASSIGNMENT OF FUNCTION RETURN

The return value of a function needs to be assigned immediately, before any other logic of the routine executes. Although I tend to think that professional programmers are positive and upbeat, you should be pessimistic about the return value at this stage of the routine. For example, if your routine returns a Boolean value of True for success, and False for failure, assume the worst from the beginning.

```
DoSomeWork = False
```

INITIALIZATION

This section contains all local, static, module, and global variables that require initialization before the body of the routine begins. Actually, I often delay the initialization of some variables until later in the logic, especially when they are reset repeatedly in a loop construct. Still, you should set as many variables as possible to their initial values. Visual Basic does perform some variable initialization for you (such as setting numeric values to zero). When in doubt, be verbose.

BODY OF LOGIC

The code. Along with the introductory comment, this section is absolutely required.

FINAL ASSIGNMENT OF FUNCTION RETURN

If your function's return value has not yet been set to its final value, do so as the last statement of your logic.

EXIT FROM LOGIC

This section includes a final Exit Sub, Exit Function, or Exit Property statement. If your routine has no GoSub or Error handlers, omit this section.

GOSUB HANDLER(S)

If you use GoSub statements in your routine, all of the "subroutine within a subroutine" sections should appear here, each with a descriptive line label and comment. Place a blank line before each handler's line label for clarity.

ERROR HANDLER(S)

The standard error handler is the last thing to appear in your routine before the End Sub, End Function, or End Property statement. Any routine that does anything even the least bit dangerous needs a standard error handler. For example, any routine that performs database access absolutely must have a standard error handler. The great thing about this handler is that it is practically a cut-and-paste insertion into your source code. There will be times when you need a more complex version of the standard error handler, but that should be the exception rather than the rule.

```
ErrorHandler:
    GeneralError "frmProcess.cmdOK_Click", Err, Error$
    Resume Next
```

That's all there is to it. Whether you use Resume Next or Exit Sub/Function/Property is a design decision, and that may vary from routine to routine. "GeneralError" is a routine I include in all of my applications that accepts three arguments: 1) the name of the routine where the error occurred, 2) the error number, and 3) the text of the error. For debugging purposes, I load up the third argument with the current state of key variables. The actual logic of GeneralError depends on the needs of the application. Often, this routine simply displays a message box announcing the error to the user.

```
Public Sub GeneralError (sRoutine As String, _
        lError As Long, sError As String)
    ' ----- Display an error to the user
    On Error Resume Next
    MsgBox "Error " & lError & " occurred in routine '" & _
        sRoutine & "'.  Please inform your system " & _
        "administrator.  The error message is:" & _
        vbLf & vbLf & sError, vbOKOnly + vbExclamation, _
        "Error"
End Sub
```

I have also had this routine display the message in a text control so that the user could copy the text of the message. Global state variables can be displayed in the message, and you can even save the error message in a database or local file.

FOOTING

This section contains only the closing End Sub, End Function, or End Property.

Summary

Perhaps you feel that you were just hit over the head with a two-by-four of rules and regulations. This was a long chapter, and it did come with more than its share of guidelines for writing source code. The professional programmer adapts coding style and standards not only to some predetermined list of precepts, but also to the needs of the user and other programmers involved in a project. Still, a good list of standards gives you a sure footing on the road to programming discipline. If you have formerly been tossed about by the winds of programming change, then declare with me this day your intention to conform your source code to a set of professional standards.

Commenting and Style

A whole chapter on commenting? Yes, a whole chapter about comments, *and style*. Comments are a touchy subject with many programmers. Some think they are a waste of time, while others add so many remarks to their code that you are not sure if there is any code at all.

Commenting deserves a whole chapter because—and I might as well shock you right from the start of the chapter—around 10 percent of a professional Visual Basic program should be comment lines. Therefore, it seems right that about 10 percent of this book be devoted to such a "remarkable" subject.

Before delving deeper into the chapter, let us look at some common ideas about using commenting and style when programming.

The Top 10 Misconceptions about Commenting and Style

1. Comments are extraneous since you can always understand the logic by looking at the code.
2. Indenting just wastes disk space.
3. I don't have time to add comments.
4. What does it matter how sloppy the code is? I'm not selling the source code.
5. Adding comments doesn't make the code run any better.
6. Hey man, don't bother me. This is my trademark coding style.
7. I comment every line of code. It makes the program so readable.
8. If there's a bug, I'll be able to fix it. It's not like I'm going to forget what this function does.
9. I'll go back later and add in the comments.
10. It's job security. If others can understand my code, they don't need me.

What Are Commenting and Style?

Although comments and style are closely linked, we will keep them somewhat separate throughout this chapter. Each section discusses commenting, followed by style.

What Is Commenting?

Comments are a descriptive method of conveying the thoughts of the programmer at the time a section of code is written. A program with comments is actually the mingling of two programming languages within a single body of code. In my case, the two languages are Visual Basic and English.

Writing programs in a high-level language, such as Visual Basic, is really for the convenience of the programmer and anyone else who looks at the source code. The CPU has no use for the source code; it only cares about your program once it is compiled down to machine code. You could always write your applications in assembly language, and they would probably run with more efficiency. But it is cumbersome to write a full Windows application in assembly language, and it is a slow read when compared to the same application written in a higher-level language. Comments are another high-level language in which programs are written. There are two main differences between comments and Visual Basic logic statements: 1) the comments are (or should be) clearer than the code, and 2) there is no compiler available for the remarks.

Comments are to a program what sleep is to a person. As I mentioned earlier, a good program should contain about 10 percent comments. The average person spends one-third of life sleeping. Sleep is not the goal or focus of one's life, just as comments are not the goal or focus of one's code. Still, both sleep and comments serve important purposes. They both bring refreshment and vitality, and they both (when done properly) result in a clearer life (or program).

What Is Style?

Style is that personal touch, that organizational structure, that only you can bring to a block of code. Although the topic of this entire book is style, in this chapter style refers to the aesthetic appearance of the source code itself, not the style of the program logic, nor the style of the application user interface.

The Visual Basic development environment imposes a certain amount of style on your code whether you wish it to or not. All keywords are forced into mixed case whenever you add or modify a line of code. Extra space is also removed from most lines with three notable exceptions: the whitespace before in-line comments, the whitespace before As clauses, and spaces after the multi-statement separator (":"). Still, most aspects of coding style are left up to the programmer.

Style includes, but is not limited to, the following aesthetic features of code sections:

- Placement, frequency, and appearance of comments
- Indentation
- Capitalization of identifiers and literal strings
- Use of blank lines within code
- Use of parentheses around conditions and expressions
- Use of line continuations ("_")

Why Use Commenting and Style?

By the time you finish this chapter, you will realize that I am quite pleased when I see a program with clear comments and style. Although your number-one reason for employing commenting and style should not be to please Tim Patrick, there is a certain amount of integrity gained when your work is appreciated by your peers. In addition to integrity, there are many practical reasons for applying a full and consistent manner of style and commenting.

Why Include Comments?

Although some programmers see no value in adding comments to their code, the professional Visual Basic programmer employs a higher standard in his or her programs. Some of the practical reasons for incorporating comment documentation in your code include the following.

Description of Purpose

You always add a subroutine or function to a program with a purpose in mind. Remarks allow you to express that purpose to anyone who wishes to read your thoughts. Comments give you a chance to justify the code you wrote, even if the justification is directed only at your own sense of discipline.

Readability

Comments enhance the readability of your code by providing an alternate method, apart from the code itself, to express the logic of a code section. It is true that some code is immediately clear without remarks of any kind. Yet applications written to fill the business needs of your customers will probably involve complex calculations and user interactions. Bringing clarity to these sections through descriptive comments will make the initial programming, and maintenance programming later on, more satisfying.

Second Memory

When you have complete responsibility over a project's design and implementation, it is easy to say, "I know everything about this program. I wrote it." While that may be a true statement today, just wait until a year from now when the users spring on you the list of modifications they have been saving up until funding was available. I guarantee that you will have forgotten some parts of the application, especially if you worked on other projects in the meantime.

Unlike your memory, comments written at the same time as the code do not forget. Even when a section of code is somewhat familiar, well-written comments can save you the trouble of reading every line of code to understand the logic. If you have to find a bug in unfamiliar code, comments can help you narrow down the problem quickly. And even better than your memory, they remain with the code when you have moved on to other projects. This makes the life of maintenance programmers (and everyone is a maintenance programmer at some time) easier.

Logic Clarity

I always recommend writing your comments at the same time as you write the logic of the code. This way, you can clarify your thoughts about the flow of a routine or section. Remarks require you to write all of your code twice, once in Visual Basic, and once in your native tongue. They are much like the redundant safety systems installed on airplanes. If the main system fails, it is comforting to know that the backup system is there.

Identification

Comments let you identify important pieces of information that may otherwise be buried in documentation, or even undocumented. Most programmers naturally put their name in their code (at least code of which they are proud). Other items that can be identified in the code include the user or manager who requested a modification to the original specification, the source from which an algorithm or data was obtained, and the features of a special input or output device with which the application was designed to work.

Code Reviews

Some companies require that all applications pass through a code review, a formal critique of the program by other knowledgeable programmers, to confirm the correctness of the application logic. I have been involved in a few such reviews, and it is almost always the case that the person conducting the review has no involvement with the application under review. In a few cases, I was in meetings where non-Visual Basic programmers reviewed Visual Basic code. Although this is not an ideal situation, this makes the presence of in-code documentation vital. Although many procedural and event-driven languages share a similar syntax, the code alone is not always immediately understandable to other programmers. Comments make the translation simple.

Future Modifications

Comments make future application modifications easier by introducing the next programmer to the thought process behind sections of code. If you have thought out future enhancements in advance, you can include remarks in your code that direct other programmers to the locations within the code where modifications should be focused.

It is also important to alert programmers, whether yourself or others, to relationships in sections of your code that are not adjacent. For example, I like to include support for status bar help when the user is browsing the menu items of the main application window, such as the "Exits the application" message in Figure 3–1.

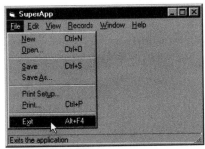

Figure 3–1   *Status bar help when using menus.*

Apart from the Windows subclassing code necessary to make this feature work, I maintain a list of constants for each menu item for which a message will appear. The subclassing callback function that checks for interactive menu selection calls a function named GetMenuMessageString() that returns a string message based on the highlighted menu item's constant. If I ever need to add a new menu item (and constant), I also need to update the function that returns the strings. Therefore, I add a comment with my menu constants that reminds me to make this update.

```
' ----- When adding new menu items, be sure to update the
'       GetMenuMessageString() routine as well.
```

```
Public Const MNU_FILE_NEW = 1
Public Const MNU_FILE_OPEN = 2
   ...
```

Why Use Style?

Like commenting, style benefits the programmer, not the computer. That is not completely true, since the use of consistent style and commenting can result in a clearer thought process, which in turn has a positive influence on the code. Still, the primary beneficiary of good coding style is the programmer. And also as with comments, there are many practical reasons to employ good coding style in your applications.

Readability

Coding style improves the readability of your code by giving it a clean, consistent, and uncluttered look. This helps the programmer and the reviewer in visually scanning the code when looking for problems.

Grouping of Logic

By placing blank lines between logically related groups of statements, you clearly show your algorithmic intentions. Adding too many or too few blank lines can give your code a sparse or cramped feeling, and make it more difficult to trace. Indentation similarly shows the subordinate relationship between statements. Although when to indent is partially dictated by the traditional use of control statements, Visual Basic allows you to employ any indentation style you wish to use (except for line labels). Using consistent and logical indentation provides a quick visual image of the course of the logic.

Guarantee of Program Flow

Although Visual Basic does not require the use of parentheses around most expressions, it is a good idea to group conditions and mathematical expressions within parentheses so that there is no mistake, either to the compiler or interpreter, or to the programmer, about the manner in which to interpret an expression.

How to Comment

Comments say a lot not only about a program, but about a programmer. The lack of same also says much about you as a programmer. If you get nothing else out of this section, please remember this: put *useful* comments in your code. This simple statement is probably one of the most argued aspects of programming. It ranks right up there with the use of the GoTo statement.

There are six different types of comments used within source code. Each type is identified by one of the six main "question" words used in English: *who, what, where, when, why*, and *how*. This common method of listing the six question words also happens to be the order of significance for comments, from least to greatest. As you write your application, keep asking yourself these six questions about your code, and then write comments that answer the questions.

Who

Who comments identify the person or persons who author or make modifications to the application. Within the range of comments that can be added to the code, these rank low on the significance scale. There are three places where *who* comments appear in a program. The first is at the top of each module's Declarations section. This *who* comment identifies the primary programmer(s) who developed the application. It may also declare ownership of the application.

```
' ----- Appointment book application
'         by Tim Patrick
'         Copyright (c) 2000 by MyCompany, Inc.
```

The second use of *who* comments comes in the form of block modification logs. Most programmers are familiar with these long lists of dates and initials of the programmers who made modifications to a source code file. These logs most often occur in the Declarations section of a source code module. Personally, I find these logs to be useless when they appear within the code. Somehow, everyone who adds to the log feels compelled to keep their comments to a single, short line, which is far too little space to write an adequate description of a change that needed a comment. If possible, modification logs should be maintained in documentation outside of the source code, in a place accessible to all programmers on a project. In addition, meaningful modification comments can be written when checking source code modules in to a source code control system. Still, some companies or managers require the use of in-code modification logs. When they are used, they need to be complete.

```
' Modification History
' --------------------
' 01/18/1998   Tim Patrick     Added the SummarizeData routine
'                              and use it to update the new
'                              lblResults label.
' 01/20/1998   Tim Patrick     Took out that buggy
'                              SummarizeData routine and the
'                              meaningless lblResults label.
'                              What was I thinking?
```

The third type of *who* comments, and the most unnecessary, are in-line change notices. These comments consist of a programmer's name (or initials) and a date of code modification.

```
For nCounter = 1 to 10
    anResult(nCounter) = anSource(nCounter)   ' TSP 2/15/95
Next nCounter
```

As you can see by the sample code, the *who* comment hanging off the second line gives no meaningful information. I know that a programmer with the initials TSP made a change on February 15, 1995 (years ago!). I may even know who TSP is. Yet I have no idea why such a change was made, or what the change was. When you make a change that alters the logic of the code, add or modify the associated *how* comment, described later in this section.

What

What comments identify some object in the source code, typically a variable or set of variables. Although they may take any form, they generally appear at the end of a declaration line, and give additional meaning to the element being identified.

```
Dim sPhone As String      ' Home phone number
```

I rarely use *what* comments if I think that the variable is self-describing. Yet I know many programmers who wince at the thought of leaving any variable without an identifying comment. If you believe that another programmer would not immediately understand the use of the variable from its name or from other comments, then by all means add a *what* comment.

I once converted a database application from Visual Basic 3.0 to the latest version of the language. In a few places within the code, a date field in the database would be assigned to a date several decades ago. It was always the same date, and I thought it might be the birthday of the original programmer. When I asked the developer, he confirmed that it was his birthday. But even more important, he explained why it was used, resulting in the following *what* comment.

```
' ----- This date is assigned to database date fields
'          instead of leaving them as NULL.  SQL compares on
'          NULL dates are slow because indexes cannot be used.
Public Const DB_NULL_DATE = "01-Jan-1951"
```

Where

Where comments indicate the location of additional information outside the source code. They are also used to identify code obtained from someone other than the developer. Often the location identified by *where* comments is documentation maintained by the development team or user community. These comments are usually ignored by anyone looking at the code. Yet they are of the utmost importance when a routine obtained from another source is found to contain errors. If the source of the logic is fully identified, comparisons to the original can facilitate a solution to the problem.

```
' ----- This encryption algorithm was originally written by
'       the Super Secret Software Society.  The web site
'       is, well, perhaps that is a secret too.  No, I will
'       tell you.  It is:
'          http://www.supersecret.org/ssss_enc_algorithm.htm
```

When

Now we come to one of my favorite types of comments, and I must admit that I use it with more frequency than is warranted. The *when* comment is used to identify a time in the future when a section of code will need modification, and what that modification must be. This comment is always identified with a special mark that is found in no other place within the code, and therefore searching for these comments is quick.

```
' !!! When the user opens a new file, store the name in the
'     registry, and also in the File menu for quick access.
```

In this example comment, assume that the code to open a file has already been written. This comment reminds the programmer to add at some time in the future, and at the place where the comment appears, code to update the registry. Notice the triple exclamation point mark at the start of the comment. A standard marker such as this is always used for *when* comments. Periodically, you search through the code looking for this marker to see if you left any modifications unfinished before the program is delivered to the user.

Although these comments are called *when* comments, they often contain no date information. The when is any convenient or important time in the future when modification is needed. What is never missing from a *when* comment is the full description of the modification to be made. Never use the marker alone without a descriptive comment. Believe me, you will forget why you added the marker, and you will remove it. Then your user will call you to tell you what you forgot to add.

Why

Along with *how* comments, *why* comments are the most important type of comment you can add to your source code. *Why* comments describe the purpose of a section of code, a routine, a module, or an entire application. This remark provides the *raison d'être* of a block of code, giving a defense for the existence of the code. *Why* comments always appear at the beginning of a logical grouping of source code, and they are always general in nature. They describe "why" the code that follows is significant within the application.

The most common location for *why* comments is at the beginning of a subroutine or function.

```
Public Function FToC (fsFahrenheit As Single) As Single
    ' ----- This function converts a Fahrenheit temperature
    '            to Celsius using the formula: c=(f-32)/1.8
```

Why comments are important because they provide the most direct means of communicating the intent of your logic to the reader of the source code. This is especially relevant when *you* are the reader of the source code, and you have forgotten what a routine was supposed to do (yet does not!). *Why* comments are the bulkiest of the six types of comments, and with good reason. They convey the most important remark information. For the programmer, especially the maintenance programmer, they are often more important than the source code itself.

Why comments allow your source code to be read like a book. They are the "Cliff Notes" of your source code, giving a reasonable and correct summary of your logic in a clear, concise format. In order to maintain clarity, always use precise, descriptive language (including correct grammar), and always be verbose. Also, when making changes to the source code, do not neglect to modify the descriptive logic of the *why* (and *how*) comments.

For most simple subroutines, functions, and Declaration sections, you will only have a single *why* comment, although for complicated routines, you may have several such block comments. Make the most of each of these comments by communicating your thoughts distinctly and completely.

How

How comments are written hand in hand with *why* comments. While a *why* comment might appear only once at the beginning of a routine or large section of code, *how* comments appear every few lines, giving a blow-by-blow description of the logic. Although each *how* comment is terse, when taken as a whole, they tell the story of an algorithm that makes for gripping reading.

The following function, a simple date verification routine, shows *why* and *how* comments in action.

```
Public Function VerifyDate(sTypedDate As String) As Date
    ' ----- This function converts a text date entered by
    '           the user into a true Date.  The user can enter
    '           a date in any format recognized by the CDate()
    '           function.  Also, numeric dates in the format
    '           mmddyy or mmddyyyy are accepted.  If no date is
    '           supplied, or if the date is invalid, then
    '           return today's date.
    Dim sWork As String
```

```
' ----- Assume an invalid date and use today's date
On Error Resume Next
VerifyDate = Date
sWork = Trim$(sTypedDate)

If (IsNumeric(sWork)) Then
    ' ----- Check for a 6- or 8-digit date
    If (Len(sWork) = 6) Or (Len(sWork) = 8) Then
        ' ----- Assume a format of mmddyy or mmddyyyy
        VerifyDate = CDate(Left$(sWork, 2) & "/" _
            & Mid$(sWork, 3, 2) & "/" & Mid$(sWork, 5))

        ' !!! What if month or day are out of range?
        '     What about Y2K issues on two-digit years?
    End If
ElseIf (IsDate(sWork)) Then
    ' ----- The user entered a valid date.  Use it.
    ' !!! What about Y2K issues on two-digit years?
    VerifyDate = CDate(sWork)
End If
End Function
```

As you can see, the *why* comment at the beginning of the routine is quite substantial, while the *how* comments sprinkled throughout the logic are short and very matter-of-fact. (I also threw in some *when* comments for good measure.) While *why* comments are generic, *how* comments are specific.

How Many Comments?

Although you may feel comfortable with the six types of comments, there is still the question of how many comments to add to your application. Too many comments can obscure the code, while too few comments can make some complex routines incomprehensible. When deciding how many remarks to add to your source code, ask yourself, "If I took away the code and left only the comments, would another programmer still know exactly what I wanted to do in this routine or section of code?" When you can answer "Yes" to this question for a given routine, then you have added the correct number of comments.

It is also important to write your comments at the appropriate times. Fortunately, the times when comments should be written are few: either before writing the actual code, or during the coding process. Adding comments to your source code after it is written is not an acceptable professional programming practice. If you delay your remarks, you will most likely delay them indefinitely.

It is best to add the comments while you type the logic statements. This method is the least disruptive to your thought process; once an algorithm takes hold, it is difficult to let it go until you reach the end. Writing your remarks during such surges of inspiration gives confirmation to the correctness of the logic. When you encounter a more difficult routine, you may find it convenient to write out the *why* and some of the *how* comments in advance of writing the code itself. This solidifies the logic of the routine in English before moving into Visual Basic.

How to Employ Style

As a segue into the topic of style, let us discuss the style of comments. Comments provide a level of readability to the code in the programmer's native language. Since source code is really just an ordered arrangement of words and symbols, it is important to set your comments apart from the rest of the source code so that they can be perused quickly. One way of doing this is to place blank lines before and after all comments and the code associated with those comments. However, this gives a disjointed feeling to the code, and you are never sure if a free-floating comment is just that, or if it really remarks on the logic statements that follow it.

A better method for separating out the comments is to use some typographical device that draws the eye of the reader. Earlier I mentioned the use of the *when* comment marker ("!!!") to draw attention to sections of incomplete code. Likewise, standard comments are marked with some noticeable symbol. Although the symbol you choose is based on your particular style, I recommend a series of dashes or asterisks to distinguish the comments. I always use a set of five dashes on the first line of a block comment to announce to the world, "Hey, here's a comment."

```
' ----- This routine adds the correct amount of coffee
'       grounds to the coffee maker, allowing the
'       remainder of the application to work in a more
'       peaceful manner.
```

Even single-line comments need to be marked. In fact, except for comments that appear on the same line as logic statements (such as *what* comments), all comments should be marked so as to stand out from the rest of the code. Never leave a comment "unmarked." Such comments are hidden from view and decrease readability. When you work within the Visual Basic development environment, this does not seem like a big deal, since the comments are displayed in a different color from the rest of the code. Still, there are times when nothing satisfies like a good black-and-white printout, and then your comments will blend in with the code itself.

Correct

```
' ----- I am a comment, hear me roar.
```

Incorrect

```
'I am a comment, hear me squeak.
```

Now you may be asking, "When do I get to add *my* style? Visual Basic auto-formats most of my code." It is true that other languages, such as C++, give the programmer absolute power over the formatting of the source code. Yet an unprofessional programmer can make as much of a mess of a Visual Basic program as a C++ programmer can make in that language. Therefore, we round out this chapter in style by discussing some methods of utilizing good style within your source code.

Indentation

Indentation is a pure style issue, since the amount of indentation you use on each statement of your application neither adds to nor detracts from the performance of the program. The program ignores all whitespace at the start of each line (although Visual Basic does impose a limit on the number of space characters that can begin a line—256). All indentation is really for the programmer's benefit. Therefore, use it well. All logic lines and comments that are subordinate to some other line should be indented under that line. That is, all code within loops and conditions should be indented within the appropriate control structures. This also means that the only lines of code that should appear flush left within a routine are line labels.

```
' ----- Check each customer's status
Do While Not (rsInfo.EOF)
    If (rsInfo!CustStatus = STATUS_DELIQUENT) And _
            (rsInfo!CustType = TYPE_FREQUENT) Then
        ' ----- Let the customer know how we feel
        rsInfo.Edit
        rsInfo!SendMail = True
        rsInfo!MailComment = "Shame on you."
        rsInfo.Update
    End If
    rsInfo.MoveNext
Loop
```

In this sample code, each line of code that is subordinate to another is indented "one level" under the dominant line of code. When indenting lines broken with the line continuation character ("_"), if the full logical line will have no subordinate lines, indent the continued lines one level from the first line. If the full logical line will have subordinate lines (as with the If statement in the sample code block), indent the continued lines two levels from the first line, then indent the subordinate code one level from the first line. The indentation of a Select Case statement follows this system. Case statements are subordinate to the Select Case statement, and the code within a Case section is subordinate to the Case statement itself.

```
Select Case (nMedia)
    Case MEDIA_TV, MEDIA_RADIO
        HandleBroadcastMedia nMedia
    Case MEDIA_PRINT, MEDIA_WEB
        HandlePrintMedia nMedia
    Case Else
        HandleSimpleMedia nMedia
End Select
```

Incorrect use of indentation can jade the reader's view of the code. The human eye naturally tends toward properly aligned objects. Since the left edge of a block of code is more in alignment than the right edge, the eye will move toward the left edge, and it will visually group basic units of logic by their indentation level. If you incorrectly indent your logic, you disarm the natural inclination of the eye.

```
If Len(sTest) = 0 And bConductTest = True Then Exit Sub
    sResult = DoSomeWork(sTest)
    txtShowResult.Text = sResult
    If (sResult = "ABC") Then
    lblAlphabet.Visible = True
    lblNumber.Visible = False
End If
```

At first glance this code may appear to be properly indented, but it is not. The first If statement contains its own Then clause, and therefore has no subordinate logic lines. Yet it appears that it has several such subsidiary lines. The trailing End If is supposed to be paired with the second If statement. This is how Visual Basic will interpret the code, but someone scanning this block of code, especially if it is part of a large routine that is being scanned quickly, may miss the Then clause and assume that all indented lines will be ignored when the first condition fails.

Visual Basic provides a default indentation level of four spaces when you use the Tab key to indent your code. I highly recommend using this suggested value, although your style may draw you to three or five spaces. Using only one or two spaces for indentation does not provide enough visual depth to define the subordinate relationships within the source code. If several programmers work on the same code, choose the same value for everyone so that indentation remains consistent throughout the application.

We will speak a little more about indentation when discussing line continuation characters later in this chapter.

Capitalization of Identifiers and Literal Strings

Traditionally, routine and variable names in Visual Basic are written in a mixed-case style, while constants are all upper case with underscores separating the significant words of the identifier. The forms that identifiers take are discussed in full in Chapter 9, *Declaration Standards*.

Use of Blank Lines within Code

Like indentation, blank lines provide no performance gain or loss. They exist only as a measure of readability within the source code, so you can add as many or as few as you wish. (Visual Basic 6.0 imposes a limit of 65,534 lines per module, but if you are bumping up against this limit, you probably need to rethink the division of code among your modules.)

Use blank lines to visually group logical sections of code, or to break up single sections into bite-sized chunks. If you follow the guidelines set out earlier in this chapter about the placement of comments, then it is easy to know where to put your blank lines: put one blank line before each block comment, except those that start a subordinate section. That is, always precede a comment block with a blank line except when the comment is the first line of an indented block. Also, never use a blank line as the last line of an indented block.

When including line labels, place a blank line before the label, but not after the label.

```
    . . .
    MyRoutine = True
    Exit Function

ErrorHandler:
    GeneralError "MyRoutine", Err, Error$
    Resume Next
End Function
```

If your line label appears within a block of code that needs to be visually grouped, it is all right to remove the leading blank line since the indentation of the label will draw attention to it.

Use of Parentheses around Conditions and Expressions

The use or lack of parentheses is the one area of style that can actually change the final executable. Visual Basic, like all procedural languages, specifies a precedence and order of evaluation by which all operations within a single statement are processed. Back in my days as a C programmer, I frequently turned to page 49 in the first edition of Kernighan and Ritchie's book *The C Programming Language*. I still remember the page number because of the frequency of reference. This page spells out the precise ranking and direction of evaluation for each operator identified in the C language. The table comprises half a page, and lists 36 distinct identifiers with their precedence.

Visual Basic has fewer operators than C, but it also has rules for evaluating expressions. (You can read these rules yourself by looking up "precedence" in the on-line help.) Most of the rules are common, such as evaluating multiplication before addition. Yet I do not know all of the rules by heart, just

44   Chapter 3 •   Commenting and Style

as I did not know the rules in C (and hence I memorized instead the page number). This is where the importance of parentheses comes in. The Visual Basic on-line help gives this useful comment under the heading of "Operator Precedence."

> Parentheses can be used to override the order of precedence and force some parts of an expression to be evaluated before others. Operations within parentheses are always performed before those outside. Within parentheses, however, operator precedence is maintained.

Because so few programmers know the order by heart, it is important to use parentheses to explicitly declare to all readers exactly what your intentions are for a statement. I always use sufficient parentheses to make it clear *to me* exactly how Visual Basic will evaluate it. For example,

```
If Not bFail And bTest Then
```

is quite different from

```
If Not (bFail And bTest) Then
```

Parentheses are your friends, the type that stand over your shoulder while you work, constantly asking you in their silent, conscience-bound manner, "Are you sure that expression is correct?" And with friends like these, well, you know the rest.

Use of Line Continuation Characters

Visual Basic 4.0 introduced the concept of line continuation characters. These underscores, when placed at the end of a line of code (or even a comment), allow you to continue a single Visual Basic statement onto multiple source code lines. There are times, especially in some If statements, when it is not reasonable to divide up a statement into multiple logic statements. Yet holding down the right-arrow key to find the correct place to make a modification in a 400-character statement is bothersome. Welcome line continuation!

Although Visual Basic allows you to continue comment lines with underscores, do not be enticed by this practice. It makes it virtually impossible to correctly trace printed source code. Each comment line should start with its own comment character (') or Rem statement (does anyone still use Rem?).

Visual Basic 4.0 allowed up to 10 line continuations per logical statement, which was later increased to 25. However, you should still stay close to the version 4.0 limit. If a statement requires more than 10 line continuations, it is probably not well designed. If you think there is a valid exception to this guideline, then feel free to line-continue away. Keep in mind that the Visual Basic environment does not allow you to add or remove line continuation characters when actively running and debugging your program.

When using line continuation, always indent continued lines under the first line by a single level of indent (that is, four characters). When continuing If, While, and other statements that begin subordinate blocks, indent continued lines by two indent levels (eight characters) so that the first subordinate line is visually distinct from the continued line(s). The following example shows both types of line continuation indentation.

```
If (nFirstBase = BASE_PLAYER) _
        And (nSecondBase = BASE_PLAYER) _
        And (nThirdBase = BASE_PLAYER) _
        And (nHit = HOME_RUN) Then
    ' ----- More excitement for grand slam home runs
    lblGrandSlam.Visible = True
    objTeam(nWhichTeam).Fans.Chear fansTheWaveYes, _
        fansTheMacarenaNo
End If
```

Use of Multi-Statement Lines

Visual Basic uses the colon character (":") as a multiple statement divider, allowing you to place more than one logical statement on a physical line. Use this operator with caution, as it can easily mask problems. It does have one useful stylistic function: it saves vertical space, especially when you perform the same two or three statements over and over again throughout your routine. For example, you may have a routine that performs a lot of error checking on a database recordset. When an error or other appropriate condition occurs, you close the recordset and return to the calling routine. If you do this often, it may be convenient to combine the standard statements in a single line.

```
If bFail Then rsData.Close: bGood = False: Exit Function
```

Automatically Generated Source Code

Microsoft supplies with Visual Basic several "wizards" that generate useful code quickly. Other vendors provide similar tools that generate advanced source code in a fraction of the time it would take to write the code from scratch. Since this generated code does not come from your own hands, it is most likely the case that it retains a different style from the rest of your code. While you could pass through the code and convert it to your own style, it is more efficient to simply declare to the world that the included code is generated and leave it at that. In the Declarations section of the generated module, add a comment such as the following.

```
' ----- NOTICE ----- NOTICE ----- NOTICE ----- NOTICE -----
'       The code in this module was generated by a source
'       code "wizard" tool.  Any changes made to this
'       module may be lost if this module is re-generated
'       at a later date.
' ----- NOTICE ----- NOTICE ----- NOTICE ----- NOTICE -----
```

Summary

Since a picture can say a thousand words, let us look at a routine written in good and bad style. First, the bad, or even the ugly.

```
Function GetString(s1 As String, s2 As String, n)
Dim t1, t2, i, t3 As Long
t1 = 1
If (n > 1) Then
  For i = 1 To n - 1
    t1 = InStr(t1, s1, s2): If t1 = 0 Then Exit Function
    t1 = t1 + Len(s2)
  Next
End If
If t1 > Len(s1) Then Exit Function
t3 = InStr(t1, s1, s2)
If t3 = 0 Then t2 = Len(s1) Else t2 = t3 - 1
GetString = Mid(s1, t1, t2 - t1 + 1)
End Function
```

The only nice thing I can say about this routine is that it works, but how? It has at least the following stylistic and logic problems:

- Three of the four local variables (t1, t2, and i), and one of the arguments (n), use the default data type (possibly Variant).
- Identifiers are meaningless. Even the function name gives little hint as to the purpose of the routine.
- No return type for the function is defined.
- There are no comments to make the logic of the code clear.
- Indentation makes all of the code seem to run together.
- Blank lines are eliminated, removing any hint of logic grouping.
- Assumptions are made about default values of variables.

Compare that late-night monologue with the following cleaned-up code.

```
Public Function GetSubString(sOrigString As String, _
       sDelim As String, nWhichField As Integer) As String
    ' ----- This function extracts a sub-string from a
    '         larger delimited string, using sDelim as the
    '         delimeter.  For example:
    '             GetSubString("A;B;C", ";", 2)
    '         returns "B", the second semicolon-
    '         separated string.
    Dim lStartPos As Long
    Dim lEndPos As Long
    Dim lCounter As Long
    Dim lTempPos As Long

    ' ----- Handle some boundary conditions
```

```
GetSubString = ""
If (nWhichField <= 0) Then Exit Function
If (Len(sOrigString) = 0) Then Exit Function

' ----- Get the starting position of the field we care
'       about.  Skip over (nWhichField - 1) delimeters
'       to find the right field.
lStartPos = 1
For lCounter = 1 To (nWhichField - 1)
    ' ----- Find the start of the next field
    lStartPos = InStr(lStartPos, sOrigString, sDelim)
    If (lStartPos = 0) Then Exit Function
    lStartPos = lStartPos + Len(sDelim)
Next lCounter

' ----- If we went past all of the fields, then return
'       an empty string
If (lStartPos > Len(sOrigString)) Then Exit Function

' ----- Get the ending position of the field
lTempPos = InStr(lStartPos, sOrigString, sDelim)
If (lTempPos = 0) Then
    lEndPos = Len(sOrigString)
Else
    lEndPos = lTempPos - 1
End If

' ----- Now extract and return the field
GetSubString = Mid$(sOrigString, lStartPos, _
    lEndPos - lStartPos + 1)
End Function
```

While this function may seem more wordy and less efficient at first glance, it is more professional. Also, I would have a much better chance at finding a bug in the latter version than in the former.

Style is a difficult animal to tame. When computers first came onto the scene, a chapter on style would have been out of place, since the ability to add character to source code was next to impossible. Today, good style is not only useful, it differentiates the amateur programmer from the professional.

User Interface Consistency

The topic of user interface consistency and organization, in contrast to the other topics covered in this book, is actually quite popular. Entire books are written about it, including a few volumes from Microsoft. It is the one area of your coding style where your users and customers will actually have something significant to say as well. And why not? Most users will never look at your source code, but they will have to stare at your application's user interface all the time.

This is not to say that you can ignore all other aspects of the application besides the user interface. While a good user interface is important, it is the logic and internal structure of your application that makes an application capable of "interfacing" with a user. If the TextBox control did not have any code behind it to display characters in response to the user typing on the keyboard, it would just be a rectangle on the screen. Still, to the user, the visual interface *is the application*. Therefore, it is essential that it be high in both quality and consistency.

This chapter provides a high-level overview of user interface topics. For a more detailed discussion on individual elements of the user interface, read Chapter 11, *Control and User Interface Standards*.

What Is User Interface Consistency?

User interface consistency is accomplished by meeting the expectations of the end user in the usability of the application. Most Visual Basic applications are created to allow the user to manipulate data (often from a database) in one manner or another. If the program makes it possible to manipulate the data in a way that seems clear and natural to the typical user, then it is consistent in its user interface.

The user interface does not consist only of forms and controls. In fact, there are three primary forms of user interfaces found in Visual Basic applications.

- **Visual interface.** The Visual interface is what is usually referred to as the user interface. This interface consists of forms, controls, Web pages, printouts, and any other form of communication between the application and the user, whether visible or audible.
- **Data interface.** The Data interface is used when opening or saving user data files, or when the application is in communication with a database system. The user cannot directly see this interface, although it can often be inferred through the presence of data files on a floppy disk, hard disk, or network server.
- **Technical interface.** Some interfaces are essential to your application, although they are rarely, if ever, noticed by the user. The Technical interface includes the use of configuration files and registry settings, and the ability of an application to be extended through the use of "add ins" (as can be done with Visual Basic itself).

Without these interfaces, an application could not successfully communicate with the user, and would be of no value. But the presence of these interfaces alone does not make an application's user interface consistent. If you start a new Visual Basic project, and drop a text box and command button on Form1, you have a working application with a user interface. But such an interface is insufficient to solve your user's complex business problems.

The user interface, the placement and order of forms and controls, and the ease of use of the application all indicate the type of organization found within the program. True user interface consistency exists in three realms: the realm of the user, the realm of the application itself, and realm of the system, where other software applications exist.

Consistency with the User

Often, the Visual Basic programmer will write an application either to replace an existing legacy application, or to automate a process presently done only on paper. Because of this, the users are already familiar with the process of carrying out the work to be done. The only thing they lack is a quality tool to assist them in that work. Is that not why you were called in the first place? Because your users may already be familiar with the goals of the application, it is your job to develop an application that clearly and consistently meets those goals. This is done by applying consistency and organization to the application.

When your program is complete, a user well trained in whatever business area to which your program applies should be able to sit right down and, without too much assistance, start using your application to solve problems. When the task that your application performs is complex, the amount of training will need to be increased. But even with an increased need for training, the user should be able to say, "Oh, that's obvious" throughout your application. A consistent user interface is the medium through which this understanding proceeds.

Consistency within the Application

When an application possesses consistency in presentation and internal organization, users can move from one part of the application to another and feel that they are using an application where all the parts were designed in the same way. This is not too difficult when a program is built by a single person, although projects that take one person more than six months to develop can show signs of an evolving understanding of the user interface. Adherence to consistency is especially important in applications developed by multiple programmers. Each programmer may think he or she has a better way of presenting information to the user than the other programmers do, but it will be only the user who suffers when a lack of understanding arises due to inconsistent organization.

Consistency with Other Applications

User interface consistency within an application also expands to include similarities with other applications familiar to the user. When you plan for this level of consistency within the application from the beginning, the user gets a head start on the usage of the program by approaching it with some understanding of how "those Windows programs" work. For example, many applications include a toolbar with standard menus and buttons for cut, copy, and paste operations, as shown in Figure 4–1.

| Figure 4–1 | *Typical Edit menu and matching toolbar buttons.* |

If your application supports these features, you should be consistent with other applications in the wording and position of the menus, and in the images used in the toolbar. Meeting your users' expectations though this brand of user interface consistency increases their understanding of the new solutions wrought by your hand.

Why Maintain User Interface Consistency?

It is all about the user. In most cases, you will never have to use the program that you are thrusting on others, except to diagnose and resolve application errors. Your users, on the other hand, will use your program regularly. They depend on you to provide a system that is consistent from the initial Start menu click to the final File Exit maneuver. Your users' needs will be vast. By providing a consistent user interface, you fulfill the expectations of the user in many areas, including the following.

Accomplishment of a Task

If the user did not need some task improved, simplified, or solved, you would not have been called in the first place. The user interface of an application must permit the user to accomplish the task for which the application was originally designed. If the application you write is rather complex, many different users may be able to accomplish a variety of tasks with a single application user interface. This is often the case when an "enterprise-wide" system is written in Visual Basic. An enterprise-wide system is one that is designed to meet most or all of the unique business needs of an organization or organizational subset. While such a system may consist of multiple (even dozens) individual Visual Basic applications, it is still considered a single user interface.

To be consistent, your user interface must allow the users to accomplish a task in a manner that they would expect the task to be done. Providing a solution that is incomprehensible to the user is the same as providing no solution at all. This is why it is so essential to involve the user in the planning of your application (as is discussed in Chapter 7, *Planning*). Just because *you* can perform some task through your application does not mean that you have provided a consistent interface. You can design entire Web sites using only Notepad, but this tool would fall short of the expectation of most users interested in building Web pages of their own.

Access to Information

All applications manage, accept, and present information, whether that information is of a business significance (such as an enterprise-wide database application) or personal (such as a game). The type of information and the method by which the information is managed is important to you as the programmer. The ability to access that same information in a reasonable manner is important to the user and, therefore, to you as well. Any unreasonable burden in accessing the user's data information must be removed. Yet what may be a burden in one system will seem insignificant to another user. One system may require that a customer's record appear on the screen within one second of entering the customer's phone number. Another system may consider speed to be less important as long as certain records are restricted by adequate security constraints. All of these aspects are part of the user's need for user interface consistency.

Increase in Productivity

Business activities went on quite well before the introduction of computers into the workplace. If a manual system is efficient, accurate, and simple, then there is little incentive to migrate the activity to an automated computer system. However, many aspects of daily business life, and personal life as well, can be performed with more efficiency on a computer. Often software applications are designed with the express purpose of increasing user productivity.

Your users expect and deserve highly efficient, straightforward, and productive software applications. If you provide a Visual Basic program that increases the user's time in performing a task, then you have not met one of the user's most basic needs. The adage "Time is money" is a reality in the workplace. Supplying a customer with a cumbersome application that decreases productivity is the same as stealing the customer's money.

There are some minor exceptions to this consideration, times when a user may be willing to give up performance in exchange for other benefits. For example, it may take additional time to perform an automated transaction via software that performs high-quality encryption and decryption. But if the user's number-one priority is the secrecy and security of the data during the transaction, then speed may be a secondary concern.

Increase in Accuracy

"To err is human; to really mess things up requires a computer." We laugh at such a statement, but it was surely written by someone who had just been the victim of an errant software application. People do make mistakes, even in fully manual systems. While they will continue to make those mistakes when presented with a piece of software, they may be unaware of how their missteps can be multiplied through improper processing on the part of the application. One small user error can truly lead to multiple data failures that "really mess things up."

A consistent user interface includes features that increase user accuracy. Such features intercept invalid data entry supplied by the user. These features also prevent isolated application errors from infecting other parts of the system or data.

Integration with Existing Workflow

Whether you are developing a small departmental software application, or a program that manages all data for a company, the user expects that your software will conform to existing policies and procedures. Granted, some procedures may be modified to take advantage of new productivity gains now available through the use of the application. However, care must be taken in the development of the program to make the transition to your new system comfortable. Duplicating existing workflow activities, using industry terminology, and providing familiar visual images and cues to the user helps meet the complex needs of your customer.

How to Maintain User Interface Consistency

This section lists some of the more important aspects of user interface consistency. Some Visual Basic applications may require specialized user interface components that are "non-standard" because of the needs of the users. Yet even in these instances, consistency can and should exist. This section is divided into the three realms listed in the "What Is" section of this chapter: the user, the application, and other applications.

Consistency with the User

Every application must be consistent with the needs of the user. If you need to write a quick emergency program within an hour, other considerations such as consistency with other software applications will be pushed to the back in deference to meeting the immediate needs of the user. In all non-emergency cases, consistency with the user is the first among the three coequal realms.

SINGLE WINDOW FOCUS

The user's primary access to the components of your application starts from a single window. This window may be an MDI (multi-document interface) window as with the default view in the Visual Basic Integrated Development Environment (Figure 4–2), or an SDI (single-document interface) window as with the Windows Notepad application (Figure 4–3). Even back in the days of Visual Basic 3, despite having code, form, property, project, and other windows all over the screen, the development environment had the menu bar as the primary starting point.

This primary window, called the "main" window, represents the application to the user, even if most of the work in the application is performed in a subsidiary form. In an MDI application, the user cannot help but notice the main window, since all aspects of the application (except possibly some toolbars) appear within its confines. Yet even in an SDI application, it should be obvious which form is the starting point for all activities within the program. The main form is a place to which the user can return when nothing else seems to be going right in the application (even if the problems represent user error), a starting point for retrieving and supplying data. The main form

Figure 4-2   *An MDI application (Visual Basic).*

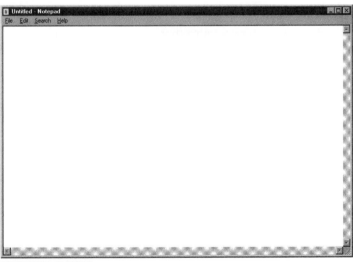

Figure 4-3   *An SDI application (Notepad).*

always has a method for obtaining on-line help, if available. Even if the main form is not currently accessible (perhaps because one or more modal forms are active), the user knows that if he just clicks all of the Cancel buttons, suddenly the main form will appear. Think of the main form as a type of security blanket.

MAKE STANDARD FEATURES OBVIOUS

Never hide important information behind secret keystrokes. All essential features within an application must be accessible through visible means, either through menu selection, through a button, or through some other clear visible interface. Having a keystroke combination, such as Shift+F1, as the only means for obtaining or entering some information is a practice to be avoided at all costs. Not only does it require that existing users remember meaningless technical information above and beyond their productivity requirements, it also forces new users to learn the equivalent of secret handshakes to use your application.

In the same way, do not use drag-and-drop as the primary means of acting on data within your application. (There are exceptions to this rule, such as drawing programs.) It may be the best way of transferring information between your application and another application, and it may be the method of choice within the application itself, but it should never be the primary method. Like hidden key combinations, it requires users to guess at the correct method of using your application to finish their work. I once inherited an application with a form that looked similar to the form in Figure 4–4.

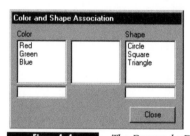

Figure 4–4   *The Bermuda Dialog: Still a Mystery.*

Three list boxes, two text boxes (below the Color and Shape lists), and one button. I knew how to use the Close button, but I had no idea what the rest of the form was for. The users infrequently accessed this form, so they had forgotten how to use it. In addition to this, there was no documentation on how to use the form, and I will give you three guesses about the quality and clarity of the source code. I asked one of the original programmers about it (fortunately he was still around), and he let me in on the secret. It seems that you are supposed to pick an item in the first list (the Color list), then drag shapes between the other two lists. When a shape is in the middle list, it is associated with the selected color. When the shape is in the rightmost list, it is not associated with the selected color. You can add new colors and shapes to the lists by typing a color or shape name in the appropriate text box, then pressing the Enter key.

In addition to its lack of adequate documentation, this form suffers from four main problems.

- It hides functionality by making it unclear how to associate a color with a shape.
- It uses a non-standard method to enter new colors and shapes into the lists.
- It provides no method to cancel a change once it has been performed.
- There is no method for removing unused colors and shapes.

There are many ways to fix a form like this, and it must be fixed, or more correctly, replaced. In this case, I rewrote this form to look like Figure 4–5.

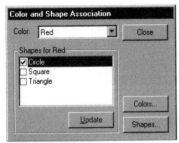

Figure 4–5 *The Bermuda Dialog: Mystery Solved.*

This version simplifies the association process between colors and shapes. You can make changes to the shape associations for a color, but they are not saved until you click the Update button. (If you attempt to close without updating changes, you are warned first.) The addition and removal of colors and shapes is moved to other forms, indicated by the Colors... and Shapes... buttons. Although some training may be needed for entry-level users to employ this form, it should be obvious to more Windows-savvy users since it possesses functionality similar to that found in other applications' forms.

PROGRESSIVELY DISPLAY INFORMATION

Unless a user absolutely demands it, do not place too many visible controls on a single form. How many is too many? That is hard to say. I have never counted a specific number that is on the border between too many and just right. But if you have a form that is beyond the old VGA 640 by 480, and you are running out of space on your form, you may need to think about reorganizing. Using the Visual Basic supplied "tab" control is a simple way to leave all of the controls on the same form, but still give the form a less cluttered look. You may also wish to move less important and more optional pieces of information to subsidiary forms.

Both methods have a common goal, that of progressively displaying information to the user. At first, only display those fields that are most important to the user, either for presenting or for gathering information. If the user needs more, he or she can click on a tab or a button to access the additional data fields. In either case, full information is only a click away. The new Color and Shape Association form in the previous item is an example of this divide-and-conquer methodology. The primary purpose of the form is to associate colors and shapes. A secondary purpose of the form is to manage the lists of available colors and shapes. Since this was not the primary use of the form, this feature was moved onto subsidiary forms accessed through the Colors... and Shapes... buttons.

LOGICALLY GROUP INFORMATION

Information that belongs together logically should be displayed together physically on a form. Whether such controls are grouped together in a frame control or not is dependent on the use of the information. Personally, I tend to stay away from the frame control, and when I do use it, I limit myself to only one per dialog. Still, the needs of the application may require more concrete groupings among data controls, especially on complex forms. Above all, the user should be able to see from the organization of a form that the presentation or gathering of information flows naturally through the organization of the controls.

ASSUME BAD DATA

Always assume that your user's data is bad. From the first release of your application, you can be assured that your users will enter all types of invalid data into all fields on your forms. Fortunately, most controls limit the damage that can be done, such as the ListBox control, which allows a user to select only an item currently in the list. However, other controls, especially TextBox controls, open up a whole new world for your users to attack your application. Therefore, be sure to add sufficient data checking code to your forms. If you have any routine where raw data entered by the user will be passed (directly or indirectly) to that routine, check the incoming data.

Most programmers writing more than a "quick fix" application make some attempt to validate the data entered by the user. There are two places where data validation can occur: when the user enters the data (Data Entry Validation), and when you use the data (Data Usage Validation).

Data entry validation occurs within the KeyPress, Change, LostFocus, DragDrop, and other similar events that are triggered by the user actively working with the control. Although such validation is useful for guiding the user toward correct data entry, you cannot depend on these events to correctly validate your information. For example, consider the following code, tied to a TextBox field.

```
Private Sub txtNumber_KeyPress(KeyAscii As Integer)
    ' ----- Limit the input to numbers and backspaces
    If (KeyAscii = vbKeyBack) Then Exit Sub
    If (InStr("0123456789", Chr$(KeyAscii)) = 0) Then
        KeyAscii = 0
    End If
End Sub
```

Generally, such code is useful to weed out all unwanted characters. However, it is quite easy for the troublesome user to enter non-digits within this field. If you cannot quite picture such a scenario, take a look at Figure 4–6 (the Shortcut menu of a TextBox control).

Figure 4–6   *Pasting to a TextBox control.*

What is in that clipboard buffer, anyway? Could it be letters? "Of course, the KeyPress event will weed out those nasty letters, won't it?" Actually, it will not weed them out. Try it!

Data entry validation is a good way to remind your users of the type of data they need to enter. Yet it is insufficient for true data validation.

Data usage validation occurs when the user has finished entering the data and it is ready to be used, saved, or manipulated by the application. Often, this occurs when the user clicks the OK button on a data entry form. When data usage validation occurs, all data fields are checked for correctness and completeness. Because the validation is delayed until all data entry is complete, invalid relationships between different data fields can also be considered.

Data usage validation is usually preferred over data entry validation. However, there are applications where data usage validation is neither practical nor possible. In these cases, the programmer must make do with data entry validation. If you are limited in this way, be very cautious about the quality of data entered by the user, as one wrong keystroke can wreak havoc on the underlying data.

CHOOSE CLARITY OVER EFFICIENCY

If you have to make a choice between clarity and efficiency in the user interface, always side with a clear presentation. However, it is possible to clearly document an efficient (but unclear) form in a way that is easier to understand than the equivalent inefficient (but clear) form. If you need to present a form that is inherently difficult to understand, minimize the confusion by sufficiently documenting the purpose and methodology employed in the form. Yet such situations should almost never arise. If you find that you are often compensating for confusing user interface elements, break up the complexity into more manageable pieces. Divide complex forms into tabbed sections, or even multiple forms, to enhance user understanding.

Consistency within the Application

When constructing a physical building, consistency in design and construction ensures a stable and usable edifice. While the decorations of each room within the building may differ, the manner in which the rooms are created remains constant throughout. The same is true when designing and constructing a software application. Consistency, internal and external, under the canopy of the user interface, presents the user with a stable constant from form to form.

AVOID SENDKEYS

Never use SendKeys to perform the internal actions of your application. Back in the early days of Visual Basic (before version 4), it was difficult to get multiple forms to interact. The introduction of form-based public functions solved all that, but a lot of Visual Basic code still remains that employs various methods to account for the lack of public functions. One method used to make two forms interact was to use the SendKeys keyword from one form to perform actions on another form.

In one application I worked on, the original programmer had placed visible command buttons on various forms, but positioned them so that the buttons could not be seen or accessed by the user. At first I was puzzled at the use of these buttons. Then I found references in other forms that used these buttons, such as the following section of code.

```
frmFriend.lblKeyValue = lKeyValue
frmFriend.Show
frmFriend.cmdRefresh.SetFocus
SendKeys "%R"
```

In this example, you need to imagine that the form frmFriend was already visible as a modeless or parent form before this code executed. The frmFriend form had a button with the text "Refresh," so that an Alt+R key combination would perform a click event on the button. The code above allowed another form to simulate a click on this button, which would perform some important work based on the value of the label lblKeyValue. It was an ingenious method at the time. But now such code is obsolete; the frmFriend code should now provide a public function with a syntax such as the following:

```
Public Sub RefreshFromKey (lKeyValue As Long)
```

SendKeys is useful, but there is no guarantee of the timing in which the keystrokes will be processed. If you send a long string of keys to another form (or even to the form with the SendKeys statement), and several of these keys cause Visual Basic events to fire, you will not be able to control whether the keys sent after the event-causing key will occur before or after the event occurs. Thus, the programmer no longer has control over that section of the application, and runs the risk of introducing errors into the application or its data.

The SendKeys statement should only be used to send keyboard commands to other applications. Within a Visual Basic application, all SendKeys statements should be replaced with the appropriate public functions or similar procedures.

NEVER DEPEND ON TRANSITION EVENTS

The transition events within Visual Basic include GotFocus, LostFocus, Mouse-Move, Activate, and Deactivate. While these events are useful for providing features in your application based on user actions, they all lack the guarantee of timely execution. This is especially true for the GotFocus and LostFocus events. Consider the simple form pictured in Figure 4–7.

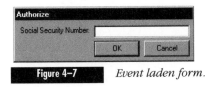

Figure 4–7   *Event laden form.*

Consider the following code fragments associated with this form.

```
Private Sub txtSSN_LostFocus ()
    ' ----- Format the SSN nicely
    txtSSN.Text = Format$(txtSSN.Text, "###-##-####")
End Sub

Private Sub cmdOK_Click ()
    ' ----- Check for a good number
    If (Len(txtSSN.Text) <> 11) Then
        MsgBox "Enter a valid social security number.", _
            vbOKOnly + vbExclamation, "Authorize"
        Exit Sub
    End If
```

```
      ' ----- Save the data
      ...
End Sub
```

Of course, the code as it is written is not sufficient to correctly test for a valid social security number. However, if the user typed in a nine-digit number (without hyphens), and clicked the OK button with the mouse, the user would receive the "Enter a valid social security number" message most of the time, *but not every time*. The problem with this code is that Visual Basic will not ensure that the LostFocus event will fire before the Click event, or even that they will occur in the reverse order. To improve your chances, insert a DoEvents statement as the first line in the cmdOK_Click event.

Transition events should never be used for major processing activities. Only use such events for simple data formatting tasks, or when a piece of user data must be immediately verified, long before the OK button is clicked. If you use transition events for major data processing, you will lose control over the order in which important data processing steps occur. This can lead to user confusion, and data corruption.

AVOID MODELESS FORMS

I once maintained an application that had over 100 forms, most of which were available as modeless forms from the menus on the main form. Although you could return to the main form from any other modeless form by using the Alt+M key sequence (a documented standard within the application), there was no requirement that any form be closed, even when a form modified data that depended on data in another form being unchanged. Needless to say, most of the users quickly became confused after bringing up and not closing four or five modeless forms. Most users were entry-level employees with little previous technical training. The ability to use unlimited modeless forms presented them with information overload, reducing their effectiveness within the application.

Modeless forms are great, especially for toolbars, property pages, or any other data that is dependent on another main form. They are also the form of choice for MDI applications, where each child of the MDI parent is a modeless form. Yet the overuse of modeless forms can quickly lead to interface confusion. There is such a thing as "too much of a good thing," even when it is your great user interface. When possible, use modal forms when you cannot justify the need for a form to be modeless.

I must warn you that this advice differs slightly from the suggestions found in the *Microsoft Windows User Experience* book. On page 209, it is stated, "Because modal secondary windows restrict the user's choice, limit their use...." However, in that book, Microsoft differentiates between "primary" and "secondary" forms, where secondary forms are additional forms for presenting, gathering, and using additional information in conjunction with the primary data collection and presentation form. The example they give is a Find dialog that allows the user to switch back and forth between the main form (such as a word processing page) and the Find form. In this case, the Find form is a "secondary" form that assists the primary form. Toolbars and property pages also fall into this "secondary" category.

When I recommend the avoidance of modeless form, I refer to modeless "primary" forms, forms that represent the primary path within an application to gather and present information. Where possible, the user should not be presented with alternate, simultaneous methods of entering primary information. If you are developing a Visual Basic MDI application, each document (MDI child) represents a unique primary window that has its own primary path through the application. In a way, each document represents a different application. Still, within such an application, primary modeless windows should be used with great restraint, as the user may confuse the association between a secondary window and a primary document window.

LOOK ALIKE, WORK ALIKE

When designing the forms and interfaces for your application, use features in a way that breeds familiarity in the user. The base Pavlovian response to look-alike forms and controls can help a user through new application territory.

NEVER HARD-CODE LOCATIONS

Never hard-code the locations of external resources. All database references (whether from ODBC, ADO, OLE DB, or some other technology), all configuration files, all data files, and all on-line help files should have their locations identified outside of the application, instead of within the source code. The system registry or an application configuration file (an INI file) is a great place to store these locations, which can (and will!) change based on the whim of the user. Storing the location information for these resources also makes it easier to quickly switch back and forth between a production and test version of the application's data.

MAKE FILE FORMATS CONVENIENT

If you are writing an application that will store its information in a proprietary, secret file format, and it needs to be that way for security purposes, then feel free to skip to the next item. However, most applications do not need such a high level of secrecy. In the standard case, the layout of any data or configuration files used by your application should be relatively easy to navigate by a technical person. Specifically, if another programmer needs to trace down a problem that relates to the way your application references its data files, and you are not around to help, you need to make it somewhat easy for the technician to diagnose the problem. Personally, I suggest that all data of a non-binary nature be stored in INI-style data files.

While INI files are not as speedy as direct file access calls, and even though they have been given a bad rap since the invention of the system registry, they are actually a very useful data tool for Visual Basic applications. Even though Microsoft laid down the law in stating that all applications should begin to use the system registry instead of INI files for configuration information, it continues to use INI-like files for data storage purposes in its own applications. If you have used Microsoft Visual SourceSafe to store versioned copies of your application source code, you may have noticed the SCC files it creates in your source code directory. These files are nothing more than INI files with an SCC extension. The amount of data stored in these files is quite small, so the INI format is the perfect medium for information storage and retrieval.

If your data files will be quite large (more than, say, 100K), you may want to consider a specialized file format, even if it is still text-based. Of course, applications that manipulate common or proprietary graphic formats will have no choice but to use a binary format for persistent storage. Whatever method you choose, be sure to create a consistent and well-thought-out format. If you have customers like I have had, you will be back to write a program that has different functionality, but uses the same files as the original program you wrote for that customer. Then you will be thankful that your file format is easy to use.

There is one thing that you should be aware of when using INI files, which is especially true for INI files found in the Windows directory. Some versions of Microsoft Windows cache the configuration information found in these files. If you access an INI file from your application using either GetPrivateProfileString or GetPrivateProfileInt, modify the INI file externally (using Notepad), and then run the application again, you may notice that your INI file changes have no impact on your application. In order to clear the cache that Windows keeps in memory, you need to issue the API statement WritePrivateProfileString with special arguments.

```
Call WritePrivateProfileString(0&, 0&, 0&, "myapp.ini")
```

This statement will clear the active INI cache found in memory for that file. If you use INI-style files in your application, include this statement in the Sub Main routine of your program.

If the data supplied by your application will be used with other applications, especially if those applications exist on non-Windows platforms, XML (Extensible Markup Language) is an excellent data medium. The self-describing nature of XML makes it quite useful for sharing data between multiple applications, especially if those applications were not originally designed to communicate with each other. When using XML data files, document all expectations about the structure of the files used or generated by your application.

Consistency with Other Applications

It is possible for a program to be a failure even if it looks and works like other popular applications. However, a programmer who takes the time to make a program consistent with other applications generally puts equal effort into all three user interface consistency realms.

CONSIDER THE OFFICIAL USER INTERFACE GUIDELINES

When Microsoft released Windows 95, it also published a handy reference guide for user interface development, *The Windows Interface Guidelines for Software Design*. This useful volume tells you everything you would ever want to know (and more) about Windows application user interface design. It goes into great detail about the use of the common controls that were available when the book was published, how to use them, how large to make them, how close to place them to other controls, where and when to use them in windows, what to call them in your documentation, how to discuss them with your users, and on and on and on. As a reference book, it is not designed as a relaxing Sunday afternoon day-in-the-park novel. However, it is an excellent and very visual work on consistent user interface design.

Just before the release of Windows 2000, Microsoft released an updated version of this book, renamed *Microsoft Windows User Experience*. This volume includes discussions of new features and modified standards created since the release of Windows 95. Along with this new book comes a useful Internet resource on Microsoft's Web site, located at msdn.microsoft.com/ui/. This site contains helpful articles, examples, and resources to assist you in achieving a clean and consistent application interface.

LEARN FROM OTHER PROGRAMS

Learn from the user interfaces of popular off-the-shelf applications. In addition to Microsoft, there are scores of large software companies that sell millions of popular software titles. Since these companies desire to have more customers purchase their wares, and also to have existing customers upgrade to newer versions, they spend a lot of money on user testing of software. In exchange for free software, ordinary people are asked to try out a new piece of software, and then give their honest opinion about it.

Even if you do not have the money to spend on such research, you can take advantage of the efforts of these companies. Their applications bear the changes noted by such user testing. By examining their products and looking at how those products communicate data and information to the user, you should be able to determine the best way to present that information yourself.

Many software products already have a common look and feel. Because of the design of the Windows operating system, most application windows have a standard title bar and resizable borders. More and more applications have toolbars just below the menu bar, and sometimes a status bar with recessed cells along the bottom of the main window. If it is important that your users have one-click access to frequently used features, consider a toolbar that looks like the toolbars found in popular applications. Place terse but useful status information in a status bar along the bottom edge of your main window, as is done in WordPad (Figure 4–8).

Figure 4–8   *WordPad status bar.*

Use key combinations and data gathering techniques found in applications with which your users will already be familiar. Perhaps you are designing an ActiveX control for your main application that looks like a standard drop-down combo box (Style property set to 0), but that allows the user to enter a city name. When you click the down button to the right of the control, it displays a map of the region in a drop-down window, and the user can click on the city to store the name of the city in the text portion of the control. (Pretty neat!) Ordinary combo boxes and the date picker control both use the Alt+Down key combination to access the drop-down portion of the control. You should also implement this keyboard feature in your control. This addition will increase familiarity with your control, even before your users have seen your application.

PLACE CONTROLS IN FAMILIAR PLACES

When you place your controls on a form, arrange them in ways that are familiar to your users. For example, when placing the OK and Cancel buttons on a dialog form, place them either in the upper-right corner of the dialog with the OK button above the Cancel button, or along the bottom edge of your dialog with the OK button to the left of the Cancel button. Never place the Cancel button to the left of the OK button, since most programs have the OK button on the left, as shown in Figure 4–9. You will only frustrate users who are used to clicking the rightmost button when they want to abandon their changes.

Figure 4–9   *Never do this!*

On a side note, you should never use both a Close and a Cancel button on a single form. Their usage will be quickly confused. In general, you should use Cancel when the user has a chance to abandon any unsaved changes.

This button usually appears with a related OK button. A Close button should also abandon any unsaved changes, but it should be used when there is only a single button to dismiss the form (instead of the two-button OK/Cancel variation). If your form allows you to save information without dismissing the form, and it sports a Cancel button, the caption of this button should be changed to Close after the first set of data is saved.

INCLUDE ON-LINE HELP

Always integrate on-line help into your application. The user should be able to press the F1 key from any form in your application and view the on-line help for the application, preferably at the page that discusses the active form. (The exception to this is the Main form, which may display the Contents page when F1 is pressed.) If you are working on a small application, and your customer does not feel that there is a need for on-line help, then go with the wishes of your customer. However, medium and large projects should always include some form of on-line documentation.

USE STANDARD COLORS

I do not understand why some programmers insist on mixing purple, orange, hot pink, and olive green all on the same form. Perhaps it is genetic, but I rather think it stems from a desire to wow the user. If you are lured by this temptation, resist! Most users will not share such a sense of artistry. Instead, they will be distracted from using the application to its fullest potential.

Summary

Be consistent. This is the most important suggestion for user interface organization, and hence its meaning is included in the chapter title. When your user moves from one part of your application to another, or between your application and other applications he or she may use, the user needs to feel comfortable with the usability of your program. If you are inconsistent in the way that you present and gather information in various parts of your application, the user may be inconsistent in the quality of data entered into the system.

Documentation

Apart from the application itself, the documentation you supply with an application is the most visible portion of the program. Therefore, it is vital that the documentation be as professional as the software. This chapter discusses the various forms of documentation that are an integral part of any quality Visual Basic project.

What Is Documentation?

Documentation is the human-language version of your application's source code and user interface. Such documentation comes in various forms, each of which is intended for a unique audience. All these forms of software documentation share a common goal: to make the reader familiar with the application.

There are two primary types of documentation, *internal* documentation and *external* documentation. Internal documentation includes those reference materials that are written for those who will have access to the application source code or design components, such as a database designer. These writings assume a certain level of technical knowledge and expertise on the part of the reader. If the reader is interested in the source code of your application, the internal documentation should blend very well with the comments found within the application code.

External documentation puts the focus on the user. Users come in various levels of expertise, from the computer novice to the knowledgeable system administrator. These writings provide all users with the information needed to correctly and efficiently use your application at each user's proper level.

Both types of documentation share common attributes that define works of quality. Professional documentation should consist of at least these attributes, which I like to call "the Seven Cs."

- **Clear.** Each document needs to be clear to the intended audience. While a technical discussion of an application's internal design may have little impact on the end user, it should speak volumes to a maintenance programmer who will make modifications to your source code. Each document needs to be worded and arranged in a manner that gives a clear understanding of the topic to the reader.
- **Concise.** Einstein once said, "Everything should be as simple as possible—but not simpler." Documentation should be neither too wordy nor too terse. Although determining the correct amount of information to place in each form of documentation is sometimes a difficult task, it is necessary. And your readers will thank you for your effort.
- **Complete.** Perhaps the most important attribute of application documentation, the need to provide complete information to the reader about an application is, unfortunately, an often overlooked component of technical writing. Although your application may be free of problems, if your users are unable to use the program because of incomplete documentation, they will surely report problem after problem.
- **Correct.** Documentation is useless if it does not reflect the true nature of your application. Professional documentation is always up to date, or is supplied with an addendum.
- **Crafted.** Professional documentation is never an afterthought of an application. Rather, it is designed into the application from the very start. Technical documentation naturally flows from the design and implementation process. End-user documentation, although usually written during the later stages of program development, has its roots in the original user considerations that made the application necessary in the first place.
- **Convenient.** The information contained within the internal and external documentation should always be accessible to the user when it is most needed. While the programmer does not need to be concerned about where the user misplaced his or her User's Guide, there should always be adequate documentation available from the computer itself. Well-designed indices and tables, such as a table of contents, should be placed within all significant writings.
- **Complementary.** The documentation supplied with your application should complement the application itself. When modifications are made that alter the original use of one or more components of your Visual Basic application, the documentation needs to be changed to reflect these updates.

Why Document?

I recently purchased a small cabinet for my kitchen that required full assembly. Although all of the pieces and parts were accounted for, the instructions were quite difficult to follow. The manufacturer, in an effort to make the cabinet available in as many countries and cultures as possible, left the instructions completely free of words. There were plenty of pictures, and I was able to complete the project with the supplied directions, but the task would have proceeded more smoothly (and without having to redo a few steps) if the documentation had been better. In this chapter on documentation, the correct question then is not "Why Document?" but "Why Provide Quality Documentation?"

I did a quick unscientific survey of my friends who are programmers, and it seems that documenting—actually, writing in any form whatsoever—is a painful task. The only thing that seemed to have more ill will attached to it was debugging. It is my conviction that the animosity tied to both of these stems from the same source: the belief that *my* application is complete and correct all by itself. Debugging is a tedious task, and I am always a little frustrated when a portion of my program fails to work as planned. How much greater is my apprehension level when a *user* finds the problem. "What do you mean there is something wrong with the program? Are you sure you clicked the right thing? Well, I told you not to click the OK button until you filled in that field."

The avoidance of documentation may also come from that same defensive posture. Those who have made computer programming their career choice need the sense of fulfillment that comes from a job well done, even if the job is not, in truth, well done. "The program, *my* program, is so easy to use that it doesn't require a User's Guide." "If you really knew how to program, you would be able to understand my source code without any technical crutches."

While there may be twangs of dislike when it comes to written documentation, the professional Visual Basic programmer knows that such writings are simply an extension of the Visual Basic application. Documentation is necessary to any quality application. Even the simplest, smallest application, if it is to be used for more than one day, needs to have documentation, even if that is only a few sentences typed into Notepad, or displayed in a MsgBox dialog.

Documentation really has two purposes: support for the technical staff, and support for the users of the application.

Technical Support

That is, confirmation and support of the application for the technical staff, including the primary programmer. This purpose is especially true of internal documentation. Documentation is a copy of the components of your application, but expressed in another language. Like any language translation task, the desire to provide an accurate translation of the original is paramount. The documentation, therefore, is a duplicate copy of your source code's intent, albeit in a form that cannot be compiled. When there is doubt or disagreement about the correct implementation or usage of a portion of the application, the documentation is a second source of confirmation as to the correct operation of the program, from either the technical side or the user side.

Technical support also comes in the form of a permanent memory. Like source code comments, documentation provides a form of written memory that maintains an accurate history of the purpose of an application for those times when human memory fails. For this reason, every effort needs to be made to keep documentation in the most up-to-date form possible.

User Support

The external portion of your documentation will be read primarily by the users. The end user generally does not have the technical skills of the programmer who built the application. In fact, some programs are written for users with no prior computer experience, especially experience with GUI-based systems. If you have no other reason to supply quality documentation, do so for your users, the beneficiaries of your programming savvy.

Users are heartless with applications. I am not sure if it is intentional, or if diet somehow plays a role in it, but users have a secret mean streak that makes them want to destroy every aspect of your program. This is especially true of those who love to use your application; they will be the first to find and report actual problems. Although you cannot force a user to read your documentation, the documentation you provide gives constructive information on the proper use and configuration of the program. Sometimes, indicating the proper page number in a manual will solve the immediate problems of the user.

The complexity (or perceived complexity) of modern operating systems adds to the novice user's frustration level. I have watched a distraught user click a dozen times on an application window, ignoring the Message Box that covered the window with its cheerful OK/Cancel selection. The actions that we do without thinking are often seen as overly complex to the end user. This is especially true of applications that we write ourselves. ("Isn't it obvious that you need to click Update before you click Close?" "Here's the problem. You tried to put commas and a dollar sign in your number." "You can't click the OK button until you enter a four-digit year.") When you cannot be there to help your users in person, professional documentation guides them through the sometimes complex operations they must master to complete their work.

How to Document

Professional Visual Basic documentation deals with the *quality*, the *style*, and the *content* of the writing.

Quality: Always Professional

One of the first Windows applications I purchased was a popular Personal Information Manager (PIM). The first thing I did, after ripping the shrink wrap off the package and running SETUP.EXE, was to sit down with the sizable user's guide and start reading. Sure, the writing was a little dry compared to a Tom Clancy novel, but what impressed me about this manual was the totality in which it described the application. The PIM, while generally easy to use, included features that would satisfy the most demanding and technically astute user. Once I started using the application, I did find a few places where the documentation was incomplete, but those areas were very isolated. Above all, the manuals supplied with the program were professional.

Professional documentation is always grammatically correct. Professional documentation never has spelling errors. Professional documentation is always clear. You would expect these aspects to be true of Microsoft's own documentation supplied with Visual Basic. In the same way, your users expect these aspects to be true of your documentation.

Always proofread your manuals to confirm that they are correct, and that they fall in line with the Seven Cs. Ask yourself the following questions when reviewing the documentation:

- **Clear.** Will someone reading my documentation without the program be able to understand the purpose and basic usage of the application? Is it clear from the external documentation what the business needs of the user are?
- **Concise.** Does the manual get to the point right away? Is it too wordy? Must the user jump all over the document, or between several documents, to find the most important information?
- **Complete.** Is every feature and configuration option described in at least one place in the external documentation? Is every source component, file, modification rule, and database element described in the internal documentation? Will the user be calling me because the manual states that you can perform such-and-such a feature, but provides no instructions to do so? If I am unable to continue with this project, will someone be able to use my documentation to quickly resume the work?
- **Correct.** Does the documentation accurately reflect the current state of the program? Have I included all last-minute modifications in the documentation or addendum? Has the modification history log been checked for overlooked features? Have all registry entries, configuration files, and database objects been fully documented?
- **Crafted.** Does the documentation demonstrate in written form the original (or modified) intent of the application? Is each document written correctly for its intended audience?

- **Convenient.** Are the indices complete? Is it clear which manual should be referenced to find a particular piece of information about the program? Are the most important documents accessible on-line?
- **Complementary.** Does the documentation feel like it belongs with the application? (For example, if you are writing a program for entertainment purposes, is the manual entertaining?) Does the organization of the manuals follow the usage of the application?

Documentation is essential to any professional product. When I provide a formal project estimate to a customer, I always include documentation as a separate line item in the estimate. I find that good documentation will consume about 15 percent of a project's timeline. Therefore, I take the original project estimate, and add 15 percent for generating all forms of internal and external documentation.

Style: From General to Specific to General

Good documentation is not that difficult to produce if you keep in mind its primary purpose: to support those who use and maintain your application. When you write your documentation, write for others, not for yourself. Of course, the readers of your manuals will range in technical aptitude from novice to expert. Your documentation needs to anticipate all of their needs.

Good documentation conveys the purpose of your application to the reader. As we all remember from our speeches in high school, we are to "tell them what you're going to tell them, then tell them, then tell them what you told them." In the same way, documentation should reinforce the primary message of your program. (Reference manuals are the exception to this rule, as they get into the details from page one.)

The first section of each work in your documentation collection should include a brief description of the application and its purpose. Also discuss why the document currently in the reader's hands is needed in the first place; if you cannot find a purpose in a document, then leave it unwritten. Discuss immediately any assumptions made about the reader, especially technical prerequisites. Since this is not a mystery novel, provide a brief summary of the entire content of the document. Finally, finish this introductory section with any typographical and technical conventions that are used in the work.

The body of the document should go into great detail about its topic. Leave no stone unturned in your effort to reveal all aspects of the application to the reader. Be sure to describe the application from the viewpoint of both the untrained user and the expert. When all of the internal and external documentation for your product is placed on a shelf, that shelf should contain the complete body of knowledge for your application, inside and out.

End each volume (or even each section within the volume) with a rousing summary of the preceding content. This summary can take various forms, including a prose summary, review questions and answers, tutorial sessions, and even a topical outline of the book.

Keep in mind that you are writing to an audience that did not write the application. Therefore, you must provide as much background into the purpose of your product, and the solutions it provides, as possible.

Content: Types of Internal Documentation

There are several important forms of internal documentation that your project should include.

SOURCE CODE COMMENTS

The importance of source code comments cannot be overstated. That is why this book contains an entire chapter on the topic. Chapter 3, *Commenting and Style*, gives a complete overview of the purpose and use of this form of internal documentation.

STANDARDS GUIDE

During the design phase of your application, a set of implementation standards should be defined. Whether this set of guidelines exists for all projects in your company, or is adjusted for each project, it is an essential internal document. This manual lists the coding and documentation conventions that impact every line of code and every word of documentation. The book you are currently reading will often be sufficient as a standards guide.

MODIFICATION LOG

Beginning with the very first line of code typed into the Visual Basic IDE, a log of all major modifications needs to be maintained religiously. I personally like to keep a Microsoft Word document containing summary paragraphs of all modifications made within each compiled revision of a project. Because the source code control system keeps track of the line-by-line changes that I make to each version of an application, my modification log is relatively short and quick to read (Figure 5–1).

If you need more control over the modification log, a simple database can be created for the task. There are also several high-quality third-party products designed specifically to track application revisions. If a file or database used by the application is changed structurally in a way that would cause previous versions of the application to fail, this must be clearly documented in the modification log. You may wish to keep a separate modification log that tracks structural changes to database or file resources.

For medium and large projects (and possibly small projects as well), the modification log needs to be tied to some form of source code control. All of the major code management products on the market (including Visual SourceSafe,

> **Version 1.2.0 of Super Tic Tac Toe, released on September 18, 2000, includes these changes:**
>
> • Added the [Winners] application section to the ttt.ini configuration file. Each key within this section is in the form "xxxx=yyy,zzz,www" where xxx is the name of the winner, yyy is the number of wins, zzz is the number of losses, and www is the number of draws.
> • The application now displays and saves game information about each user of the program in the [Winners] section of the ttt.ini file.
> • The main form flashes in a rainbow pattern when the user wins.

Figure 5–1   *Sample modification log entry.*

shipped with some versions of Visual Basic) provide a place to include modification log comments with all updates to the code database. These entries should either refer to the master modification log, or should contain a short summary of the appropriate section of the log itself. You will save yourself a lot of headaches if you carefully maintain this log of changes. In any significant project, you will most likely hear a user say, "Hey, this used to work last week. Why did you break it?" Keeping an accurate and complete log of all modifications, and tracking the code changes with a source code control system, is the right way to solve upgrade issues. Be sure to keep it up to date from the very first day because there is little chance of re-creating it at some later time.

ISSUE AND BUG LOG

Like the modification log, the issue and bug log is maintained throughout the development of your application. Unlike the modification log, the issue and bug log will (hopefully) become smaller and smaller as you approach the release of your program, and application issues are resolved. This log can be maintained in a spreadsheet, word processor, database, or any other utility that can be easily accessed by all members of the technical staff. Each entry in the issue and bug log will contain key pieces of information about each issue, such as the date when the issue was reported, the importance of the issue, the user who reported the issue, a full description of the issue, a list of steps needed to reproduce the issue, the name of the person assigned to fix the issue, the date when the issue was fixed (including application version in a post-release fix), and a short description of the solution. Not every project will require all of these elements. For instance, if you are the only developer on the project, then there is no need to list the name of the person who will fix each problem.

You may wish to group your issue and bug lists into different areas of activity (such as documentation and source code), or by priority and urgency level.

Table 5.1	Example Issue and Bug Log		
ID	**Description**	**Reported**	**Fixed**
✓ 82	The order entry form crashes if the promised ship date contains an invalid date.	5/2/2000	5/5/2000
83	Add new customer form to the on-line help.	5/3/2000	
✓ 84	Add new customer form to the user's guide.	5/3/2000	5/5/2000

CHECKLISTS

Visual Basic allows you to write easy-to-use programs very quickly, but professional software applications will generally go way beyond simple dragging and dropping of controls onto forms. Besides the application itself, a programmer must understand and build context-sensitive on-line help, create a setup program with user-configurable options, develop and deploy databases, write useful documentation, design and integrate predefined and *ad hoc* reporting features, *et cetera*. With all of these tasks it is easy to forget important steps or leave various components with a level of inconsistency. Checklists provide a method by which consistency can be applied throughout your application. Build a standard set of items to add to your checklist at the beginning of each project, and group them by the different types of tasks you will perform in the development of your application. For example, as you finish each form within your application, you may wish to scan through these and other elements of your "form completion checklist." (Figure 5–2.)

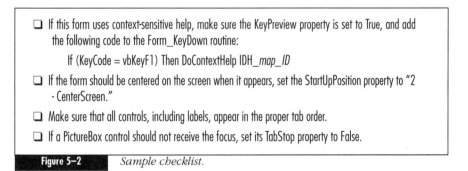

❑ If this form uses context-sensitive help, make sure the KeyPreview property is set to True, and add the following code to the Form_KeyDown routine:

```
If (KeyCode = vbKeyF1) Then DoContextHelp IDH_map_ID
```

❑ If the form should be centered on the screen when it appears, set the StartUpPosition property to "2 - CenterScreen."

❑ Make sure that all controls, including labels, appear in the proper tab order.

❑ If a PictureBox control should not receive the focus, set its TabStop property to False.

Figure 5–2   *Sample checklist.*

It is difficult to come up with a checklist that will meet all possible programming scenarios, so often you have to create the checklist as you go. You can create checklists for different types of tasks such as control and form development, methods of interacting with the user, documentation, and on-line help.

RESOURCE KIT

The mother of all internal documents, the resource kit is the be-all and end-all of technical information about the application. Unlike the very public *Windows xx Resource Kit* volumes, this document is meant for those who are intimately involved with the development of the application. Therefore, it is essential that this manual be continually updated with all relevant technical information as the project progresses. Some sections that may be found in the resource kit include the following.

- Purpose, scope, and functionality of the application as agreed upon by the user.
- Summaries of all source code modules.
- Locations of all development files and directories.
- Full descriptions of all registry entries and configuration files relevant to the application.
- A full layout of the names, versions, and locations of all installed files for the delivered product.
- Descriptions of and relationships between all database objects used within the components of the application.
- Contact names and phone numbers for third-party supplied products used in the application.

The resource kit is a complex document, tying together all aspects of the technical side of a professional Visual Basic project. It is vital that this document be an integral part of the design and development process. A well-designed application will have a resource kit that is almost complete before the first line of code is written. All technical principals must have at least read-only access to this document, and its location must be common knowledge.

For a medium-sized database application, the resource kit may contain the following sections:

- **Cover Page.** The name and ownership information for the application.
- **Table of Contents.** Generated by the word processor.
- **Overview.** A brief (no more than two pages) description of the application and the reasons why it was written.
- **Source File Locations.** A hierarchical view of all important directories and files used in the development of the application, as shown in Table 5.2. Some files, such as Visual Basic "frx" files, can be described collectively.
- **Destination File Locations.** The files and directories added or modified through the installation or use of the application on a user's system. If possible, include Visual Basic supplied files, and other third-party files.
- **Database Tables and Objects.** An alphabetical listing of all database tables (with field descriptions) used by the application and its related

Table 5.2	Sample Source File Locations Table

File or Directory	Description
Source Code	The source code for the Voila application.
Main.frm	The main form, listing all customers.
Details.frm	The details form, used to enter customer data.
*.frx	Binary data for Visual Basic forms.
Voila.vbp	Visual Basic project file.
Help	On-line help documents
Voila.hpj	The WinHelp project file.
Voila.rtf	The source document for the on-line help.
Images	Bitmaps used from the Voila.rtf document.
Documents	Important documents created for Voila
ResourceKit.doc	This document.

reports and features, as well as views, queries, stored procedures, security rights, and other database objects needed by the application. For tables and fields, use a grid format similar to the Table Design view found within Microsoft Access, with the primary key clearly marked (Figure 5–3).

- **File Formats.** A description of the contents of any file needed by the application, including configuration (INI) files.
- **Registry Entries.** A description of any registry entries used or modified by the application. Those entries modified by Visual Basic during installation or by a third-party ActiveX control need not be documented.
- **On-line Help Mappings.** If you use Map IDs to enable context-sensitive help in your application, those IDs are listed here.
- **Contact Information.** Technical and primary user contacts, and information on third-party products used in the application.

Customer—The master list of all customers.

Field	Type	Description
ID	Long Integer	Primary key. Required.
FullName	Text(50)	Last name, first name. Required.
ProfileType	Long Integer	The type of customer based on buying habits. Foreign reference to CodeProfile.ID. NULL if the type is not defined. Optional.

Other objects used by this table:

- **seqCustomer**—Sequence to generate Customer.ID field values.
- **trgCustomer**—Trigger that adds Customer.ID to new records.
- **idxCutomerID**—Primary key index: ID ASC.
- **idxCustomerName**—Non-unique name index: FullName ASC.

Figure 5–3   *Sample Database Tables and Objects section.*

Content: Types of External Documentation

The following forms of external documentation are not only important, but your users will often expect that they be included with your delivered application.

ON-LINE HELP

When your users are in need of technical assistance, the first place they will look (after calling your technical support number!) will be the on-line help. It is imperative that this document be complete and accurate. If possible, include the entire content of all other external documents somewhere within the on-line help system supplied with your application.

The on-line help must be easy to navigate, the index must be complete, and the look and feel of the on-line help should be similar to that of other products on the market. A user should not have to guess at how to find information about your application. At the very minimum, you should have at least one page of on-line help for each form within your application, which gives a short description of every data entry control on the form. Pressing the F1 key from a form will bring up the on-line help for that form. (F1 from the main form, if your application has a "main" form, may bring up the contents or introduction page instead of the help for the main form.) Also include pages that give overviews of the application and its major features, keyboard shortcuts, usage tips, copyright and credits for the application, and information on how to obtain technical support for the product.

The on-line help should be the best resource your users have, and they should always leave the help screen with the feeling that their questions were answered. For small projects, I have always found the RTF features found in most word processors to be sufficient for writing pre-HTMLHelp documents. For medium and large applications, I highly recommend that you invest in a third-party help authoring application. These applications (if they are professional) allow you to focus on the content of your help document, instead of trying to remember which footnote goes where.

On-line documentation now extends into cyberspace. If you are planning to include some of your content on a Web page (such as a knowledge base), be sure to provide information that is as complete, as convenient, and as professional as the application itself. There is nothing more frustrating than a poor application that has even poorer electronic support.

USER'S GUIDE

The user's guide for your application will be the primary chance for you to test out your prose-writing ability. User guides are written for the most general of all audiences using your application. When developing this document, keep in mind the "general to specific to general" outline presented earlier. As long as your application is not intended for a purely technical clientele, you should be able to give your application and user's guide to someone who is unfamiliar with the purpose of the application, and he or she should be able to explain accurately the usage and intention of the program.

If your application uses data entry forms, include a section or chapter for each form that the user will encounter. Explain the purpose of the form, and describe each of the controls on the form in a way that will be relevant to the user (Figure 5–4).

If the user will also be handling all configuration and administrative tasks, be sure to include these topics (such as the installation of the application) in this guide, or refer the reader to the administrative manual. If you have only one paper manual supplied with your application, it should be a user's guide. It is possible to provide the actual contents of the user's guide only on-line, and supply a "Getting Started" manual with your product that directs the reader to the full documentation available through on-line help.

REFERENCE MANUAL

If your application includes user- or administrator-programmable features, you should also include a reference manual to provide quick lookups of the details of those features. Just like the *Visual Basic Language Reference*, your reference manual should include every exposed feature of your application in alphabetical order. Each entry should be similar in style, and without exception the information covered in each entry must be clear and complete. Make frequent use of the "See Also" section heading when appropriate.

Customer Properties Form

Use the Customer Properties form to add new customers to the system, or to update information about an existing customer. You can access this form for new customers by selecting the New menu item on the Customer menu of the Main form. To view existing customers in this form, use the Customer Lookup form to locate the desired customer.

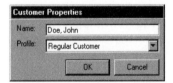

The fields on the Customer Properties form include:

- **Name** (Text entry field). Enter the name of the customer, up to 50 characters, in last name, first name order. You must supply a customer name.

- **Profile** (Drop-down list). Select the appropriate customer profile from the list of profile types. This list is defined by the system administrator through the Profile Type Maintenance form. If a profile does not apply to a customer at this time, select "<No Profile Specified>," which should be the first entry in the list. You must make a selection from this list.

- **OK**. To save your changes and return to the previous form, click the **OK** button. You will be prompted to make any needed corrections.

- **Cancel**. To abandon any changes and return to the previous form, click the **Cancel** button.

Figure 5–4   *Sample user's guide page.*

ADVANCED TOPICS GUIDE

If your application contains features that may be too intimidating for the average user, place the descriptions of those components into a separate guide for advanced users. This guide should be similar in format to the primary user's guide.

ADMINISTRATION AND CONFIGURATION GUIDES

Some applications are designed to be used concurrently by a team of users, all manipulating a common store of information. Database applications are a common area of Visual Basic development, and it is not uncommon to have administrative personnel, other than the "data users," who are responsible for the installation, configuration, and maintenance of the application and its database component. Under such circumstances, a separate administrative guide can be included, covering those topics of special interest to the administrative staff, but that would never be the concern of the ordinary user.

The administration and configuration guides can actually be a collection of different guides, each geared toward a different administrative branch. For example, you may have one manual that discusses the network portions of your application for the Network Administrator, and another manual for the Database Administrator (DBA) that discusses periodic maintenance of the data store.

GRAPHICS AND ARTWORK

Any artwork included in your on-line or printed documentation should be professional looking, and the colors should be "normal." I struggle in this area because, although I consider myself to be an artist in the work of Visual Basic source code, I have no aptitude for the fine arts. I have trouble drawing recognizable stick figures. Still, I can recognize when something looks somewhat professional. With the introduction of the World Wide Web and its flashy graphics, users are accustomed to professional visual presentations. If you include art or drawings in your documentation, be sure to have them purchased from or drawn by someone with talent.

Summary

Little things mean a lot. Although the development of application documentation is a big thing in the mind of the programmer, it should be a small thing to the user. Users simply expect quality documentation to be there if and when they need it. Printing disk labels and putting the customer's logo on the documentation (for custom applications) are nice touches. Still, the content of your documentation is the key, and your users and technical staff may forget all of the nice things you did if you are unable to deliver on your promise of professional documentation.

I still remember when my coworker purchased a Macintosh only a few days after it was released back in 1984. With an ear-to-ear grin on his face, he exclaimed, "I haven't had time to look at the manuals yet; I've been so busy *using* the computer." A well-written application may be quite usable without any documentation, but a low-quality program will not get any better just because the user's guide is well written. Documentation is not a replacement for a working application. When an application is so tedious that it cannot be used without documentation, it is time to take a look at the correctness of the application itself.

Foundation

Professional programming is not simply an activity, a method for building great code. Much more than that, it is a mindset, a way of thinking and acting that has as its focus the satisfaction and productivity of the user of the software. This mindset is much like a deep-seated compass, directing you through the sea of programming choices. As you read through this section of the book, do not think primarily about the changes you may choose to make to your coding style. Rather, think about the attitude that surrounds great programmers.

Discipline

The first aspect of professionalism, discipline, is an internal characteristic that is visible in the external activities of the programmer. This chapter discusses the meaning of discipline, the reasons why it is important, and some activities that can help bring it about.

What Is Discipline?

Discipline is an ominous word. Perhaps our cultural tendency to equate discipline with punishment causes us to wince at the very thought of doing anything in a disciplined manner. Even my Webster's dictionary lists "punishment" as the first definition of the word. Yet discipline carries so much more significance with it. In this text, I will use another definition of the word: "training that corrects, focuses, or perfects the mental faculties or moral character." This definition is well suited to the programmer. Let us look at the words of this definition in more detail.

Discipline Is Training

Nobody is born with an innate knowledge of various programming languages. Such skills must be learned and require much study, and today's computer saturated world affords many opportunities for good training. A *formal computer science education* is a strong foundation upon which a sound understanding of software solutions can be built. University-level computer science courses teach you not only how to program in various languages, but how to solve real-world problems independent of your choice of language. Knowing how the hardware works, and how software communicates with the hardware through machine code, may seem a bit dry, but such information provides clues on how to write your applications using the best structure possible. Other topics taught include data and program organization, computer architecture, operating system and language development, and approaches to programming such as procedural and object-oriented programming.

Formal training is not always an option, especially when your job suddenly requires you to write a program by a rapidly approaching deadline. If you need to enhance your skills in a language or methodology, *tutorial or self-study* is an excellent option. Today's computer training market is large and varied, and the shelves at the bookstore down the street groan from the weight of programming language tutorials. You can find books and CDs on various languages, like Visual Basic, as well as books that focus on key software market application development such as graphics and games programming. You can also learn from the numerous software training companies that offer one-week courses in languages and applications.

While formal education and self-study are beneficial for the programmer, disciplined training is much more than just learning the ABCs of a software language. Programming is not an end in itself; you write programs to achieve another purpose. Olympic athletes train year after year for the chance to compete with like-minded people from around the world. Does a runner spend all of those years thinking, "I just love running seven or eight hours a day, and returning home exhausted. That's all that I need in life?" Of course not. All investment in training is focused on a goal. For the athlete, that goal may be a gold medal, the admiration of his or her peers, or some other tangible or intangible result. The training is the path to that goal, but it is not the goal itself.

In the same way, training to develop applications is not done just to become trained. Rather, there is a prize to be gained. There are not many gold medals handed out for bug-free programming, but there are still benefits. These benefits include customer satisfaction, a regular salary, the respect of your peers, etc. Although the professional programmer does seek to improve his or her skills through training, the purpose of the training is not simply to become a better programmer. The purpose of the training is to meet the needs of people, both the needs of the programmer and the needs of the user.

Discipline Corrects

"Correct" is a very nice word, but in programming circles, it is usually said in the context of other words such as "bug," "error," and my personal favorite, "post-implementation issue." Programmers, even the best ones, spend a sizable amount of time correcting coding problems. Such activity, although unpleasant, is at the very heart of discipline. Experience is an excellent teacher after all, and nothing drives a lesson home like a big, fat mistake.

When we fix bugs in our code, we are really fixing *in ourselves* solutions that we will use again and again in future programs. If we are disciplined enough to learn from our mistakes, then we will be one step closer to writing correct code the next time.

Only through the continual application of discipline can bugs become a stepping stone instead of a stumbling block. My high school chemistry teacher announced to our class at least once per week, "Accidents are planned." His point was clear: Plan not to have accidents. Take steps in advance of the activity to prevent problems from occurring. If you are trying to think of a word that sums up this idea, it is—it must be firmly implanted in your mind by now—"discipline." As with training, correction is not an end in itself, but it is a required step in achieving professional programming solutions. With an attitude of discipline, past errors can be effective preparation for larger hurdles still to come.

Discipline Focuses

Programming can be a lot of fun, but it can also be draining. Distractions abound for the programmer who is stuck on a boring or complex piece of code. Walk down the aisles of any software company and you will see computer screens quickly change from a green-background Solitaire game to a code editor as the sound of your feet passes by. The World Wide Web is a great research tool, but it is also a fantastic time waster when you need to (or want to) turn your thoughts elsewhere. I once had a supervisor tell me, "I expect about 10 percent of my programmers' days to be wasted." He did not say it with bitterness, but with honesty. He knew from experience that developers sometimes find it hard to stay focused on a software task.

Professional programming is more work than typical programming, and it requires more focus and more attention to detail. Visual Basic takes away a lot of the overhead associated with Windows programming, but there is still much work to do. Besides the main program itself, a Windows program often includes on-line help, user and administrative documentation, installation programs, registry configuration, and other little tasks that must be done routinely, consistently, and correctly. All of this requires a lot of focus on the part of the programmer and others involved in developing a software application. Tracking all of the details for a project can often feel like the man at the circus who tries to balance 10 spinning plates on poles. He can do it, but he must never lose his focus.

Like training and correction, focus is an important aspect of discipline. Staying focused does not mean non-stop activity from design to delivery of a program. Rather, it is a guarantee that certain important, routine chores will be completed when needed. When I see someone working frantically on a piece of code, I do not think about focus, but about busyness. When I see a program where all forms have the same look and feel, produce consistent, expected results, and are backed up with clear, concise documentation, then I think, "That programmer is focused."

Discipline Perfects

Try as we might, the perfect program remains elusive. Even if we find and fix all known bugs, there are still usability and interface problems with which we, or our users, must contend. And of course there are always more features to add. With each new feature and each new program the skills needed to fulfill the requirements of the user are honed and improved.

In the realm of programming, "perfection" is a relative term. What may be the perfect application for one person is rubbish for another. I often debate the merits of one popular word processor over another that my coworker uses, and he just as adamantly defends the superiority of his word processor over mine. The user plays a large role in determining what makes a program perfect. The key feature of a perfect program is *usability*. Is the program easy to use? Is the application useful for completing the work that the user needs to perform? Is using the program better than "the way we used to do it"? Is it easy for other programmers to maintain the code? Is the program documented well? All of these questions are issues of application usability, from the standpoint of both the user and the developer. Perfect programs are usable by all parties involved.

While you could attempt to write a perfect program by the sheer force of your will, a better way is to use a disciplined approach. Since the truly perfect program is not attainable, you need to ask yourself, "What does this program need to have to appear perfect to those who will use it?" Then you bring about those features or traits through methodical, focused programming. I discuss how to do this in the section "How to Instill Discipline."

Discipline Affects the Mental Faculties

How many times have you heard, "Oh, you're a programmer? Wow, you must be smart." We all secretly enjoy hearing others say it, but of course we deny it. Yet the question still remains, "Do you have to be really smart to be a programmer?" The correct answer is "No." You do not need to be really smart to be a programmer; you need to be really disciplined. Programming is not about being smart. It is about breaking down a task into its smallest components or steps. (This is especially true of assembly language programming.)

My eighth-grade English teacher gave our class a simple assignment one day. "Class," she said over her horn-rimmed bifocals, "I want you to write down the instructions for making a peanut butter and jelly sandwich. You need to write it clearly enough so that someone who has never made a sandwich before will be able to accomplish the task." For the next 20 minutes we teased our papers with the basics of PB & J creation. Imagine our horror when the teacher was able to find large gaps in our sandwich construction process. Most of the students wrote, "Spread the peanut butter on one slice of bread, and the jelly on the other," but we never preceded the instruction with "Using a knife...." It may seem silly in this world of accomplished sandwich makers that we would have to tell anyone to use a knife. When you write a program, however, you must be that detailed. Unless there is a library or API call available to perform a task, you must tell the computer in excruciating detail what you want it to do. It does not take a smart person to do that. It takes a careful, thoughtful, disciplined programmer.

I am not saying that a roomful of stupid people could write an award-winning application. What I am saying is that mental faculties in the programming world are only partially judged by how intelligent you are. A more important use of our mental resources is to program by a structured, comprehensive method that brings about the most solid programs possible.

Discipline Affects Moral Character

Software development may not seem like a moral activity. However, for the professional programmer, code design and authoring are just two of the many daily tasks driven by moral character. Discipline is an attitude that touches all areas of one's life. You cannot be disciplined in only one area of your life. Like blood flowing through all the capillaries of the body, discipline flows through all activities and thoughts of a person. I will expand on this topic in Chapter 8, *Ethics*.

Why Be Disciplined?

When we want to enhance our muscular strength, we exercise: a process of using our muscles to perform work. Those same muscles that perform the work are strengthened little by little so that they can carry out even more work. In the same way, the exercise of discipline amplifies our overall level of discipline.

The more involved one is in disciplined activity, the more growth in personal discipline will occur. Because discipline both builds and is supported by mental faculties and moral character, it is the primary attribute of the professional programmer. Without discipline, one cannot truly be a professional programmer.

You may be asking yourself, "Why do I need to be disciplined when my programs run fine now?" There are many good reasons why you need to program in a disciplined manner, and better yet, there are no good reasons why you should avoid discipline. The following list of reasons for pursuing the way of discipline is by no means exhaustive, but it should give you the encouragement you need to begin the process.

Discipline Results in Professional Programs

Professional programming is a central theme of this book, and discipline is the key to professional programming activity. Because disciplined programmers pay careful attention to the details of a project, the final application is consistent, well organized, and problem-free. If bugs are discovered, they are eradicated quickly and easily because sufficient technical documentation, including code commenting, is readily available. The customer is satisfied because the program works as expected, and it is delivered on time.

Discipline Reduces Development Pressures

Most stress that arises from the development process comes in the form of unmet deadlines. I once spent three years working on an 18-month project. You can be sure that the stress level in that development group significantly increased as the months wore on. If you could find a way to reduce the chances of missed deadlines, would you do it? Disciplined programming is one such way. The activities of discipline give you a guideline that you can follow throughout the development process. It begins in the design process where time limits are established. If thoughtful, carefully crafted timelines are drafted, and implementation is carried out in a disciplined fashion, then even when obstacles arise, they can be dealt with in a timely manner.

Discipline Increases Application Satisfaction

All parties involved in the application are satisfied, including the developer and the user. The disciplined programmer determines in advance exactly what the user wants and needs, even if the user is not initially sure what is needed. Naturally, when the customer is satisfied, the developer is satisfied.

Discipline Prepares You for Advanced Programming

Pull out a copy of a program you wrote three years ago and critique it. If you wrote that program today, would you implement it differently? Now turn the question around. Three years from now, what techniques will you employ to write programs? Of course this question cannot be answered directly since it would involve knowledge of future events. But you can still prepare for programming tasks to come through disciplined programming practices in the present.

When I use a program that is well written, I ask myself, "How did they (the developers of the program) implement it? What is the structure of the application's logic? Do I have what it takes to write such a program?" Consider a large-scale application like the Visual Basic development environment. The number of pieces that comprise it can make your head spin. I really enjoy the feature that automatically displays the syntax of a subroutine or function in a ToolTip window as you type the statement. This seemingly small feature involves many individual programming methods and implementations working in harmony. How do you catalog all of the routines available to the user for quick access? How do you communicate with ActiveX controls to query the syntax of their methods and properties? How you ascertain the current argument being entered by the programmer when a single source code statement may contain multiple, nested functions, broken onto multiple lines? The developers who wrote this portion of Visual Basic had to carefully consider these and other questions before they started their implementation.

As users become more demanding in terms of the features they want in their software, the ability to handle advanced programming tasks becomes even more important. Disciplined programming prepares you to tackle these tasks. Although some concepts in advanced applications can be understood only through wrestling with the algorithms day after day, most of the difficulty in implementing any complicated application has to do with the ability to structure and organize the code. Time spent disciplining yourself on less involved applications will supply you with the skills needed to handle applications of any size and complexity.

Discipline Attracts the Admiration of Your Peers

While the user will be happy with a working application, writing solid code will also gain you the accolades and admiration of other software developers. Programs written in a disciplined manner announce to the programming community, "This program works very well."

I would be remiss if I implied that all programmers will respect your work if it is produced in a disciplined manner. On the contrary, it has been my experience that a certain percentage of programmers care neither for disciplined, professional programming practices, nor for other programmers who display these habits. Until these programmers come to realize the importance of professionalism in their software and in their interactions with others, nothing you can do will command their respect.

How to Instill Discipline

Indeed, how is discipline instilled? Discipline is a recursive activity; the more you work in a disciplined manner, the more disciplined you become. The main way of instilling discipline is by acting in a disciplined manner. But how do you get started? How do you "pull yourself up by your bootstraps"? What if you, like me, are not disciplined? Although my parents brought me up well, discipline was not always my highest priority. My childhood home had an old but usable upright piano. I loved to tickle the ivories, and I could play various one- and two-finger tunes that I heard on the radio. When I was about six years old my parents decided that it would be a good idea if I took some piano lessons. I thought it was a groovy idea (this was the 1970s) and dreamed of actually using three or more fingers at once. But after a few weeks it was obvious that I did not like to practice, and I was not improving at all. After two months, I asked my parents if I could quit the lessons.

Of course my parents encouraged me to continue with the lessons, but I was obstinate. I put the books and the flash cards behind me and went back to hunt-and-peck music. I did not learn much about the piano during those two months, and I learned nothing about discipline. As I look back, I see that a general disregard for discipline extended to my indolent behavior at the piano. I was not a bad child, but study and discipline were not very important to me.

Fortunately, discipline is not something that is only acquired as a child. Discipline can be learned at any age. And it does not depend primarily on will power. That is very important, especially for programmers like myself who lack will power in many areas of life. Discipline is an attitude, a mindset, that does not come from the will, but from the character (some would say, "from the spirit"). A strategy for molding that character is needed, including the establishment of a routine, and the improvement of your methods.

Establishing a Routine

A friend once told me that habits, both good and bad, become ingrained in our minds after they are performed 29 times. I do not know how true this statement is, and I cannot expand on any magical qualities of the number 29, but it is true that repetitive activity does result in habits. You can instill good, disciplined habits in your programming practice by establishing a routine, a standard course in which you navigate your way through successful projects.

Establishing a routine means that you do things in the same manner time and time again. Discipline is difficult if each day gives no chance for regularity. Just like habits, discipline becomes fixed if it is reinforced. Such repetition appears at many different levels within a project. Your company may already have some methods of application design and implementation drafted. Following these rules each and every time you write an application will ingrain the method in your mind.

The best way to establish a routine is to document how you are going to act in a routine fashion. I document my routine through checklists, to-do lists, and a catalog of code portions that I use often.

By establishing a routine, you enhance your common sense and intuition. By repeating the same methods again and again, you become an expert in your style of programming. Like Pavlov's dogs, you salivate (in a programmer's metaphorical sense) over the thought of writing a section of code so that the user experiences consistency. Actually, if the user does not even notice the use of the application, you have received your best compliment in the area of application consistency.

Improving Your Methods

In his book *The Seven Habits of Highly Effective People*, Steven Covey explains the importance of being "proactive" instead of "reactive." A reactive person is controlled by his or her situation, always reacting suddenly to life. These reactions are often "too little too late." A proactive person takes steps to handle problems before they occur. The professional programmer has many areas available in which a proactive approach to application development can be forged. These skills can be summed up in the "three Rs" of improvement, namely reading, research, and refinement.

Reading is a skill that, for many like myself, requires more than the average amount of discipline. Yet application development, especially development which is done in a graphical user interface, demands much in the way of reading. There are so many Windows-based technologies now available, and new ones being created daily, that you must always have a book (or a CD) at hand for access to the latest information about this API or that standard. Fortunately, there is no shortage of good and bad books on the subject of computers.

The importance of reading up-to-date technical texts and journals cannot be emphasized enough. I have worked for companies where the programmers were satisfied to continue work on 30-year-old technology, never thinking of delving into new technology. Line editors and drab text interfaces were enough for their daily bread. Yet even among businesses that develop on non-graphical operating systems, the desire for easy-to-use and easy-to-manage applications is important. For those who have programmed for decades, thoughts of retirement and a stable life may draw them away from more adventurous programming tasks. But for the professional programmer, new methods of development and program implementation are always of interest. Keeping current with one or two programming journals is a must for staying "with it."

Although there is more than enough to read today, there are also more improved tools to extract only the portions of the texts that are really important. *Research* is the skill of using those tools and references to solve problems and learn new techniques. Many important computing references and journals are now available on compact disc, or in part or in whole on the Internet. Most of these references come with a search tool to help you narrow the scope of the documents you need.

In addition to reading and research, *refinement* of your programming skills is a must for improving your development practices. Refinement requires you to focus on the details of a project. When you refine, you bring out the beauty of the application, placing your personal mark of quality on the program as a whole. Think of yourself as a sculptor. You start with an overgrown slab of marble, and you chop away large sections that mold the rough form of the shape you desire. Then you move to the details, carefully considering the sections that will be the most satisfying to the viewer. Refinement often takes place over the course of several applications.

Summary

Discipline is a serious matter, but it need not be burdensome. Through the tools of routine and method, you can more than meet the important challenge of professional Visual Basic programming. And when you look back, you will wonder how you ever wrote programs without discipline.

Planning

It is amazing how little things can have such a large impact. I realize the truth of this facet of life every time I take my car into the shop. On one trip across the Midwest, I had to wait with my broken car for five hours before I learned that a valve the size of a quarter had failed. Planning is one of those little things that can have a big effect. This chapter discusses the importance of planning, and gives some tips on what to plan for in your Visual Basic projects.

What Is Planning?

Planning is nothing more than deciding in advance what you will do. Shall we move on to the next section? Ah, but if planning is so simple to define, why do we have so much trouble making a plan? The reason is simple: planning is difficult. Properly performed, planning should be one of the most difficult components of any project. Still, just because something is not pleasant does not mean it should not be done. In fact, good planning can make the remaining portion of the project a breeze. If you have seen *Mary Poppins* recently, you may recall her words of advice: "Well begun is half done."

Planning is especially difficult in Visual Basic because Microsoft, in developing Visual Basic, made it so easy for anyone to create useful Windows applications. In truth, the amount of planning required for a project will vary only slightly from one programming language to another. Yet the comparative simplicity of Visual Basic masks the true need for adequate planning, especially in medium and large projects.

Planning involves two very important steps: 1) taking something apart, and 2) putting it back together again. I learned this lesson from my son. When he was about six months old, he was given a small set of Duplo blocks with which to amuse himself. At first, he just picked at the blocks, not knowing what they were other than colorful distractions. When he was old enough and strong enough to play with toys in both hands, he began to pull apart the Duplo blocks that I had assembled.

After many weeks of dismantling all of my great Duplo projects, he finally discovered that Duplo blocks could be put together. He would take a red block in his left hand, and a blue block in his right hand, and carefully ease them together. He still needed a little help in getting the pieces to snap together, but I could see the wheels spinning in his head as he thought about ways to join the colorful components.

Planning involves the very same process of taking a problem apart (the user's need for a software solution), and putting it back together (deciding on a course of action to implement the solution). Both steps are essential for planning to have its desired effect.

Taking the Problem Apart

The first half of a plan involves asking a lot of questions, and doing a lot of research: no programming, flowcharting, or algorithm design is considered at this time. Let us say that your boss comes into your office and says, "George," (let us also say that your name is George), "our employees in the Information Tracking Department need a program to help them keep track of information. I am putting you in charge of the project, and I want you to plan out the project for approval." Now what do you do? Simple: you take the problem apart.

The first step in taking any problem apart is to actually find out what the problem is. The supervisor in this example was extremely vague. Now is the time to start asking questions.

- What type of information does the Information Tracking Department need to track?
- When do they need the program completed?
- What type of computers do they use (operating system, performance, etc.)?

Even if all of these questions are answered to your satisfaction, there is one very important question that needs to be asked before the problem can be fully disassembled: *What does the user need to do his or her job?*

This is the most vital question to ask in the planning process. Unless you know what the user needs, you probably cannot supply a useful utility for his or her work. This question is not always easy to answer, even for the potential user, but it must be answered before planning can continue.

Make sure it is the user's needs you understand, and not the supposed needs dictated by someone else. I once worked on a project where many pieces of information needed to be collected on customers. The person who described the program to be written told me that the information needed to appear in certain logical groupings. However, when I delivered the first prototype to the users, all I received were complaints. The program did not meet their needs at all. In fact, the program, as designed, would have increased the time it took them to do their jobs. What went wrong? I relied on the needs of someone other than the users. The users had no need for the logical groupings that I had designed. Instead, they needed to enter the data in chronological order based on when the data was received. Although the modifications were not dramatic, I was forced to rewrite a portion of the program logic to meet the needs of the real customer.

Along with the questions comes research, a tool to help you answer the questions. Much of the research will revolve around understanding the purpose and nature of the user's work. Once you understand the needs of the user, you can begin to take apart the problem into small, Duplo-like pieces. Instead of colors, these pieces have names like "data," "owner," and "security." We will discuss the actual components, and methods of research, in more detail later in the section "How to Plan."

Putting the Solution Together

Once you have the pieces of the user's problem there in front of you, it is not always obvious how to piece them together properly, but the second part of planning requires that you do just that. A pile of Duplo blocks always looks like a pile of Duplo blocks, no matter what shape they were in before they were dismantled. Along with pieces of the user needs are other pieces, such as "schedule," "programming language," and that one piece that always looks like it is too small to fit, "budget." The Duplo blocks do not always end up in the same shape when they are reassembled. Once all the pieces are there in front of you, you may see a better way to put them together. How do you decide the best way to put them back together? What you need is guidance.

When I was about 10 years old, I was given a very large Erector set. It had hundreds of pieces (thousands if you included all of the little screws and washers). My sister and I built many fun projects, but there were two creations that we could not accomplish. The inside of the Erector set's lid displayed a **WORKING RECORD PLAYER** and a **THREE FOOT WALKING ROBOT, WITH EYES THAT GLOW!** How we longed to play our 78rpm records on a machine of our own making, and watch our friends stare in awe as the walking robot glided across the room, holding them in its transfixing gaze. Alas, we were never able to build those marvels because the instructions for building them were missing from the box when we received the set. In other words, the plans for the project were missing. We probably could have built a robot of some sort, but we clearly could not see how the myriad of parts could be assembled into a working record player. Without the correct plans, the correct result could not be accomplished.

A plan is a guide, a set of instructions for building all aspects of a project. It lays down in clear terms what work is to be done, how it is to be done, and when it is to be done. This guide may be large or small, depending on the size of the project itself, but the plan must still exist to ensure proper completion of the project. Once you have all of the pieces of the project before you, you assemble them into a coherent, organized plan. Just as a list of Erector set parts would not be useful in assembling a record player, so also a list of user needs does not give direction in completing a project. The pieces must be put together in a way that fully describes the steps and pieces needed to build the project. When such a plan is complete, it will provide the guidance—the instructions—that all parties (users, developers, managers, etc.) will look to for project-related information.

Why Plan?

Let's face it, planning seems like a waste of time. You already know what you want the program to do, and what you want it to look like. What more is there to plan? "The users do not know what they want, so why ask them? And there is a deadline that has to be met. If you take the time to plan, you may not have time to finish the project itself, and then where will the users be? The customer will never pay for time that is not dedicated to coding. Therefore, planning (and documentation) must be excluded from the project."

I have heard all of these excuses for not taking the time to plan. Some of them, I am sorry to say, were heard coming from my own mouth. Planning often does seem like a waste of time, especially in one-person projects. Even with this book I was tempted to jump right into writing without taking time to organize what I wanted to say. Yet I have read many books where it was clear that the author took no time to organize the information into a coherent order. Even more numerous than books are the number of programs I have used that were maddening in their disorganization and incompleteness. The fact is, you can almost always tell when programmers did not invest time in planning before they put their hands to the keyboard. There are very few people who can write a perfect program without a plan, and I am not one of them. I depend on plans if only to keep me honest to the specifications I agreed upon with the user.

I recently attended a programming conference where one of the speakers announced, "You plan it, you architect it, then you develop it." He could not have been more correct about putting planning as the first step in developing applications. And the reasons for developing a good plan are abundant.

Understanding the User's Needs

The most important reason to plan is to gain a clear understanding of the user's software needs. This is not to say that the user always has the final say on all design aspects. Often a developer or manager will have insight into factors (either in the computer system or in potential workflow interruptions in other departments) that the user cannot foresee. Often the majority of a project is easy to see, but only those who immerse themselves in the daily routine of a task know its true esoteric facets and idiosyncrasies. If you only deliver the major features, and not the important hidden details, you may make the user's work more difficult than it needs to be.

Understanding the user's needs also gives you a chance to understand what features the user requires *right now*. The user may bring a list of requirements that would rival a letter to Santa. If either time or money is a limiting factor in the development process, it may be necessary to trim this wish list. But which features do you exclude? By designing a plan with the user, you can determine which portions of the application can be postponed until later revisions.

It is important to include the user in the process of developing the plan. I have been in design meetings where a user would announce, "It doesn't matter what I say; the IS department is just going to give us what they want anyway." Often this is not said in anger, but with a sense of defeat that comes with experience. The professional programmer includes the user in the most important aspects of the development process, and as the first step in the process, planning is that most important step.

Standardization

Projects, especially medium and large projects, need a structure of support to succeed. The planning process provides a perfect environment in which to build such a support structure. Not only are the key players identified during the formative stages of a project, but planning also gives a team the chance to standardize and document implementation methods. This is crucial for projects that involve more than one programmer, but even projects with only a single developer benefit from the firm foundation that a plan of standardization provides.

When standards are established from the start and communicated to all of the developers, the opportunity for producing a quality program is greatly enhanced.

Goals and Milestones

How long does it take to write a professional Visual Basic program? How can you tell at any given time if you will be able to complete the application by the time the user requires it? You can always make a good guess, but without the proper establishment of goals and milestones up front, your guesses may not be "good" at all. Goals and milestones are essential in a project, not only to give you practice in using a project management tool. They are important for instilling discipline, the topic of the previous chapter, and the primary fountain from which the spring of professional programming flows.

Goals provide a measurement of the completeness of the application. A program is not complete simply because it has all the features originally planned. A complete program also fills a need for the user. Goals can bring this about because they provide direction and focus throughout the development and implementation process. Some goals, such as "meet budgetary limits," may have management or the technical staff in mind. But the most important goals that must be met have to do with the user. An example of a goal may be, "Reduce the time it takes the user to process one customer order by three days." As you can see, goals pinpoint areas that will be affected by the implementation of the Visual Basic application, yet they are still quite general in scope.

Milestones are also general in nature, and are used to indicate time-based requirements from the start of a project. Realistic milestones are the best indicator of progress throughout a project. Milestones can be placed on a per-feature, per-time-interval, or per-person basis, or a combination of all of these. It is often useful to use a project management application to organize your milestones once you have determined the major features and people involved in the project.

Milestones and goals must be established during the planning phase of a project. Establishing goals and milestones helps prevent costly delays and the infamous "scope creep" (the list of features and tasks that continues to grow long after the project is started) that can beset almost any project.

Anticipating Surprises and Risks

It is difficult to anticipate every problem that you may encounter during the implementation of your project. This is especially true when other vendors supply large parts of an application. Although Visual Basic makes it easy to write complex Windows applications, not every portion of an application may originate in Visual Basic code. Databases, ActiveX controls, networking software and hardware, report generators, and other components of your application may have been purchased off-the-shelf, or selected to continue compatibility with other in-house applications. Proper planning does not remove surprises and risks, but a little research up front can save hours (or days!) of frustration because some component refuses to integrate with your 50,000-line Visual Basic program.

How to Plan

There are many different types of Visual Basic projects, and therefore, there are many different methods of project planning. You can break down the universe of all Visual Basic projects into small, medium, and large projects. Another way of differentiating projects is by primary purpose: database storage and retrieval, file utility, productivity package, game software, and the list goes on.

The reality of different ways of planning an implementation is demonstrated by counting the number of books available on the subject of software systems planning. Most of these books present a solid, start-to-finish methodology for planning all aspects of a project. This section, with all its brevity, does not attempt to compete with those volumes, all of which describe valid, real-world tasks for the design of a software project. Still, when you reach the end of this chapter, you should understand how the professional Visual Basic programmer plans a program.

As with discipline, planning is not simply a tool that the programmer keeps locked away for especially tricky projects. It is part of a professional attitude, a temperament that guides the professional programmer through the early stages of the design and implementation process. Although a team of users, managers, and programmers can all agree on a plan, planning is actually a very personal thing that bubbles up from inside you. It springs from a desire to present to the user the highest quality application that meets his or her needs.

When you are in the planning phase of a project, there is often a feeling that "real work" will never commence for all the up-front discussion and organization that needs to be done. (Sometimes the real work never does get done. One of my customers had a large non-Visual Basic project they were planning in one of their departments. After two years of planning, they scrapped the entire project.) But time well spent in shaping the overall project will be appreciated when the truly difficult portions of the project are attacked. Planning is hard work, but it is not a difficult process. As was mentioned earlier, it involves taking something apart, and putting it back together again. As a practical matter, we can reorganize these two steps into four different tasks or components.

Understand What the User Needs

This component corresponds to the step of taking the problem apart that was discussed earlier in this chapter. Planning is the art of determining how to fulfill the computing needs of a user. The best way to meet those needs is to first understand those needs. It is during the planning phase that that understanding occurs. Until you can say, "I understand how a Windows application can help the user do his or her job," you have not properly planned.

When determining the parts of the user's workflow, you need to continually ask yourself questions of understanding:

- Do I understand how the user does his job?
- Do I understand what type of information is being collected?
- Do I understand how the user interacts with other departments and external agencies?

You could conceivably come up with hundreds of similarly relevant questions. Understanding the full needs of the user is at the heart of the planning component of a project. Once you truly understand how the user does his or her job, you are ready to implement. This does not mean that you can do the user's job. Some jobs are quite complex, and many of the tasks that a user may perform would fall outside the scope of a computing project. Yet if you were asked to describe the job function of your user, you should be able to meet the challenge with the ease of discussing your own job description.

There are a multitude of methods for developing an understanding of workflow, including:

- **Interviewing the user.** Talking to the user about his or her job, what tasks are performed daily, and what could be best automated with a software application.
- **Observing the user.** Watching the user perform his or her job, and taking notes in areas where the process could be improved through the use of software.
- **"Being" the user.** Trying your hand at performing the user's job. This method is not always possible, especially if the user's job is quite complex or risky.
- **Researching the user.** If the user's job is common within an industry, you may be able to obtain generic documentation about the types of tasks that are performed in that job role.

Generally you can use a combination of these methods, and other methods that are applicable in the user's particular industry. No matter which method you choose, your goal is simple: find out how the user performs his or her job. Understand the job function; "be" the job function. You can write a fairly decent program without going to this level of understanding, but the professional programmer will seek out all ways to write a program that best meets the needs of the user.

There are a few areas you should focus on when attempting to discern the job functions of the user.

- **Data and Information.** Data refers to the raw numbers and words with which a user or department works. That data becomes information when it is put within the context of its purpose. Understanding the various pieces of data in use is very important, but understanding the information—the meaning and use of the data—is essential to the success of the program. Understanding the data and information is especially important because your Visual Basic application will be primarily concerned with managing and communicating meaning with that data.
- **Ownership and Security.** Which person or department is responsible for the integrity and security of the data? Can everyone access the data, or only those with a certain job function? Often in large organizations,

there are specific roles for working with the data. Some users only enter data, and are not permitted to perform analysis or maintenance functions on previously entered data. Other users have supervisory capabilities over all aspects of the system. In some instances, a portion or all of the data may be made available to external agencies (perhaps on a World Wide Web site). Understanding the relationships between the different types of users and the data they are allowed to manage must be built in to the application from the very start if it is to be coherent. In addition to the business ownership of the data, the technical ownership must also be considered. Once you finish writing the application, who will maintain it and upgrade it? How will additional features (such as *ad hoc* reports) be handled? If you are unsure about the technical competence of the user, you may need to supply additional utilities and documentation beyond the amount needed for the application to be supported by an Information Systems department.

- **Schedule and Sequence.** Are tasks performed in a specific order? Once one task is performed, must the next item be completed within a limited amount of time? Perhaps there are processes that need to occur at regular intervals, whether hourly, monthly, or yearly. If you only consider what the user does on a typical day, you may miss those special circumstances that only happen, say, at "year end."
- **Pragmatic Issues.** What are the practical issues that need to be considered when performing the job? For example, if you were designing an order entry system for a fast food restaurant, you might want to design the application to reduce the number of keystrokes, or even replace the keyboard with a touch screen. These issues can be determined only by a careful understanding of the daily tasks of the user.

Determine the Project Scope

This component is actually a mini-step that occurs between "taking the problem apart" and "putting the solution together." It offers a chance to take a step back from the pieces you have in front of you, sort them out, and take a deep breath before diving into the next step.

Determining the project scope could also be called "limiting the scope," since any project can include an infinite number of features and extensions. The role of the professional programmer in this phase is, with the user, to choose which of the user's needs will be met by the implementation of this application, and to what extent those needs will be met. This task is not limited to large projects. Even a small project, if not properly limited in scope, can become a medium project before the final product is delivered.

Once the scope of the project is determined, it should not be changed. In fact, the limits of the project should be documented and signed by representatives of the user and technical sides of the project if possible. Although not a true contract, this written "statement of work" conveys the importance of the established scope. This scope must not be altered unless both parties agree to an adjustment of cost, quality, or schedule. Generally this is unacceptable, since a slippage of cost or schedule is viewed by the user as a failure, and a slippage on quality should always be viewed by the professional Visual Basic programmer as taboo. However, if some emergency does arise during implementation that requires a modification to the scope, be sure to fully document the modification to scope, and inform all interested parties that such a modification has been made. "Scope creep" is the term given to any project that suffers from an ever-changing list of features and extensions. Scope creep is a constant danger in any project, and once it appears, it can result in a slow, painful sickness (or even death) of the project.

When deciding which components to include or exclude, keep thinking to yourself, "plan for limited functionality, allow for unlimited extensibility." Although your project will be limited by agreement in the features it provides, that should not stop you from building in features that make later enhancement of the application simple and clear. One way to prepare for extensibility from the start is to build an object view of the data being managed by the application. If your data warrants such a structure, you can design one or more COM (Component Object Model) interfaces to the data and methods of your application. Although these interfaces need not be implemented in your application immediately, they do pave the way for future augmentation of the program by defining a clear understanding of the data relationships within the application. Starting with Visual Basic 5, Microsoft included many useful documents for designing and implementing COM interfaces. COM is beyond the scope (pun intended) of this book, but there are many good books for designing and implementing COM-enabled Visual Basic applications.

Limiting the scope of the application takes fortitude, on the part of both the user and the programmer. The user must have a firm grasp of the features that are possible in a computer application. Although the user is not required to be fully computer literate, he or she should understand some basic processing concepts. The concepts needed will vary by project, but may include database terminology (records, tables, fields) or document management terms (document, folder, linked information).

The user will begin to better understand the software solution being built through the timely accomplishment of project milestones, such as beta releases. During these times of discovery, the user may see ways in which the application could be enhanced through the addition of new features. This newfound excitement on the part of the user creates pressure to change the scope of the project before the final release. Resist this pressure! Fortitude on the part of the programmer comes in the form of enforcing limits defined in the scope document. For medium to large projects, the programmer usually has management available to assist in this task, but even when management is present, the programmer must make the case for keeping the scope, once defined, as immutable as possible. When changes to scope are later suggested, the programmer should look for all possible alternatives, such as the addition of a second phase to make all modifications requested after the scope is defined.

Organize the Project

This component of planning corresponds to the step of putting the solution together. This is where the traditional aspects of planning are performed by the professional programmer. Specific methods may differ by project type and corporate decree, but they often include identification of the major user interface components, field-level design of database tables, and preliminary sketching of essential algorithms. As was mentioned earlier, there are many high-quality books on the subject of planning methods, and these should be referenced, especially in large projects.

It is during this phase of planning that all design documents are produced. For large projects, prototypes may result as well. What is most important for the professional programmer during this phase is that he or she is able to communicate in written or programmatic form a full understanding of the needs of the user. Organizing the project is really organizing the needs of the user into a usable application. Once this step is complete, the programmer should be able to hear the user say, "Yes, you really do understand what I need to do my job." In order to demonstrate this understanding, you should write a one-page summary of the application to be developed. The user is not required to understand all of the technical jargon that may appear in the detailed project plan, but the one-page summary of the project should be clear to anyone who reads it and has an understanding of the basic job functions of the user.

Review the Project

This step occurs after delivery of the completed application. Although this component does not take place during the planning phase, it is an important step in planning for the professional programmer. Project review involves taking an inventory of progress during the project, and comparing it to the project plan. All of this is done with the purpose of developing better plans for the next project to come along.

Project review is a way to plan for planning. By taking the time to review places where a plan fell short of its intent, you cement in your mind the best methods and tools for developing high quality plans, and in turn, high-quality projects. My high school chemistry teacher repeatedly told our class, "Accidents are planned." He emphasized this statement both before *and* *after* laboratory exercises to keep us continually on guard against dangerous situations. Project review gives the same warning: "If you make the same mistake again next time, you planned to do it."

Perhaps you will find it tedious to relive the past, especially when the user is already satisfied with the quality product you delivered. Yet such review, which is considered a form of research, yields great advantages in future projects, even unrelated projects.

When reviewing a project, look for the following:

- What surprises were revealed during implementation that were never thought of during the planning phase?
- Which elements took longer than expected? Which elements took only a fraction of the planned time?
- What tools provided useful implementation benefits? Which tools did you toss in the trash during implementation?
- To what extent does the finished program resemble the single-page description you penned during the planning phase?
- To what extent does the finished program resemble the overall project plan?
- To what extent did involvement from the users, managers, or technical staff help or hinder the project?
- If you could start the entire project over again, what would you do differently?

Summary

Planning is often bittersweet. Most programmers actually enjoy the thought of solving a meaty problem with nothing other than their own brain to aid them. Planning in this context is viewed as an encumbrance to the task of development. Yet the sweetness comes when the quality of the overall project is realized even before the development begins. Trust me, the user is even more interested in having you write the program than you are (whether this is admitted to or not). Like discipline, once a routine of planning is instituted, it becomes a relished part of the development process, like a salad before the main course. Properly performed, planning enhances the development adventure.

Ethics

Ethics is a part of any good philosophical world-view. In this chapter, we will discuss ethics from the viewpoint of the professional Visual Basic programmer.

The fact that this chapter comes third in line after the chapters on discipline and planning should not lead you to believe that it is third in importance after the other two. As you will read, discipline and planning work because the professional programmer adheres to a system of ethics.

What Is Ethics?

As with most words, the dictionary definition of ethics is much simpler than the concept itself. Ethics and morality are among the big ideas of human history. "What is right?" is a question that could be considered as important as "Why am I here?" Although entire libraries can be filled with all of the books written on the topic of ethics, we will limit ourselves to a few key aspects as they pertain to professional programming. Ethics, in this context, is the part of a person's world-view that deals with right and wrong actions and attitudes.

Ethics Is Part of a World-View

Although the discussion of ethics in this book is limited to its effect on programming practices, ethics itself cannot be so limited. Ethics is part of a person's *world-view*, an individual's complete system of understanding and belief about the world. Each ethical decision made by a person comes from his or her overall conviction about how the world is or should be structured.

For many people, ethics is an extension of their deeply held religious beliefs. Religiously based ethical beliefs are often codified in sacred writings. The Ten Commandments is a good example of a written code of ethics. Whether your world-view is religiously based or not, you still have one, and part of the world-view is your system of ethics. It is important to understand the type of ethics that you adhere to, although most people have not found a need to consciously enumerate their ethical beliefs.

Consider the plight of software bootleggers. Soon after I posted a question to a programming newsgroup, my e-mail address was added to a mailing list where I could receive the latest information about obtaining software at prices that were a steal (literally). The pirates who sent out these mailings tried to convey their virtuous duty by writing statements such as, "Help put the American software makers to shame, who have been robbing from consumers for years. Buy copied software from me." Yet their unethical world-view shows them for what they really are: thieves. Although they made bold claims about their righteous position in relation to American software companies who "rob" the consumer, what were they doing but stealing from software companies? Their words were false because they did not match the beliefs that had their source in their world-view, and their ethical position.

Discipline and planning are supported by your world-view. For example, discipline is not something you indulge in only when you sit down at the keyboard to type a program. Instead, the manner of discipline you put forth in your programming life generally matches the discipline you put forth in all areas of your life. The same is true of planning, and other areas of your life that overflow from your world-view and your system of ethics, although you seldom stop to consider it. You can think of ethics as radio waves. These waves travel through your body without your having to know that they exist. In the same permeating way, ethics affects every part of your being, and it especially affects your work behavior.

Ethics Deals with Right and Wrong Actions

Although ethics is a part of your internal world-view, the system of ethics you hold to will be noticed by others through your actions. If part of your ethics says, "I will not steal," but you steal anyway, this will be noticed by others, especially by the person who is the victim of your ethical lapse. Your right or wrong actions are the most visible source of how others view your ethical beliefs.

Ethics Deals with Right and Wrong Attitudes

Right and wrong actions are important, but as you may have noticed by now, the attitude of the professional programmer takes precedence over mere actions. Attitudes, like yeast added to dough, give rise to the true content of our ethical character when played out in our actions.

Attitudes are very powerful forces, especially during times of emotional tension, when they can overpower actions such as restraint, politeness, and calm. Because of this, it is important to have attitudes that are professional, taking cues from the "right" side of the ethical "right-wrong" continuum. Attitudes can be masked by more appropriate actions. For example, you may have an attitude along the lines of, "This customer doesn't know a Window from a widget. I can skimp on the coding and they will never know the difference." But your actions (and your words) may state during the design phase, "I will work my hardest to give you the best program that meets all of your needs." Such a dichotomy is a problem, especially since attitudes are stronger than actions. When you are not paying attention, your true attitude may squeak out, much to the customer's chagrin.

Why Have Ethics?

For those who draw their ethics from religion, the reason for holding to right ethical beliefs can be as simple as, "Because God demands it," or "Because it is written in scripture." Having a deity behind your beliefs can give you that extra stability you need when you are in a position to compromise your ethical convictions. Still, many programmers do not rely on religious belief for their ethics. For these people, a practical answer will have to suit them.

Fortunately, there is a very practical response to the statement, "Why have ethics." The answer can be summed up in one word: *trust*. Ethics establishes an atmosphere of trust, trust between you and the customer, trust between you and your employer (if you have one), and trust within yourself. This trust is essential as a professional Visual Basic programmer, for it is by this trust that you will be remembered.

I once worked for a customer who had several systems for tracking various aspects of customer records. One of the systems was programmed by a man named Sam (not his real name). Although Sam had not been there for over a year, his name was brought up so frequently, you would have thought that he was still employed. Almost daily you would hear statements like, "Oh, here's some more rotten code that Sam wrote," or "Where is that Sam? I would like to wring the neck of the so-called programmer who wrote this report," or "I think Sam took that part of the source code with him, so we can't change it. It's just like him to do that." It was clear from those statements that, not only was Sam disliked, he was also not trusted. Sam would not be asked to fix any of the code that he left in shambles, even though he may have an understanding of the design. The customer had lost so much trust in Sam (and they had lost time and money as well), they would not consider his work as having much value at all.

The trust you convey through your ethics is clearly displayed in the programs you produce. If you write your programs well, they will be in use long after you have moved on to other projects. If you write your programs ethically, as a professional programmer will, your applications will speak well of you even when you are forgotten.

How to Have Ethics

Ethics is a vast subject, but there are a few key attributes of right ethical behavior that are especially relevant to the professional programmer. The remainder of this chapter discusses five of those attributes.

Honesty

For the professional programmer, honesty is the most important ethical attribute you can possess. Honesty greatly affects our agreements with others, and a large part of the programmer's job (especially during the design phase of a project) focuses on agreements. Honesty is noticed by the customer and others, and so is dishonesty. As a programmer, you interact with many people, including your employer, your coworkers, your customer/users, and even yourself. Honesty in all these relationships is vital to professional programming.

Some examples of where honesty is important include the following programmer tasks:

- **Honesty about your skill level.** The professional programmer is very skilled in many tasks, but the world of software changes so fast that no single person can maintain up-to-date information on all aspects of software tools and development. Even Visual Basic brings its own constant learning curve with the release of each new version. When you are asked about the programming skills you possess, be honest. Let your employer know what tasks you are and are not capable of performing. This includes telling yourself honestly if you are self-employed. Being honest about your skills can save you a lot of headaches later when you have to explain why you were not able to complete correctly one or more portions of an application. Still, being honest does not mean being negative about the skills you do not possess. The professional programmer is constantly learning new tools and new techniques to give the user the best possible software. Although you may not know how to perform some programming method now, you know the rate at which you can acquire new skills. Let those who question you know this great news as well.
- **Honesty about a project estimate.** Estimates are difficult to produce because they not only involve educated guesses about routine aspects of a project, but also conjecture about components for which no comparable programming work has previously been performed. On top of this, the numbers are often "modified" so that the customer will not experience an

extreme degree of sticker shock. This modification puts the programmer in the dangerous situation of having to explain later why the project went over budget. If you are responsible for the estimate presented to the user, do not play the hours modification game with the customer. Be honest about the time you believe it will take to produce a quality application. If your customer is uneasy about the overall cost, see if there are ways in which the estimate can be made more palatable, possibly by trimming off a few unneeded features, or by reducing the unit cost of the billed time.

- **Honesty about cost and schedule overruns.** Be honest about the possibility and the limitations of cost overruns. The contracts my company makes with customers almost always include a clause that allows a project to exceed the original estimate by up to 15 percent, in case any unexpected or unforeseen problems arise during development of the application. The customer is expected to pay all reasonable costs up to this point. If the cost of development moves beyond this 15 percent due to issues not caused by the actions or neglect of the customer, my company absorbs the loss. If the customer makes requests that move the cost beyond the initial estimate, the customer pays. This honesty up front makes all parties happy. Because no one wants the project to go over budget, honest estimates are delivered and accepted before work begins.

- **Honesty about a schedule.** Honesty about schedule refers both to the original schedule estimate, and alterations of the schedule caused by modifications to the project after development begins. Honesty in the original schedule coincides with an honest estimate, as discussed in the previous item. All parties agree on a schedule up front, and pledge to maintain that schedule. If an honest schedule is presented before development, the two things that can allow the schedule to slip are unexpected problems arising after development begins, and modifications to the project plan after development begins. The former event is, by nature, impossible to foresee, and once such problems occur, steps must be taken that attempt to minimize or eliminate the effect that the problem has on the project. A more pressing issue is the second one, where someone (often the user) asks for modifications to the original estimate. If these modifications are accepted into the project, you must be honest about the effect they will have on the schedule (and the cost). Be direct about any extensions to the delivery time of the project, and clearly document all modification requests. Maintain relevant e-mail requests, and for large projects, only allow modifications with appropriate management signatures. This honest approach keeps everyone on schedule, and expectations unambiguous.

- **Honesty about provided features.** Being honest about the features that will appear in an application starts during the planning phase. In the previous chapter on planning, I stressed the importance of understanding the needs of the user. If you do not understand some aspect about the user's task, be honest about it, and obtain a clear understanding before planning ends. Then you will be able to provide those features that are most needed by the user. Giving the user the features he or she needs is important. Giving the user features you know he or she will never use just so you can increase the cost or lengthen the schedule is unethical. A professional programmer does not engage in such activity, or have such an attitude. However, you may know of extra features that will be beneficial to the user over time, and explaining these benefits to the user is a good idea.

- **Honesty about problems when they arise.** If problems do occur, be honest about them as soon as necessary. "As soon as possible" is not the right expression because you should take some time to determine the nature and extent of the problem before concerning everyone about it. Still, keeping silent for too long about an issue during development can have disastrous consequences later on.

- **Honesty about expectations.** Be clear about what you expect from the user. That is, confirm with the users that their involvement is not optional, but required, to deliver a quality application. This will be especially important when problems occur in the application. Many users do not understand (or care) how to provide adequate diagnostic information. Does this sound familiar?

> **Tech:** Thank you for calling Very Soft Ware technical support. How can I help you?
> **User:** Your program crashes when I use it.
> **Tech:** Which of our products are you using?
> **User:** The one that crashes!
> **Tech:** Are you using our word processor or our spreadsheet?
> **User:** Well, your word processor, of course. Does your spreadsheet crash too?
> **Tech:** What were you doing when the program crashed?
> **User:** I was writing a letter.
> **Tech:** Could you be a little more specific?
> **User:** I was writing a letter *to my mother.*

Most users are not intentionally belligerent or cruel about problems. Most users just want to get their work done, and they are upset that your application stopped them from doing so. However, it is also true of most users that they do not know how to report sufficient details to diagnose the problem. Make sure you express your expectations about error reporting and other issues up front to the users. Help them to help you by supplying the materials (either in the program or externally) they need to meet your expectations. This may include supplying a standard error report form for the user to fill out in the unlikely event of a program failure.

Trust

As a programmer, you have a great advantage over the user: a clear understanding about how a software program works. The customer (or user) often knows nothing about programming, and sometimes knows little about how to use a computer. Although training can overcome some of the gaps in the users' understanding, they still must trust in you enough to write the program that best meets their needs. Never take advantage of a user's lack of computer knowledge to provide an inadequate software solution.

Building an atmosphere of trust is essential during all aspects of a project. If the users know that they can trust you, they will be more relaxed about conveying to you the various elements of their work, and sometimes they will entrust you with information about problems in the design of their current workflow. You can use this information to create a better application for the users, even further enhancing their trust in you.

The customer is entrusting you with more than just a portion of their budget. For many Visual Basic projects, you are entrusted with the heart of the customer's business, the ability to perform a service or produce a product efficiently. Your application can mean efficiency or inefficiency, and it does make a difference to the user. Often the customer is also putting their data into your care. Misusing, damaging, or divulging that data is clearly unethical. Suggesting better ways to manage that data, however, is ethical.

Having the customer trust you is also important for your employer, especially if you are a self-employed Visual Basic programmer. Trust is a key to repeat business, and since most software firms are not charitable organizations, repeat business is desirable.

Quality

Quality is one of the important ethical traits of the professional Visual Basic programmer. Quality work announces to the world the skills of the programmer, and like a résumé, it presents in a coherent form the qualifications you possess to implement software solutions. Always be relentless to provide a quality application.

Quality is one of the three legs of the supposedly mythical "schedule-cost-quality" model. This model is deemed mythical because of the impossibility of supplying all three items to the satisfaction of a customer. The theory states that you can have any of the following:

- Short schedule, low cost, poor quality
- Short schedule, high cost, good quality
- Long schedule, low cost, good quality

However, you cannot have short schedule, low cost, and good quality. Actually, I hate this theory, and I have always fought against it, but it does seem to be true. I once received a joke award from a customer stating that I had displayed the "feasibility of the schedule-cost-quality model" because of my attempts to reduce modifications to the scope of the project once development began. Now I can look back on that moment and laugh, but at the time I received this award, I was somewhat upset and embarrassed since the customer never once approached me professionally about the serious business needs that warranted modifications to the application.

I tell you this story not to sing you a ballad of my past miseries, but to present one of the challenges of quality. If you have a customer who refuses to allow a reasonable amount of time, or a reasonable investment of funds, into a project, quality will likely suffer. It is up to you, as a professional programmer, to make it clear to the customer, and all interested parties, the importance of a quality application.

Quality is a difficult attribute to define, since what may be an important aspect of an application for one person may be overlooked by another. Still, there are some constants that run throughout all quality applications. These constants are elaborated on in the other chapters of this book, but some general aspects of a quality application to consider are:

- Meets the needs of the user
- Easy to use and understand
- Consistent interface and usage throughout the application
- Sufficient documentation and support
- High performance level
- Bug free
- Maintainable and modifiable

Ownership

Ownership for the programmer is a difficult issue, since you will rarely be the official legal owner of either the completed application or the data it manages. Even if you work alone to produce a mass-market application, your users will consider themselves to be the owners, not you. Since they paid for your product, they will be correct in that belief. Still, the programmer is not a disinterested party when the ownership of an application in development is under consideration.

During the development process, the professional programmer should consider himself or herself to be a co-owner of the application along with others who are involved in the development process. Co-ownership carries with it two important facets. The first is that you do not possess sole rights to the end product (although in some situations you may legally be the sole owner). By sharing ownership with others, you take their needs and contributions into account while development is under way.

The other component of co-ownership is that, as an owner, you bear a certain amount of responsibility for the application. The more professional you are, the more responsibility you should be willing to bear for the portions of the application under your control.

Taking ownership for a project (or the portion assigned to you) is not a "keep your hands off, it's mine" power grab. Rather, ownership evokes the desire to bring out the best in the application, just like the owner of a classic car desires to restore the vehicle to mint condition.

Once I was discussing a project I was in charge of with the customer. Several times during the conversation I described the application as "my program" (to distinguish it from other development efforts at their office). Soon the customer became agitated. "I am paying you to write that program. I own it. You will stop referring to it as 'your program.'" Perhaps I should have been more careful in my terminology, but I believe that any customer should be happy to hear their competent, professional programmers call a project "mine." Such a statement is not a claim of legal ownership, but of responsibility. The customer was accurate in identifying himself as the legal owner of the application. Yet the responsibility-based ownership of the application belonged both to the customer and to the programmer.

Humility

Humility, the last of the ethical attributes discussed in this chapter, is the most subtle of the attributes, but it can have one of the most powerful effects. Humility does not always come easy to good programmers. Hey, we are good, and others know it. That is why people ask us to write programs for them, right?

We have all met people who thought they were better than everyone else, who in truth were only mediocre at what they did at work. I have met people who were as good as their self-proclamations, but their boasting made them quite difficult to work around. The professional Visual Basic programmer is very good at programming, and the user knows it. However, that knowledge does not come about from boasting, but from the professionalism of the work.

Humility does not mean you hide the truth about your competence from others. If you did, you would be shirking your responsibility for honesty stressed earlier in this chapter. Yet the knowledge of your own skills is not something to be lorded over others. Proclaiming your qualifications with the blast of trumpets can be like erecting a brick wall over which your customers and coworkers refuse to climb.

Consider the ideas and suggestions of others, even when those suggestions run contrary to your own ideas about how an application should be designed. Once after delivering a prototype of an application to a customer, several points of difference arose. Although most of them were clarifications of the original plan and its implementation, one issue was aesthetic in nature. I had designed a form to collect basic customer information, including the full first, middle, and last name. Although I do not remember the exact field lengths any longer, I do recall that much more space was allocated for the first and last names than for the middle name. The form I presented had fields arranged similar to what is shown in Figure 8–1.

| Figure 8–1 | *The way I wanted it.* |

After the customer reviewed the application, they insisted that I visibly shorten the middle name field. Although I tried to explain about the importance of a consistent look, and even directed them to such instructions as found in the *Microsoft Windows 95 User Interface Guidelines* book, I was overruled and required to change the form (Figure 8–2).

| Figure 8–2 | *The way the customer wanted it.* |

This is where humility is necessary. Misaligned fields tend to irritate me, and I was not happy about shortening the middle name field. But the customer had a legitimate reason for modifying my design. As the one paying the money for the project, the final word rested with the customer. I was humbled, not because my design was wrong, but because the customer felt strongly enough to change one aspect of the program. This was not a loss for me, but a victory for the user.

Above all, be easy to work with. Like it or not, any programmer can be replaced. Still, it is difficult to replace a truly professional Visual Basic programmer.

Summary

Ethics is so much more than an aspect of programming. Keep in mind that if you only act ethically in one area of your life, then you are not an ethical person. Ethics is built upon the world-view of an individual, and the way you act when programming is the way you will act in other areas of your life as well.

Standards

Consistency of quality in your software applications is an essential trait. Even if you have a great attitude, and you write excellent documentation, if you lack the knowledge and ability to write good code, then the software is at risk, as is the user's data. As you now move through the standards section of this book, keep in the front of your mind the goal of building software that is consistent in quality, consistent in *high* quality.

Declaration Standards

Often thought of as the only place where standards can be applied within a program, the use of declaration plays an important part in the style of an application's source code. This chapter discusses those standards and guidelines that are employed when using declaration within the Visual Basic source code. Chapter 2, *Using Declaration*, provides a general overview of the use of declaration within a Visual Basic application.

Declaration plays an essential role in any Visual Basic application, and its use must be handled with care. As you read through this chapter, do not think of it as a set of rules to master *you*, but the description of an environment in which *you* master the data and information processed by your application.

Throughout this chapter, the term "module" refers to any type of major file component that can be added to a Visual Basic project, such as forms, ".bas" modules, user controls, property pages, and so on. The expression "code module" refers only to those files added to a project that have a ".bas" extension.

Nomenclature Standards

The use of declaration standards in Visual Basic includes both the naming of code and user interface elements (nomenclature), and the declaration and use of those elements (instantiation). This discussion of declaration begins with the nomenclature standards. Believe it or not, most elements defined within Visual Basic do not use the Hungarian standards you have heard so much about. Each of the elements described in this chapter takes its naming standards from a combination of tradition and functionality.

Nomenclature for Variables

The names given to variables within a Visual Basic application are one of the most obvious forms of declaration standards in your program. *Hungarian* naming conventions provide a method by which the name given to a variable can carry information about the type, scope, and usage of a variable. Invented by Charles Simonyi of Microsoft (a Hungarian by descent), this system of naming variables was first used for applications written in the C language. Perhaps *Hungarian* is an appropriate moniker for the system since, like many human languages, the convention comes in a variety of dialects. The dialect presented here is a distillation of several variations, with adequate room left for the addition of new entries.

A variable name is Hungarian if it is built up from four components.

```
[scope][tag]basename[qualifier]
```

Scope indicates the visibility of the variable within the application. The scope, when present, is the first component of a Hungarian variable name, and it always appears in lower case. Table 9.1 identifies the different values for the scope.

Table 9.1	Hungarian Scope Prefixes for Visual Basic
Scope	**Description**
g	A global variable, defined within the Declarations section of a module using the Public keyword. Variables of this scope are accessible from all routines within the application.
m	A module-level variable, defined within the Declarations section of the module using the Private keyword. Variables of this scope are accessible from all routines within the module, class, form, or other code file in which the variable is declared, but are hidden from other modules.
x	A local variable, defined with the Static keyword.
nothing	A local variable, defined with the Dim keyword. Variables passed into a routine through its argument list also have no scope prefix. Also, user interface control names do not require the use of a scope prefix, as they are module-level in scope by definition.

Most variables defined within a Sub, Function, or Property routine will have no scope prefix; only those local variables declared with the Static keyword need indicate the scope. All variables defined outside of a Sub, Function, or Property routine will always start with a "g" or "m" prefix. (See the "Nomenclature Exceptions" section for an exception with public class variables.)

VBScript programmers should note that all variables defined outside the confines of a Sub or Function are actually module-level in scope. However, because of the temporary nature of Visual Basic script code, concepts like "module-level" and "global-level" are not always relevant. When declaring variables in VBScript outside of a defined routine, either use the local variable declaration syntax with the Dim statement, or the module-level syntax with the Private statement (prefixing variables with "m"). Whichever method you choose, be consistent throughout your script code. All examples of VBScript declarations in this book use the Private syntax with "m" prefixes.

```
Private mnCounter
```

Tag is used to identify the type of a variable being declared. In general, tag values range from one to four characters in length, and are always lower case.

If you are declaring an array variable, the letter "a" is prefixed to the tag. For example, the declaration

```
Dim asColonies(1 To 13) As String
```

indicates a local array of 13 string variables, while

```
Dim sColony As String
```

declares storage for a single local string value. The "a" array indicator, when present, always appears before the actual tag, but after any scope prefix.

Table 9.2 presents a list of the more common tag values used in Visual Basic programming.

Table 9.2	Hungarian Tag Prefixes for Visual Basic
Tag	**Meaning**
b	Boolean data type. In Visual Basic 3.0, Boolean values were declared as Integer. Visual Basic 4.0 introduced a true Boolean data type.
by	Byte data type.
ctr	Generic control type, when a control variable can indicate more than one type of control.
dt	Date data type for handling dates or times.
fc	Currency data type.
fd	Double data type.
fs	Single data type.
h	Handle data type. In Visual Basic 3.0, handles were declared as Integer. Beginning with the 32-bit version of Visual Basic 4.0, handles are declared as Long.

Table 9.2	Hungarian Tag Prefixes for Visual Basic *(Continued)*
Tag	**Meaning**
l	Long data type (the tag is the letter *ell*).
n	Integer data type.
obj	Object data type.
s	String data type. For fixed-length strings, append the size of the string to the end of the variable name, as in sBuffer200.
va	Variant data type used for Variant Arrays.
vnt	Variant data type. In general, Variants should not be used unless no other data type will meet a particular need.

Because of the unlimited number of ActiveX components that can be added or created for use with Visual Basic, a full rendering of tags is impossible. From time to time you will have to add to the lists of tags found in this chapter. When adding new tags to the list, take care not to create conflicts with other prefix combinations. For example, if you create an ActiveX component for a chemistry application that represents a gas, do not use the tag "gas" for your new object. A declaration such as

```
Dim gasHelium As ChemGas
```

could be interpreted as a global array of string variables ("g" for global, "a" for array, "s" for string, although the declaration shows that this is truly not the case). Select a unique tag, ranging from two to five characters, that will be free from such conflicts of interpretation.

Basename is a traditional variable name, such as "CustomerName" or "ScanPosition," always in mixed case with an initial capital letter. *Qualifier* is an extension that differentiates variations in related variables. For example, lCustOrderFirst and lCustOrderLast indicate the first and last orders for a customer. The qualifiers for these variables are "First" and "Last." For the purposes of the standards described in this chapter, you can consider Qualifier to be part of Basename. When declaring variables, the combined Basename and Qualifier must be at least two characters in length.

Visual Basic, Scripting Edition, contains only a single non-object data type: Variant. It would be somewhat useless to prefix every variable in your VBScript page with the "vnt" tag, since such naming would not distinguish between the different uses of these Variants. When declaring variables in VBScript, provide names that you would give the same variables in a standard Visual Basic application. For instance, if you declare a variable that will only be used to hold a customer name, name it "sCustName" instead of "vntCustName."

Avoid negative variable names; that is, variable names containing the words "No," "Not," and other similar words, especially when using Boolean variables. It is clearer to write

```
If bReady Then
```

rather than

```
If Not(bNotReady) Then
```

Nomenclature for Constants

Constants are non-variable variables; that is, a named value that cannot be changed while the application is running. They include those programmer-defined elements created with either the Const or #Const keywords. You can also establish a constant by entering it in the Conditional Compilation Arguments field in the Visual Basic Project Properties form.

A constant name always appears with upper-case letters and digits, with underscore characters separating the significant words of the name.

```
Public Const SLICE_OF_PI = 3.1416#
```

Use a common prefix for related constants, not a suffix.

Correct
```
Private Const TAB_CUSTOMER = 1
Private Const TAB_VENDOR = 2
Private Const TAB_ORDER = 3
```

Incorrect
```
Private Const CUSTOMER_TAB = 1
Private Const VENDOR_TAB = 2
Private Const ORDER_TAB = 3
```

If you are adding constants to your project that were defined by a third party (such as those found in the API Text Viewer application supplied with Visual Basic), retain the case and style used by the original vendor.

Nomenclature for User-Defined Types

User-defined types are created by using the Type statement. The syntax of the statement includes two namable parts, the initial tag, and the variable elements that make up the data type.

```
Private Type CustomerType    ' This is the tag line
    lCustomerID As Long      ' This is an element line
    sCustomerName As String  ' This is another element
End Type
```

When naming the elements within the data type definition, follow the Hungarian naming standards for local variables listed earlier in this chapter. The data type tag ("CustomerType" in this example) appears in mixed-case text, beginning with a capital letter, and with no underscore characters. It should be short, yet descriptive. Always end the tag name with the word "Type."

Nomenclature for Enumerated Data Types

You can create enumerated lists of long integer values through the Enum statement. Like the syntax for user-defined types, the syntax of enumerated data types has two parts: an introductory tag, and a list of elements.

```
Public Enum CompassPointEnum    ' The tag line
    pntNorth = 1                ' And four element lines
    pntEast
    pntSouth
    pntWest
End Enum
```

The tag name of the data type appears in mixed-case text, with an initial capital letter, and no underscore characters. It should state clearly the purpose of the data type, although it need not be overly wordy. Always follow the tag name with the text "Enum" as shown in the "CompassPointEnum" tag name in the example.

The elements within the data type look a lot like Hungarian variable names. They are not true Hungarian names because the initial text does not identify the data type of each element (which is Long). Each element should begin with a lower-case leader, with the same leader applied to each element within the data type ("pnt" in this example). This leader is a two-to-five letter abbreviation for the type of elements being enumerated (compass "point" in the example). Follow the leader with a unique mixed-case element name. Avoiding conflicts with Hungarian variable prefixes is a good idea, but if the context of the enumerated constant set is clear, it is permissible to share prefixes with a seldom-used Hungarian prefix.

Nomenclature for Line Labels

Line labels are used as destinations for GoTo, GoSub, and On Error GoTo statements. Visual Basic allows both numeric and alphanumeric line labels, but they are treated a little differently. Alphanumeric labels must be followed by a colon (":"), while the colon is optional after a numeric label. Numeric labels can be used as reference points in error processing (via the Erl keyword), while alphanumeric labels give no such information.

Although numeric labels seem to have the advantage, they should not be used within your application. Numeric line labels are a holdover from the original versions of the BASIC language, in which every line had to start with a line number. Only use numeric labels if you need to gather additional error information with the Erl keyword. Instead of meaningless numeric labels, use alphanumeric labels with names that hint at the purpose of the label. Line labels should consist of letters and digits only, starting with an initial capital letter, and containing no underscore characters. They appear in mixed case.

```
NextIteration:
    ' ----- Continue with the next group
```

Nomenclature for Procedures

Procedures include private and public functions, subroutines, properties (Get, Let, and Set), class methods, and other similar constructs. Unlike variables, procedures do not follow the Hungarian naming standards. Instead, all procedure names appear in mixed-case type, with each significant word capitalized. Never use underscores within the procedure name.

```
Public Sub DoAUsefulAction(nMethod As Integer)
```

Events, although true procedures, do not follow the naming system described in this section since the control or class on which the event is based defines the name of the event.

```
Private Sub txtBirthdate_GotFocus()
```

Because procedure names, especially those belonging to Function and Property Get procedures, do not contain any data type information, it is imperative that you supply meaningful names to all of your procedures.

If you have two private procedures in different modules that perform basically the same function (but they cannot be logically combined into a single public procedure), provide the same name for both procedures. For example, when I create a form that provides a basic "properties" view of a logical object (such as "customer properties" or "document properties"), I generally have these three procedures defined within the form's code pane.

```
Private Sub LoadData()
    ' ----- Populate the form with data from the active
    '          record.  The module-level variable mlActiveID
    '          contains the primary key of the active record.

Private Function VerifyData() As Boolean
    ' ----- Called when the user clicks the OK button.
    '          Make sure all fields contain valid data.
    '          Return True if all data is valid, or False if
    '          there are any problems.

Private Function SaveData() As Boolean
    ' ----- Update the existing record, or add a new record
```

```
'        to the database.  Set mlActiveID to the ID of
'        the new record.  Return True on success.
```

I often have several of these properties forms within an application, and each form contains variations of these procedures, all with the names listed in this sample code. If you do reuse procedure names in this fashion, make sure that the procedures are always defined as Private to the module.

Avoid using negative names for your procedures. That is, refrain from words such as "Not" and "No" in the name of each procedure, especially those Function procedures that return a Boolean value. There is nothing more disarming than trying to decipher the return value of a negative function call.

```
If (Not ClearanceNotNeeded(sUser, bNotReady)) Then
```

Nomenclature for Declares

The Declare statement is used to access dynamic link library (DLL) procedures supplied by Microsoft, another third party, or a member of your programming team. Once declared, such API procedures act as if they were written within the Visual Basic source code itself. Because of this, the naming conventions for Declare statements closely follow those of procedures. The Declare statement has an Alias option through which you can supply the original name of the procedure as it appears in the DLL. This is useful when the procedure name conflicts with a Visual Basic keyword or other code object. It is also useful for turning procedure names that do not follow the standards of this book into compliant procedures.

```
Public Declare Sub DoSomeWork Lib "makework.dll" _
    Alias "do_some_work" (ByVal nWorkType As Integer)
```

In this example, the makework.dll library contains a subroutine named "do_some_work." Through the syntax of the Declare statement, the name was moved into the more compliant form "DoSomeWork."

Because the Declare statement accesses features that are external to the Visual Basic application, you may wish to bend the nomenclature rules in favor of overall project consistency. If you are developing your Visual Basic application in conjunction with another group using C++ or Pascal to create a DLL, using the naming conventions of the DLL routines when accessing those functions may simplify code reviews and other activities that involve both groups of programmers.

Nomenclature for User Interface Elements

The user interface in the Visual Basic development environment consists of two types of objects: work areas (forms, user control backgrounds, Report Designer backgrounds, etc.), and controls to be placed on the work areas (menus, command buttons, text fields, combo boxes, etc.). All of these components fall under the same naming standards as variables: the Hungarian naming standards. These conventions apply both to actual user interface elements, and to references to such objects within the source code of your application. In fact, within the source code, user interface elements are really just instances of object (or class) variables, so they follow all of the Hungarian standards for variables. Within the user interface itself, Hungarian names are used without the scope prefix. User interface elements are module-level in scope by definition, so the scope prefix is redundant.

Tables 9.3 through 9.8 present various lists of Hungarian prefixes for user interface and other data object elements commonly used within Visual Basic. This list is by no means complete, as there are new user interface elements created by Microsoft and other vendors every day. When you employ additional third-party controls, append your standard names for those new elements to these lists to assure consistency in naming all of your user interface elements.

The first table in this set is Table 9.3, listing the standard Hungarian names for those controls built in to the Visual Basic form designer.

Table 9.3	Hungarian Tag Prefixes for Built-In Visual Basic Controls
Tag	**Meaning**
cbo	ComboBox control, including the drop-down combo, simple combo, and drop-down list styles.
chk	CheckBox control.
cmd	CommandButton control
dir	DirListBox control. See also "drv" and "fil."
drv	DriveListBox control. See also "dir" and "fil."
fil	FileListBox control. See also "dir" and "drv."
fra	Frame control.
hsb	HScrollBar (horizontal scroll bar) control. See also "vsb."
lbl	Static Label control.
lin	Line drawing object. See also "shp."
lst	ListBox control, both standard and checkbox styles.
mnu	Menu control, including standard, pop-up, and system menus.
ole	OLE container control. If possible, include a short abbreviation of the foreign application in the control name.
opt	OptionButton control.

Table 9.3	Hungarian Tag Prefixes for Built-In Visual Basic Controls *(Continued)*
Tag	**Meaning**
pic	PictureBox control.
shp	Shape drawing object, including Rectangles, Squares, Ovals, Circles, Rounded Rectangles, and Rounded Squares. See also "lin."
tmr	Timer control.
txt	TextBox control, both single-line and multi-line styles.
vsb	VScrollBar (vertical scroll bar) control. See also "hsb."

Table 9.4 documents the Hungarian prefixes for user interface backgrounds and workspaces, those areas on which you place other controls. Also listed are naming conventions for code-only modules.

Table 9.4	Hungarian Tag Prefixes for User Interface Workspaces
Tag	**Meaning**
bas	Standard code modules, which generally have a ".bas" extension.
cls	Class modules. Do not use for variables of a generic class type.
ctl	User control module.
de	Data environment.
dob	User document module.
frm	Form module, both Single Document Interface (SDI) and Multi Document Interface (MDI) styles.
htm	DHTML pages, documents, document titles, and document bodies.
pag	Property page module.
rpt	Data report module.
wc	WebClass module.

Included in Table 9.5 are those elements available in the DHTML Page Designer. Many of the elements in this table use the same prefixes as those for standard Visual Basic form controls.

Table 9.5	Hungarian Tag Prefixes for DHTML Elements
Tag	**Meaning**
cbo	DHTML Select control.
chk	DHTML CheckBox control.

Table 9.5	Hungarian Tag Prefixes for DHTML Elements *(Continued)*
Tag	**Meaning**
cmd	DHTML Button control, ResetButton control, and SubmitButton control.
hdn	DHTML HiddenField control.
htm	DHTML pages, documents, document titles, and document bodies.
lin	DHTML HorizontalRule object.
lnk	DHTML Hyperlink object.
lst	DHTML List control.
opt	DHTML Option control.
p	DHTML paragraph ID.
pic	DHTML Image control.
tbl	DHTML tables and table bodies.
td	DHTML table cells.
tr	DHTML table rows.
txt	DHTML TextField control, TextArea control, and PasswordField control.
upl	DHTML FileUpload control.

Table 9.6 contains Hungarian prefixes for data-related objects used in writing Visual Basic data access code with any of the standard data interfaces (DAO, RDO, ADO, etc.).

Table 9.6	Hungarian Tag Prefixes for Data-Related Objects
Tag	**Meaning**
clm	RDO column object or collection.
com	ADO command object. Also for command objects within a data environment.
con	ADO connection object, DAO connection object or collection, or RDO connection object or collection. Also for connection objects within a data environment.
ctn	DAO container object or collection.
db	DAO database object or collection.
dbe	DAO database engine object, or RDO database engine object.

Table 9.6	Hungarian Tag Prefixes for Data-Related Objects *(Continued)*
Tag	**Meaning**
doc	DAO document object or collection.
dta	Intrinsic Data control, ADO Data control, or Remote Data control.
env	RDO environment object or collection. For Visual Basic data environments, use the tag "de."
err	ADO error object or collection, DAO error object or collection, or RDO error object or collection.
fld	ADO field object or collection, or DAO field object or collection.
grp	DAO group object or collection.
idx	DAO index object or collection.
obj	Generic object variable.
prm	ADO parameter object or collection, DAO parameter object or collection, or RDO parameter object or collection.
prp	ADO property object or collection, or DAO property object or collection.
qry	DAO QueryDef object or collection, or RDO query object or collection.
rec	ADO record object.
rel	DAO relation object or collection.
rs	ADO recordset object, DAO recordset object or collection, or RDO resultset object or collection. Recordset objects include table, snapshot, and dynaset-style recordsets, and all other allowed cursor types.
stm	ADO steam object.
tbl	DAO TableDef object or collection, or RDO table object or collection. Also used for DHTML tables and table bodies.
usr	DAO user object or collection.
wsp	DAO workspace object or collection.

Use Table 9.7 to name elements placed on a Report Designer workspace.

The Hungarian naming standards for many of the controls supplied by Microsoft with Visual Basic appear in Table 9.8.

Menus that are attached to forms carry additional nomenclature rules that identify the natural grouping of those menus. Prefix the names of all second-level menus, third-level menus, and so on, with the name of the menu just above it. For example, consider the menu in Figure 9–1.

Table 9.7	Hungarian Tag Prefixes for Report Designer Elements
Tag	**Meaning**
lbl	RptLabel control.
lin	RptLine drawing object.
pic	RptImage control.
rpt	Data report module.
shp	RptShape drawing object, including Rectangles, Squares, Ovals, Circles, Rounded Rectangles, and Rounded Squares.
txt	RptTextBox control and RptFunction control.

Table 9.8	Hungarian Tag Prefixes for User Interface Controls
Tag	**Meaning**
ani	Animation control.
cal	Calendar control. See also "dtp" and "mvw."
cbo	ComboBox control, including the drop-down combo, simple combo, and drop-down list styles, data bound ComboBox control ("DataCombo"), lightweight ComboBox control, or DHTML Select control. See also "icbo."
cht	MSChart control, or other controls used for bar and line charts. See also "gra."
chk	CheckBox control, lightweight CheckBox control, or DHTML CheckBox control.
clb	CoolBar control. See also "tlb."
clp	Picture Clip control. See also "img" and "pic."
cmd	CommandButton control, lightweight CommandButton control, DHTML Button control, DHTML ResetButton control, or DHTML SubmitButton control.
comm	Communications control or component.
dir	Directory List Box control. See also "drv" and "fil."
dlg	Common Dialog Box control, whether used for opening files, saving files, selecting print options, selecting colors, selecting fonts, or displaying on-line help.
drp	Data Repeater control.

Table 9.8	Hungarian Tag Prefixes for User Interface Controls *(Continued)*
Tag	**Meaning**
drv	Drive List Box control. See also "dir" and "fil."
dta	Intrinsic Data control, ADO Data control, or Remote Data control.
dtp	Date Picker control. See also "cal" and "mvw."
fil	File List Box control. See also "dir" and "drv."
fra	Frame control, lightweight Frame control, or 3D panel control.
gau	Any type of gauge control, other than the Slider control supplied with Visual Basic. See also "sld."
gra	Graph control, or any control for drawing graphs, but not charts. See also "cht."
grd	Grid control, FlexGrid control, data bound grid control, and other third-party grid controls. See also "hgrd."
hgrd	Hierarchical FlexGrid control. See also "grd."
hsb	Horizontal Scroll Bar control, lightweight Horizontal Scroll Bar control, or Flat Scroll Bar control in the horizontal orientation. See also "vsb."
icbo	Image Combo control. See also "cbo."
img	ImageList control. See also "clp" and "pic."
inet	Internet Transfer control, including FTP, Gopher, HTTP, HTTPS, and any other supported protocol. See also "skt" and "web."
lbl	Static Label control, or Report Designer RptLabel control.
lin	Line drawing object, Report Designer RptLine drawing object, or DHTML HorizontalRule object. See also "shp."
lst	ListBox control, both standard and checkbox styles, data bound ListBox control ("DataList"), lightweight ListBox control, or DHTML List control.
lvw	ListView control.
mm	Multimedia control.
mnu	Menu control, including standard, pop-up, and system menus.
mpm	MAPI message control.
mps	MAPI session control.
mvw	MonthView control. See also "cal" and "dtp."

Table 9.8	Hungarian Tag Prefixes for User Interface Controls *(Continued)*
Tag	**Meaning**
ole	OLE Container control.
opt	OptionButton control, lightweight OptionButton control, or DHTML Option control.
pic	PictureBox control, Image control, Report Designer RptImage control, or DHTML Image control. See also "clp" and "img."
prg	Progress bar control.
rtf	RichTextBox control. See also "txt."
shp	Shape drawing object, including Rectangles, Squares, Ovals, Circles, Rounded Rectangles, and Rounded Squares, or Report Designer RptShape drawing object. See also "lin."
skt	WinSock control. See also "inet" and "web."
sld	Slider control. See also "gau."
spn	Spin or UpDown control. If used with a "buddy" control (such as a text box), the remainder of the variable name following the "spn" tag should be the same as the post-tag name of the buddy control. For example, if you have a spin control that is a buddy to a text box named "txtYear," the spin control should be named "spnYear."
sts	Status Bar control.
sys	SysInfo control.
tab	Tabbed Dialog control, TabStrip control, or any third-party tabbed section control.
tlb	ToolBar control. See also "clb."
tmr	Timer control.
tvw	TreeView control.
txt	TextBox control, both single-line and multi-line styles, Masked Edit control, lightweight TextBox control, Report Designer RptTextBox control, Report Designer RptFunction control, DHTML TextField control, DHTML TextArea control, or DHTML PasswordField control. See also "rtf."
vsb	Vertical Scroll Bar control, lightweight Vertical Scroll Bar control, or Flat Scroll Bar control in the vertical orientation. See also "hsb."
web	Web Browser control. See also "inet" and "skt."

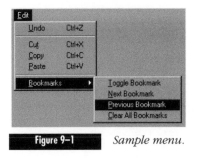

Figure 9–1 *Sample menu.*

Using such "cascading" Hungarian names for menus, the menu items for the menu in Figure 9–1 might have the names listed in Table 9.9.

Table 9.9	Sample Menu Naming Conventions
Menu Item Caption	**Menu Item Name**
Edit	mnuEdit
Undo	mnuEditUndo
(divider bar)	mnuEditBar1
Cut	mnuEditCut
Copy	mnuEditCopy
Paste	mnuEditPaste
(divider bar)	mnuEditBar2
Bookmarks	mnuEditBook
Toggle Bookmark	mnuEditBookToggle
Next Bookmark	mnuEditBookNext
Previous Bookmark	mnuEditBookPrevious
Clear All Bookmarks	mnuEditBookClear

When adding divider bars to a menu, always build the name by taking the parent's menu name, and adding the text "Bar$x$" where x is an increasing number within the parent menu's scope.

Menus can be built using control arrays, where several menus share a common name, but vary by an index number. Only use control arrays for menus where the menu items are truly related and can share a common base of code. For instance, if you have a menu with three mutually exclusive checkable items that all process similar code, they can appear in a control array. Such a control array could use code similar to the following:

```
Private Sub mnuModeChange_Click(Index As Integer)
    ' ----- The user changed the mode
    Dim nMode As Integer

    ' ----- Put a check next to the correct mode
    For nMode = MODE_FIRST To MODE_LAST
        mnuModeChange(nMode).Checked = (nMode = Index)
    Next nMode

    ' ----- Update the rest of the display
    SwitchDisplayMode Index
End Sub
```

Do not use control arrays for elements that are not directly related in their logic. For instance, the common menu items found in an Edit menu (Undo, Cut, Copy, Paste) will generally have coded functionality so different that they could not share a common algorithm. They also should not share a common event procedure.

Incorrect

```
Private Sub mnuEditAction_Click(Index As Integer)
    ' ----- This is bad code!!!
    Select Case Index
        Case 0
            ' ----- Undo related code
        Case 2
            ' ----- Cut related code
        Case 3
            ' ----- Copy related code
        Case 4
            ' ----- Paste related code
    End Select
End Sub
```

Nomenclature Exceptions

There are legitimate times when you should not strictly follow the guidelines set forth in this chapter. Fortunately, those times are few, and your inclination will be to abandon the conventions in these minor cases.

Some traditional variable names are excluded from the rules of Hungarian nomenclature. Any user-defined data type or Declare statement that you obtain from the API Text Viewer application that ships with Visual Basic, or directly from the Windows Software Development Kit (SDK), should not be altered to conform to the Hungarian dialect described in this chapter. Copy and paste the names as-is directly from the SDK or API Viewer into your code pane.

Event arguments that are generated by Visual Basic need to be left alone. For instance, the standard argument list for the MouseMove event is

```
Button As Integer, Shift As Integer, _
   X As Single, Y As Single
```

Oh, it makes my eyes hurt just looking at this list. Not a single Hungarian name in the bunch. Still, these arguments fall under the grandfather clause of variable naming; they came into existence with Visual Basic, and too many programmers depend on the consistency by which they appear in every Mouse-Move event declaration. Do not alter such names to the Hungarian standard.

When you are building a class that contains public module-level variables, name them as if they were used to name Property Get and Property Let routines. Public class variables look like properties to the user of the class; assign such variables property-like names.

Instantiation Standards

Now that you have decided on names for your variables, constants, controls, and other elements of your application, it is time to put them into active use. Instantiation is the process of adding declaration elements to your source code.

Instantiation of Variables

Because all of your modules will contain the Option Explicit statement, you are required by the Visual Basic development environment to declare every variable before use. Take care in declaring your variables, as these declarations will determine the range of values available for each variable. Declare your variables in known locations, and in a consistent manner.

Visual Basic contains six types of variable declaration: global, module, local, static, passed, and redeclared. Always place *global* variables in the Declarations section of a standard code module, never in a Form. The look of these variables is pretty consistent.

```
Public glCustomerID As Long
```

The declaration begins with the Public keyword, not the antiquated Global keyword. It is quickly followed by the letter "g," the Hungarian prefix for global variables. And if a consistent declaration head was not enough, the end of the line always contains the appropriate As clause (except in VBScript).

Module variables would almost be indistinguishable from global variables were it not for the replacement of the Public keyword with the Private keyword. They always appear in the Declarations section of the appropriate module. While Visual Basic allows you to declare these variables with the Dim keyword, always use the Private keyword instead.

```
Private msLoginName As String
```

Module variable names begin with the "m" scope prefix, and are followed by the appropriate As clause.

Your application will generally have more *local* variables than any other type. In fact, you should strive to make most of your variables local in scope. Global and module variables are convenient, but they carry risks (read all about those risks in Chapter 2). You declare local variables within a procedure. Visual Basic affords you a lot of freedom in the placement of your declared variables; you can declare a variable almost anywhere in your procedure, even as the very last line. However, spreading out your declarations in this manner makes maintenance of your source code more cumbersome. Instead, place the declaration of all local variables at the very top of your routine, just after the introductory comment.

```
Private Sub txtStatus_Change()
    ' ----- Update other fields based on the current status
    Dim sActiveStatus As String
    Dim nCounter As Integer
    ...
```

Except within VBScript code, always include the appropriate As clause, plus a useful Hungarian variable name. If you have variables in many routines that share a common purpose, give them the same name throughout your code. For example, many times you will include For loops in your source code. Instead of using a variable name such as *x* or *i* (dreadfully non-Hungarian names) as the loop variable, use nCounter, or a similar consistent name. Such consistency will make it easier for others to follow the thought process of your source code.

Static variables appear within procedures, but act like global variables, retaining their values from the end of one use of the routine to the start of the next use. Visual Basic allows you to preface the procedure declaration with the Static keyword to cause all variables within the routine to automatically assume the role of static variables. However, you should shun this method; instead, use the Static keyword before each variable that needs to be static. Do not forget to include the "x" Hungarian scope prefix before the variable name.

```
Public Function RunningTotal(nNewValue As Integer) _
        As Integer
    ' ----- Maintain a running total of values.  Return the
    '           current total on each call to the function.  If
    '           nNewValue is 0, clear the total.
    Static xnTotalSoFar As Integer

    If (nNewValue = 0) Then
        xnTotalSoFar = 0
    Else
        xnTotalSoFar = xnTotalSoFar + nNewValue
    End If
```

```
      RunningTotal = xnTotalSoFar
End Function
```

When declaring static variables in a local procedure, place them just after the declarations of local variables. The use of static variables can sometimes hide logic errors, especially when used in conjunction with recursive procedures. Use static variables, but use them carefully.

Passed variables are those that are listed as arguments of a procedure declaration. Consider the Unload event for a form.

```
Private Sub Form_Unload(Cancel As Integer)
```

This event procedure contains a single passed variable named Cancel. Variables can be passed by value (local changes to the variable are not passed up to the calling routine) or by reference (changes made to the variable are reflected in the original variable used in the calling routine). By default, all passed variables are passed by reference. It is not necessary to specify the ByRef keyword for pass-by-reference variables (although it is required in Declare statements), but you will need to use the ByVal keyword to specify pass-by-value. If you do pass in a variable by value, never modify its value within the procedure or in a subordinate procedure. Although this is allowed in Visual Basic, you should declare a separate local variable and use it instead of treating a by-value passed variable like a local variable.

Visual Basic allows you treat passed variables as optional arguments by using the Optional keyword. If you want to use the IsMissing function to test whether an optional argument was supplied, you must declare the argument as a Variant. Use the proper Hungarian prefix ("vnt") for such optional arguments.

The final type of variable is the *redeclared* variable. These are array variables that are initially declared without array subscripts using the Public, Private, or Dim statements, or as an element of a user-defined type, and then later resized using the ReDim statement.

```
Dim asDayInfo() As String
. . .
ReDim asDayInfo(1 To nDaysInMonth)
```

Visual Basic allows you to create a new variable using the ReDim statement (without an initial Public, Private, or Dim statement for that variable). Do not employ this method of variable declaration. Instead, always initially create resizable variables using a Public, Private, or Dim statement, and later resize it using the ReDim statement.

Never change the number of dimensions using the ReDim statement. If you intend to use a certain redeclared variable with two dimensions, never give it fewer than two dimensions, or more than two dimensions, when using the ReDim statement, even though this is allowed. Changing the number of dimensions throughout your source code also changes the expectations for the use of the variable. If you originally redeclare a variable with two dimensions in one routine, and later redeclare it again with three dimensions in another routine, you violate the original definition of the variable when the first ReDim statement was employed.

When declaring variables in versions of Visual Basic other than VBScript, only include a single variable with each Dim, Private, and Public statement. That is, each variable should be declared on a line by itself.

Incorrect

```
Dim nCounter As Integer, sCustName As String
```

Correct

```
Dim nCounter As Integer
Dim sCustName As String
```

Declaring variables in VBScript is a little different from the same process in other flavors of Visual Basic. With Variant being the only type of true non-object data type, the As clause is irrelevant. Still, variables are declared in VBScript for specific purposes, with some of those purposes requiring date variables, some string variables, and some numeric variables. It may be useful to visually group variables of like data type during declaration. In such cases, it is permissible to place more than one variable within the same Dim statement, but only if they start with the same Hungarian prefix.

VBScript Only

```
Private msCustName, msCustPhone, msCustCity
Private mnCounter, mnOrdersSoFar
Private mdtOrderDate, mdtShipDate
```

Instantiation of Constants

Place constant definitions in the Declarations section of a module, form, class, and so on. Although Visual Basic allows you to declare constants in any procedure, you must shun this practice. Placing all constants in the Declaration sections of your application makes the quick location of such constants easy.

Always precede the definition of a constant with either the Public or Private keyword. Private constants can appear in any Declarations section, but a Public constant must never appear in a Form module (Visual Basic will not permit such a definition). If you find a need to declare a set of related incremental numeric constants, consider an enumerated data type instead.

Like variables, constants can be declared with an As clause.

```
Public Const MAX_ADDRESSES As Integer = 12
```

The use of the As clause is optional when a type declaration character is attached to the constant's assigned value. (See the "Data Typing of Literals" section later in this chapter for a discussion of type declaration characters.) If you are declaring constants of type Currency, Double, Integer, Long, or Single, use the appropriate As clause, or follow the literal value of each constant with the appropriate type declaration character.

```
Public Const MAX_ADDRESSES = 12%
```

When declaring constants of type Boolean, Byte, Date, String, or Variant, use the As clause to correctly identify the constant.

Some versions of Visual Basic make Year 2000 compliance difficult by trimming off the first two digits of a four-digit year from literal dates appearing in the 1900s. In those versions of the Visual Basic development environment, if you type in the date literal #9/23/1999#, Visual Basic will conveniently change this to #9/23/99#. To overcome this deficiency, always enter date literals from the 1900s in string format.

```
Public Const PROCESS_BASE_DATE As Date = "1/1/1980"
```

Instantiation of User-Defined Types

User-defined data types always appear in the Declarations section of some type of module. Always include the Public or Private prefix to the data type definition, remembering that Visual Basic will not allow public user-defined types in a Form module.

Instantiation of Enumerated Data Types

Enumerated data type sets always appear in the Declarations section of a module, form, or other similar user interface class. When declaring the data type, always include the Public or Private keyword before the declaration. A Private enumerated data type can appear in any type of module, but a Public enumerated data type may only appear in the Declarations section of non-form modules.

Instantiation of Line Labels

Line labels are simple to use, and as such, the rules surrounding their use are simple too. The only real rule has to do with placement of the label. Although line labels can appear on the same line as logic statements, such lines are no longer label lines, but true logic lines. Line labels should always appear on a line of their own. Even comments should appear after the line label line.

Correct

```
DetermineResult:
```

```
' ----- Find out if processing was successful
mbResult = True
```

Incorrect

```
' ----- Find out if processing was successful
DetermineResult: mbResult = True
```

If you have a line label accessible section of code that appears in numerous procedures, use the same line label throughout the application for the similar sections. For example, if you have an error handler that appears in many of your routines, a label with a name such as "ErrorHandler" will make the label name more meaningful as someone peruses your source code.

```
ErrorHandler:
    GeneralError "frmMain.Form_Load", Err, Error$
    Resume Next
```

If you call a subroutine that has no arguments as the first statement of a multi-statement line, you will notice a display anomaly in some versions of the Visual Basic development environment. If you have a subroutine named DoSomeWork, and you write the statement

```
DoSomeWork: lblWarning.Visible = True
```

Visual Basic will correctly process this multi-statement line by first calling the DoSomeWork routine, then setting the Visible Property of the lblWarning label to True. However, the code window within the development environment will interpret the DoSomeWork component as a line label, and force the line to the left border of the code window. In order to defeat this interpretation, either avoid multi-statement lines, or use the Call statement with such routines.

```
Call DoSomeWork: lblWarning.Visible = True
```

Instantiation of Procedures

Procedures include functions, subroutines, event procedures, and the various forms of property procedures (Get, Let, and Set). It is impossible to write complex Visual Basic applications without procedures, so their declaration is key to the core functionality of your application. Procedure declarations consist of four parts: qualifiers (Public, Private, Friend, and Static), the procedure name itself, the argument list, and the return value (for Functions and Property Get procedures).

```
Public Function GuessMyAge(sName As String) As Integer
```

Always prefix your procedure declaration with either the Public, Private, or Friend keyword. Public and Private procedures can appear in any type of code module, although the use of Public form procedures should be limited to those instances where the form must interact with another form or module. The Friend keyword only appears in class module procedures, and is in some ways a combination of Public and Private. The Static keyword must never be used to qualify a procedure declaration. If you need all of the local variables within a procedure to be static in nature, declare each variable individually with the Static keyword.

Function procedures and Property Get procedures both return values of a specific type. When declaring Functions and Property Get procedures, always include an As clause to specify the return type of the procedure, even if the return type is the default Variant data type. This will make it clear to the caller of your procedure what type of data to expect. Visual Basic can also weed out some incompatible conversions of function return values into variables.

The argument list of a procedure consists of zero or more passed variable names. Each of these names must use a proper Hungarian name as if each variable were declared locally. Each of these names must also be followed by the appropriate As clause (except for ParamArray arguments). By default, all arguments are passed by reference (an implied use of the ByRef keyword). If an argument should be passed by reference, the use of the ByRef qualifier before the argument name is not needed. However, you must use the ByVal keyword if you want an argument to be passed by value. ByVal arguments must not be modified within the body of the procedure.

There are two special types of variables that can be included in the procedure argument list. Optional arguments are preceded by the Optional keyword. While you can declare an optional argument as almost any Visual Basic data type, you will not be able to use the related IsMissing function unless you declare the optional argument as a Variant. Optional arguments can include a default value.

```
Optional fsTemperature = 98.6!
```

If there is any chance that the meaning of the default value will be unclear to the reader of your source code, declare a constant indicating the default value, give it a descriptive name that makes the meaning of the constant clear, and assign this constant as the default value of the optional argument.

```
Optional fsTemperature = NORMAL_BODY_TEMP
```

The other special type of argument list variable is the parameter array variable, which is always preceded by the ParamArray keyword. Only one parameter array argument can appear in the argument list, and it must be the last argument. This argument is actually an array of Variants by definition, so it does not require the use of the As clause.

Instantiation of Declares

As mentioned in the "Nomenclature for Declares" section earlier in this chapter, the rules surrounding the use of Declare statements generally follow the format supplied by the vendor of the DLL from which you are declaring the procedure. Still, there are a few guidelines that can help make your use of Declare statements more consistent.

As to the location of Declare statements, they should all appear in the Declarations section of your primary code module. Always prefix such declares with the Public keyword. It is permissible to place Private Declare statements in other modules when you have:

- A code module, form, class, etc., that is designed to be "self-contained." Such a module can quickly be added to any new Visual Basic project, and will immediately work because it contains all coding aspects needed to correctly execute the code contained within the module.
- A class module that is designed to be "isolated" from the application in which it appears. Classes are useful for creating "black boxes" of code and data, usable through limited points of access, much like using the on and off ramps of a freeway. API calls used within the class can be declared privately within the Declarations section of the class.

The remaining standards surrounding Declare statements exist to make a statement complete and clear. Consider this commonly used API call from the API Text Viewer supplied with Visual Basic.

```
Public Declare Function SendMessage Lib "user32" _
    Alias "SendMessageA" (ByVal hwnd As Long, _
    ByVal wMsg As Long, ByVal wParam As Long, _
    ByRef lParam As Any) As Long
```

Always include the ByVal or ByRef keyword in front of each procedure argument. By default, these arguments are passed ByRef. If one of these keywords is missing for a parameter, the ByRef keyword will generally be correct. When in doubt, reference the vendor's original documentation.

If a procedure was originally declared by the vendor of the DLL as a function, do not declare it as a Sub. Correctly declare it as a Function, and either capture and ignore the return value, or use the Call keyword when using the function.

Declaration Modifiers

This final section discusses several features of the Visual Basic language that influence the use of declaration throughout portions of code, whole modules, even an entire application.

Global Options

The Declarations section of a module is the home to several important elements of a Visual Basic project. Of course, module-level and global variables and constants are found in this section, as well as user-defined data type definitions. In addition to these elements, there are several options that can be set. This section describes these options.

DEFTYPE

The DefType statements include DefBool, DefByte, DefCur, DefDate, DefDbl, DefDec, DefInt, DefLng, DefObj, DefSng, DefStr, and DefVar. These statements allow you to indicate that variables starting with a specific letter are automatically assigned to a specific data type. Procedure arguments and return values from functions and Property Get routines are also affected by these statements. For example, the statement

```
DefBool a-c
```

sets all affected elements within the module that begin with the letters a, b, or c, to the data type Boolean, unless an element is specifically typed with an As clause.

The DefType statements must not be used within a Visual Basic application. Allowing variables to be declared without As clauses permits subtle data type errors to appear, especially within medium to large Visual Basic applications.

VBScript does not use the DefType statements since the only non-object data type is Variant.

OPTION BASE

Option base is used to set the default lower bound for array subscripts to either 0 or 1. For example, the statement

```
Option Base 0
```

indicates that all arrays declared without the To clause have a lower bound of 0. A declaration of

```
Dim asName(5)
```

is the same as

```
Dim asName(0 To 5)
```

The default setting in the absence of the Option Base statement is to set the lower bound of arrays to 0.

Do not use the Option Base statement within Visual Basic. Instead, always specify the lower and upper bounds for all arrays (where subscripts are indicated at all) when they are declared with the Dim or ReDim statements.

Incorrect

```
Dim asNames(5, 10)
```

Correct

```
Dim asNames(1 To 5, 1 To 10)
```

OPTION COMPARE

The Option Compare statement specifies the sorting order for text during comparisons. The two settings, Binary and Text (the Microsoft Access version of VBA adds a Database setting), use different rules for sorting upper-case, lower-case, international, and accented characters. The default setting is Binary.

Use the Option Compare statement as needed within your application. If you choose to use it within one module, add the statement to the Declarations section of all modules. If your application makes certain assumptions about the sorting order of text, be sure to provide adequate documentation within those procedures where it makes a difference, and also within the application's Resource Kit. Some Visual Basic features, such as the InStr() function, contain arguments used to override the default comparison setting.

OPTION EXPLICIT

The Option Explicit statement requires all variables and constants used within a Visual Basic module to be declared before use. In the absence of this statement, it is possible to use variables and constants without first declaring them. The Option Explicit statement must appear as the first non-comment line of each module within your Visual Basic application. This rule also applies to VBScript pages and files.

OPTION PRIVATE MODULE

The Option Private Module statement is used within some implementations of Visual Basic for Applications to restrict the view of public module-level elements to the project in which the module appears. Use the Option Private Module statement as needed within your Visual Basic for Applications code.

Compiler Directives

Visual Basic 4.0 introduced compiler directives into the language. These statements, which always begin with the number sign ("#"), direct the Visual Basic compiler or interpreter to alter the way it processes certain sections of code. Similar directives exist in the C and C++ languages, where they are intercepted by a "pre-processor," which acts on the source code before it is seen by the real compiler.

#CONST DIRECTIVE

The #Const directive defines a compiler constant, a non-changing value for use only with other compiler directives. Visual Basic does define a few global compiler directives, but you are free to define as many as you need.

Use #Const directives as needed to define compiler constants within your application. #Const directives should always appear in the Declarations section of a module. (Even if they appear within a routine, Visual Basic interprets them as if they appeared in the Declarations section.) Like standard constants, values defined with the #Const directive should be all upper case, with underscore characters ("_") separating the key words of the constant.

Correct

```
#Const DEBUG_VERSION = 1
```

It is possible to define global compiler constants through the Project Properties dialog in the Visual Basic development environment. Document all custom compiler constants used in your application in the project's Resource Kit.

#IF, #ELSE, #ELSEIF, #END IF DIRECTIVES

The #If directive and related directives allow you to exclude Visual Basic source code from the view of the compiler or interpreter based on the values of compiler constants. Use the #If directive and related directives as needed to direct the inclusion or exclusion of code sections within your application.

Visual Basic Limitations on Declaration

Visual Basic does impose some maximum limits on the number of allowed object names through its use of the Project Name Table. This table, managed internally by Visual Basic, contains the names of all variables, procedures, constants, modules, types, and so on. The *Visual Basic Programmer's Guide* has this to say about the Project Name Table.

> *The project name table is unlimited in total size, but is limited to a total of 32K case-sensitive unique entries. If the limit is reached, reuse private identifiers in different modules to limit the number of unique entries to 32K.*

This means that the total length of all object names in your application, including some overhead, cannot exceed 32K. For most small and medium-sized projects this is not a problem. But large projects, especially those that have a large number of user-defined constants from third-party vendors, can quickly reach the limit. Although it was written for use with Visual Basic 3.0, Microsoft Knowledge Base article Q112860 discusses a method for estimating the size of this table.

If you exceed the limits of this table, your application will not run. There are two primary methods you can use to stay below this boundary.

- **Remove all unused code, variables, and constants.** The professional programmer should always be on the lookout for dead code in need of pruning. Extra code and variables add to the complexity of the source code without providing any benefit to the user. Remove such dead weight from your application.
- **Use the same names over and over for the same objects.** This is especially true for variables. When you have a local variable that serves the same purpose in several procedures, give it the same name. This not only keeps the size of the Project Name Table small, it also gives the reader of the code a quicker understanding of new routines encountered during a walk through the code. Make a list of some handy names that you will use frequently. Included in my own list are the common variables listed in Table 9.10. This reuse rule also applies to line labels, module-level variables and constants, and any other object name in your application that appears repeatedly in different procedures or modules.

Table 9.10 Common Variable Names

Variable	Type	Description
bFound	Boolean	Boolean value indicating whether a condition was met during a series of tests.
lActiveID	Long	Primary key value for the main database table in use by a procedure.
nCounter	Integer	Generic loop counter.
nPos	Integer	Return value from InStr( ) function call.
sSQL	String	String to hold SQL statements for database access.
rsInfo	Recordset	Generic Recordset variable used with ActiveX Data Objects (ADO) and Data Access Objects (DAO) programming.
sWork	String	Generic temporary string.

Data Typing of Literals

Literals include all numeric, string, and date values that are entered directly into your source code. For example, in the statement

```
nDays = 365
```

the value 365 is a literal number. Literal strings are surrounded by double-quote marks, while literal dates begin and end with number signs.

```
sMessage = "An error occurred."
dtDeclaration = #7/4/1776#
```

When you enter a date literal from the 1900s into the Visual Basic development environment, some versions of Visual Basic will strip off the first two digits of a four-digit year. To defeat this feature, enter such date literals as strings, with or without the CDate function.

```
dtAction = "9/23/1999"
   ' ----- or
dtAction = CDate("9/23/1999")
```

By default, all literals are of type Variant. Table 9.11 lists the various type declaration characters defined by Visual Basic that can be used with literals to coerce them into a different data type.

Table 9.11   Data Types and Declaration Characters

Data Type	Declaration Character	Description
Boolean		There is no declaration character available for the Boolean data type, but then again, there are only two literals, True and False. True and False literals can be assigned to variables from a variety of data types. Be aware that the Boolean data type will sometimes be converted to an integer value (-1 or 0), and sometimes to a string value ("True" or "False") when it is coerced into another data type.
Byte		Byte literals cannot be entered directly in Visual Basic. Use the CByte function instead.
Currency	@	If you are working with currency values, always use the Currency data type instead of Single or Double. Currency is not prone to the rounding errors that can occur with Single and Double values.

Table 9.11		Data Types and Declaration Characters *(Continued)*
Data Type	**Declaration Character**	**Description**
Decimal		The Decimal data type is not a true data type at this time, but is a subtype of the Variant data type.
Double	#	Double is the default format for floating point literals. Do not use Double values for currency, as they are prone to rounding errors. Use the Currency data type instead.
Integer	%	Integers are also known as "short integers" because of their small range when compared to values in the Long data type.
Long	&	Longs are also known as "long integers" because of their extended range when compared to values in the Integer data type.
Object		You cannot create an object literal, except to make an object undefined through the Nothing keyword.
Single	!	Do not use Single values for currency, as they are prone to rounding errors. Use the Currency data type instead.
String	$	It is not possible to use the "$" type declaration identifier with a string literal. Any literal appearing between double-quote marks is a string by definition.
Variant		Every literal that is not coerced with a type declaration character is automatically a Variant.

Summary

You cannot avoid declaration in a Visual Basic application. It appears each time you add a control to a form, when you call a procedure, or when you use a variable. Proper use of declaration keeps your source code readable and consistent. This chapter included the following key topics:

- Name variables using the Hungarian naming conventions, employing the scope and tag values listed in this chapter. When defining new Hungarian tags, avoid conflicts with existing combinations. Use the appropriate Public, Private, or Dim keyword to declare each variable. Always use an As clause for all variable declarations. Use Hungarian tags in VBScript as if you were using the appropriate As clause after each variable declaration.

- Constants appear in all upper case with underscore characters between each significant word. Never declare a constant within a procedure; all constant definitions appear within the Declarations section of a module, using the Public or Private keyword. Use an As clause, or a type declaration character, for clarity.

- User-defined types use an initial capital, mixed-case tag name, always ending with "Type." The elements of the type use standard local Hungarian names.

- Enumerated data types use an initial capital, mixed-case tag name, always ending with "Enum." The elements are mixed case with an initial lower-case leader, a two-to-five character abbreviation of the data type.

- Line labels use an initial capital, mixed-case name, with no underscore characters. Always place line labels on a line of their own.

- Procedures appear in mixed case with an initial capital and no underscores. All arguments and return values require As clauses. Begin the declaration with the appropriate Public, Private, or Friend keyword, but never include the Static keyword.

- Declare statements generally follow the naming rules for procedures, but for large, multi-programming-language projects, it may be best to follow the rules of the original DLL author.

- User interface elements employ local Hungarian names.

- Menu item names use a "cascading" form of Hungarian naming, where each menu item name is prefixed with the name of its parent menu.

- Reuse module-level and local variable, procedure, constant, and line label names where functionality is similar. Remove unused code and objects. These steps will keep the Project Name Table small.

- Avoid negative names for variables, constants, procedures, and other similar elements. That is, do not put the words "Not" or "No," or similar words in the element names.

- There are exceptions to the naming guidelines for traditional variable, constant, user-defined type, declare, and procedure names, and for property-like class variables.

- Do not use the DefType keywords. Always use Option Explicit as the first non-comment line of each module, page, or file in your source code. Never use Option Base. Rather, specify lower and upper bounds for all array declarations. Use Option Compare, Option Private Module, and compiler directives as needed.

- Use type declaration characters with literals for data type coercion.

Keyword Reference

This chapter provides detailed recommendations on the usage of every Visual Basic, Visual Basic for Applications, and Visual Basic, Scripting Edition, keyword. Methods, properties, and events of controls and other objects are not included, although you will find control-related information in Chapter 11, *Control and User Interface Standards*.

This chapter is meant to be read through once quickly, then used as a reference when needed. As you move through the keywords, you will begin to see patterns of rules and recommendations. Many of these patterns are listed in the summary section at the end of the chapter.

Categories

All of the Visual Basic keywords listed in this chapter are divided into categories. This short section lists all keywords that fall within each category.

Compiler Directives

#Const Directive, #If...Then...#Else Directive

Conversion Functions

Array Function, Asc Function, CBool Function, CByte Function, CCur Function, CDate Function, CDbl Function, CDec Function, Chr Function, CInt Function, CLng Function, CSng Function, CStr Function, CVar Function, CVErr Function, Hex Function, Oct Function, Str Function, StrConv Function, Val Function.

Date and Time Features

CDate Function, Date Function, Date Statement, DateAdd Function, DateDiff Function, DatePart Function, DateSerial Function, DateValue Function, Day Function, Hour Function, IsDate Function, Minute Function, Month Function, MonthName Function, Now Function, Second Function, Time Function, Time Statement, Timer Function, TimeSerial Function, TimeValue Function, Weekday Function, WeekdayName Function, Year Function.

Declaration Features

ByRef Keyword, ByVal Keyword, Call Statement, CallByName Function, Const Statement, Control Keyword, CreateObject Function, Declare Statement, DefType Statements, Dim Statement, Empty Keyword, Enum Statement, Erase Statement, Event Statement, Function Statement, GetObject Function, Global Statement, Implements Statement, IsArray Function, IsEmpty Function, IsMissing Function, IsNull Function, IsObject Function, LBound Function, Load Statement, Nothing Keyword, Null Keyword, Option Base Statement, Option Compare Statement, Option Explicit Statement, Option Private Statement, Optional Keyword, ParamArray Keyword, Private Statement, Property Get Statement, Property Let Statement, Property Set Statement, Public Statement, RaiseEvent Statement, ReDim Statement, Set Statement, Static Statement, Sub Statement, Type Statement, TypeName Function, UBound Function, Unload Statement, VarType Function.

Error Handling and Debugging Features

Debug Object, Erl Function, Err Object, Error Function, Error Statement, IsError Function, On Error Statement, Resume Statement.

File System Features

ChDir Statement, ChDrive Statement, Close Statement, CurDir Function, Dir Function, EOF Function, FileAttr Function, FileCopy Statement, FileDateTime Function, FileLen Function, FreeFile Function, Get Statement, GetAttr Function, Input # Statement, Input Function, Kill Statement, Line Input # Statement, Loc Function, Lock # Statement, LOF Function, MkDir Statement, Name Statement, Open Statement, Print # Statement, Put Statement, Reset Statement, RmDir Statement, Seek Function, Seek Statement, SetAttr Statement, Spc Function, Tab Function, Unlock # Statement, Width # Statement, Write # Statement.

Financial Features

DDB Function, FV Function, IPmt Function, IRR Function, MIRR Function, NPer Function, NPV Function, Pmt Function, PPmt Function, PV Function, Rate Function, SLN Function, SYD Function.

Flow Control Features

Choose Function, Do...Loop Statement, DoEvents Function, End Block Statement, End Statement, Exit Statement, For Each...Next Statement, For...Next Statement, GoSub...Return Statement, GoTo Statement, If...Then...Else Statement, IIf Function, On...GoSub Statement, On...GoTo Statement, Select Case Statement, Stop Statement, Switch Function, While...Wend Statement, With Statement.

Math Features

Abs Function, Atn Function, Cos Function, Exp Function, Fix Function, Int Function, IsNumeric Function, Log Function, Randomize Statement, Rnd Function, Round Function, Sgn Function, Sin Function, Sqr Function, Tan Function.

Miscellaneous Features

' Comment Operator, AddressOf Operator, App Object, AppActivate Statement, Beep Statement, Command Function, DeleteSetting Statement, Eval Function, Execute Statement, ExecuteGlobal Statement, False Keyword, GetAllSettings Function, GetLocale Function, GetRef Function, GetSetting Function, Global Object, IMEStatus Function, InputBox Function, Let Statement, LoadPicture Function, LoadResData Function, LoadResPicture Function, LoadResString Function, Me Keyword, MsgBox Function, Partition Function, QBColor Function, Rem Statement, RGB Function, SavePicture Statement, SaveSetting Statement, Screen Object, ScriptEngine Function, ScriptEngineBuildVersion Function, ScriptEngineMajorVersion Function, ScriptEngineMinorVersion Function, SendKeys Statement, SetLocale Function, Shell Function, True Keyword.

Operators

- Operator (Binary), - Operator (Unary), & Operator, * Operator, / Operator, \ Operator, ^ Operator, + Operator, < Operator, <= Operator, <> Operator, = Operator (Assignment), = Operator (Comparison), > Operator, >= Operator, And Operator, Eqv Operator, Imp Operator, Is Operator, Like Operator, Mod Operator, Not Operator, Or Operator, Xor Operator.

String Features

Environ Function, Filter Function, Format Function, FormatCurrency Function, FormatDateTime Function, FormatNumber Function, FormatPercent Function, Hex Function, InStr Function, InStrRev Function, Join Function, LCase Function, Left Function, Len Function, LoadResString Function, LSet Statement, LTrim Function, Mid Function, Mid Statement, Oct Function, Replace Function, Right Function, RSet Statement, RTrim Function, Space Function, Split

Function, Str Function, StrComp Function, StrConv Function, String Function, StrReverse Function, Trim Function, UCase Function.

Alphabetical Keyword List

The following list contains keywords intrinsic to Visual Basic, Visual Basic for Applications, and Visual Basic, Scripting Edition, that are not directly related to forms, controls, or objects.

' Comment Operator

Category	Miscellaneous Features
Availability	VB:Yes, VBA:Yes, VBScript:Yes
Purpose	Begins a source code comment line or line section.
Typical Syntax	' comment
See Also	Rem Statement

Use the comment operator (') as needed within your Visual Basic source code. When adding comments to your source code, always use the single quote comment operator; discontinue use of the Rem statement.

The syntax of Visual Basic allows you to continue any line, including a comment line, with a line continuation character (_). Do not use this method to join adjacent comment lines together.

Incorrect

```
' ----- It is very important that you read this full _
'       comment so that you can be fully informed.
```

Correct

```
' ----- It is very important that you read this full
'       comment so that you can be fully informed.
```

For full information on the use and style of comments within your source code, see Chapter 3, *Commenting and Style*.

- Operator (Binary)

Category	Operators
Availability	VB:Yes, VBA:Yes, VBScript:Yes
Purpose	Subtracts one value from another.
Typical Syntax	*expression1 - expression2*
See Also	- Operator (Unary), & Operator, * Operator, / Operator, \ Operator, ^ Operator, + Operator (Assignment), = Operator (Assignment), Mod Operator

Use the subtraction operator (-) as needed within your Visual Basic source code. When subtracting date or time values, use the DateAdd function instead of the subtraction operator.

- Operator (Unary)

Category	Operators
Availability	VB:Yes, VBA:Yes, VBScript:Yes
Purpose	Indicates the negative value of an expression.
Typical Syntax	*- expression*
See Also	- Operator (Binary), & Operator, * Operator, / Operator, \ Operator, ^ Operator, + Operator (Assignment), = Operator (Assignment), Mod Operator

Use the negation operator (-) as needed within your Visual Basic source code. Visual Basic allows you to use the negation operator before a wide variety of expressions, including numeric literals, variables, or parenthesized expressions. In complex expressions or code, the negation operator may become visibly insignificant, making it difficult to debug a section of code. In such cases, you may wish to discontinue use of the negation operator, and instead multiply the expression by -1.

#Const Directive

Category	Compiler Directives
Availability	VB:Yes, VBA:Yes, VBScript:No
Purpose	Defines a conditional compiler constant.
Typical Syntax	**#Const** *constname* = *expression*
See Also	#If...Then...#Else Directive, Const Statement

Use the #Const directive as needed within the Declarations section of your Visual Basic source code. While Visual Basic allows you to define a compiler constant anywhere within a source code file, restrict the use of the #Const directive to the Declarations section. You can also declare compiler constants through the Project Properties form within the Visual Basic development environment. Additionally, you can define these constants with command-line arguments when compiling an application through the Visual Basic shell command.

Use constant names that include only upper-case letters, digits, and underscore characters. For more information about using compiler directives, see Chapter 2, *Using Declaration*, and Chapter 9, *Declaration Standards*.

#If...Then...#Else Directive

Category	Compiler Directives
Availability	VB:Yes, VBA:Yes, VBScript:No
Purpose	Includes or excludes source code based on compiler-level conditions.

Typical Syntax	**#If** *expression* **Then**
	[*statements*]
	[**#ElseIf** *expression-n* **Then**
	[*statements*]]
	[**#Else**
	[*statements*]]
	#End If
See Also	#Const Directive, If...Then...Else Statement

Use the #If...Then...#Else directive as needed within your Visual Basic source code. Even if the #If condition is met, all of the #ElseIf and #Else expressions are evaluated. Therefore, any compiler constants used in those expressions must be defined at compile time.

For more information about using compiler directives, see Chapter 2, *Using Declaration*, and Chapter 9, *Declaration Standards*.

& *Operator*

Category	Operators
Availability	VB:Yes, VBA:Yes, VBScript:Yes
Purpose	Concatenates two expressions.
Typical Syntax	*expression1* **&** *expression2*
See Also	- Operator (Binary), - Operator (Unary), * Operator, / Operator, \ Operator, ^ Operator, + Operator, = Operator (Assignment), Mod Operator

Use the concatenation operator (&) as needed within your Visual Basic source code. Although Visual Basic permits it, do not use the addition operator (+) to concatenate two string expressions together. Use the concatenation operator instead to remove any ambiguity in the functionality of the addition operator.

Always leave at least one character of whitespace between the concatenation operator and the expression that precedes it or follows it. If you immediately follow a Long variable or a numeric literal with the & character without introducing whitespace between them, the & character will act as a type declaration character for the Long data type. Placing the & character immediately before an expression tells Visual Basic to treat the expression as a non-decimal value, such as a hexadecimal or octal value.

* *Operator*

Category	Operators
Availability	VB:Yes, VBA:Yes, VBScript:Yes
Purpose	Multiplies two values together.
Typical Syntax	*expression1* * *expression2*

See Also - Operator (Binary), - Operator (Unary), & Operator, / Operator, \ Operator, ∧ Operator, + Operator (Assignment), = Operator (Assignment), Mod Operator

Use the multiplication operator (*) as needed within your Visual Basic source code.

/ Operator

Category Operators
Availability VB:Yes, VBA:Yes, VBScript:Yes
Purpose Divides one number into another, and returns a floating point value.
Typical Syntax *expression1 / expression2*
See Also - Operator (Binary), - Operator (Unary), & Operator, * Operator, \ Operator, ∧ Operator, + Operator (Assignment), = Operator (Assignment), Mod Operator

Use the division operator (/) as needed within your Visual Basic source code. The second expression cannot be 0 (zero). If the second expression is supplied by the user, or if you think that the second expression may be zero, include appropriate code to test the second expression, and take corrective action when needed.

\ Operator

Category Operators
Availability VB:Yes, VBA:Yes, VBScript:Yes
Purpose Divides one number into another, and returns only the integer portion of the result.
Typical Syntax *expression1 \ expression2*
See Also - Operator (Binary), - Operator (Unary), & Operator, * Operator, / Operator, ∧ Operator, + Operator (Assignment), = Operator (Assignment), Fix Function, Int Function, Mod Operator, Round Function

Use the integer division operator (\ ) as needed within your Visual Basic source code. The second expression cannot be 0 (zero). If the second expression is supplied by the user, or if you think that the second expression may be zero, include appropriate code to test the second expression, and take corrective action when needed.

The integer division operator rounds the expressions before the division takes place. After the division operation, any fractional value is truncated, not rounded. If you need to use a different system of rounding or fractional truncation, consider using the division operator combined with the Fix function, the Int function, or the Round function.

^ *Operator*

Category	Operators
Availability	VB:Yes, VBA:Yes, VBScript:Yes
Purpose	Raises one value to the power of another value.
Typical Syntax	*expression1* ^ *expression2*
See Also	- Operator (Binary), - Operator (Unary), & Operator, * Operator, / Operator, \ Operator, + Operator (Assignment), = Operator (Assignment), Mod Operator

Use the exponentiation operator (^) as needed within your Visual Basic source code.

+ *Operator*

Category	Operators
Availability	VB:Yes, VBA:Yes, VBScript:Yes
Purpose	Adds one value to another.
Typical Syntax	*expression1* + *expression2*
See Also	- Operator (Binary), - Operator (Unary), & Operator, * Operator, / Operator, \ Operator, ^ Operator, = Operator (Assignment), Mod Operator

Use the addition operator (+) as needed within your Visual Basic source code. Although Visual Basic permits it, do not use the addition operator to concatenate two string expressions together. Use the concatenation operator (&) instead to remove any ambiguity in the functionality of the addition operator. When adding date or time values, use the DateAdd function instead of the addition operator.

Visual Basic does permit the use of the addition operator as a unary prefix to indicate that a value is positive. However, this syntax is redundant. Do not use the addition operator as a unary prefix.

< *Operator*

Category	Operators
Availability	VB:Yes, VBA:Yes, VBScript:Yes
Purpose	Determines if one value is less than another value.
Typical Syntax	*expression1* < *expression2*
See Also	<= Operator, <> Operator, = Operator (Comparison), > Operator, >= Operator, Is Operator, Like Operator, Option Compare Statement

Use the less than operator (<) as needed within your Visual Basic source code. The use of the Option Compare statement can affect comparisons performed with the less than operator.

<= *Operator*

Category	Operators
Availability	VB:Yes, VBA:Yes, VBScript:Yes
Purpose	Determines if one value is less than or equal to another value.
Typical Syntax	*expression1* <= *expression2*
See Also	< Operator, <> Operator, = Operator (Comparison), > Operator, >= Operator, Is Operator, Like Operator, Option Compare Statement

Use the less than or equal to operator (<=) as needed within your Visual Basic source code. Visual Basic allows you to reverse the two characters that make up the <= symbol. However, always use this operator in its documented fashion.

Incorrect

```
If (nFirst =< nSecond) Then
```

Correct

```
If (nFirst <= nSecond) Then
```

The use of the Option Compare statement can affect comparisons performed with the less than or equal to operator.

<> *Operator*

Category	Operators
Availability	VB:Yes, VBA:Yes, VBScript:Yes
Purpose	Determines if one value does not equal another value.
Typical Syntax	*expression1* <> *expression2*
See Also	< Operator, <= Operator, = Operator (Comparison), > Operator, >= Operator, Is Operator, Like Operator, Not Operator, Option Compare Statement

Use the not equal operator (<>) as needed within your Visual Basic source code. Visual Basic allows you to reverse the two characters that make up the <> symbol. However, always use this operator in its documented fashion.

Incorrect

```
If (nFirst >< nSecond) Then
```

Correct

```
If (nFirst <> nSecond) Then
```

The use of the Option Compare statement can affect comparisons performed with the not equal operator.

= *Operator (Assignment)*

Category	Operators
Availability	VB:Yes, VBA:Yes, VBScript:Yes
Purpose	Assigns an expression to a variable.
Typical Syntax	*variable = expression*
See Also	= Operator (Comparison), Let Statement, Property Get Statement, Property Let Statement, Property Set Statement, Set Statement

Use the assignment operator (=) as needed within your Visual Basic source code. If the user is supplying the expression, or if you think that the expression might fall outside the valid range for the destination variable, include appropriate code to test the expression, and take corrective action when needed.

= *Operator (Comparison)*

Category	Operators
Availability	VB:Yes, VBA:Yes, VBScript:Yes
Purpose	Determines if one value equals another value.
Typical Syntax	*expression1 = expression2*
See Also	< Operator, <= Operator, <> Operator (Comparison), > Operator, >= Operator, Is Operator, Like Operator, Not Operator, Option Compare Statement

Use the equal operator (=) as needed within your Visual Basic source code. The use of the Option Compare statement can affect comparisons performed with the equal operator. If the user is supplying one or both of the expressions, or if you think that the expressions might be incompatible in a comparison, include appropriate code to test the expressions, and take corrective action when needed.

When comparing the return value of a function that takes no arguments to another expression, always follow the function name with an empty set of parentheses. This makes the use of the function visually distinct from the use of a variable.

Correct

```
If (DoWork() = True) Then
```

Incorrect

```
If (DoWork = True) Then
```

> *Operator*

Category	Operators
Availability	VB:Yes, VBA:Yes, VBScript:Yes
Purpose	Determines if one value is greater than another value.
Typical Syntax	*expression1 > expression2*
See Also	< Operator, <= Operator, <> Operator, = Operator (Comparison), >= Operator, Is Operator, Like Operator, Option Compare Statement

Use the greater than operator (>) as needed within your Visual Basic source code. The use of the Option Compare statement can affect comparisons performed with the greater than operator.

>= *Operator*

Category	Operators
Availability	VB:Yes, VBA:Yes, VBScript:Yes
Purpose	Determines if one value is greater than or equal to another value.
Typical Syntax	*expression1 >= expression2*
See Also	< Operator, <= Operator, <> Operator, = Operator (Comparison), > Operator, Is Operator, Like Operator, Option Compare Statement

Use the greater than or equal to operator (>=) as needed within your Visual Basic source code. Visual Basic allows you to reverse the two characters that make up the >= symbol. However, always use this operator in its documented fashion.

Incorrect

```
If (nFirst => nSecond) Then
```

Correct

```
If (nFirst >= nSecond) Then
```

The use of the Option Compare statement can affect comparisons performed with the greater than or equal to operator.

Abs Function

Category	Math Features
Availability	VB:Yes, VBA:Yes, VBScript:Yes
Purpose	Returns the passed value, converting negative values to positive if needed.

Typical Syntax	**Abs(***expression***)**
See Also	Fix Function, Int Function, Round Function, Sgn Function

Use the Abs function as needed within your Visual Basic source code.

AddressOf Operator

Category	Miscellaneous Features
Availability	VB:Yes, VBA:Yes, VBScript:No
Purpose	Obtains the address of a Visual Basic procedure for use as a callback function supplied through an API call.
Typical Syntax	**AddressOf** *procedurename*
See Also	Declare Statement, Function Statement, GetRef Function, Procedure Get Statement, Procedure Let Statement, Procedure Set Statement, Sub Statement

Use the AddressOf operator as needed within your Visual Basic source code. The use of the AddressOf operator assumes a more advanced level of Visual Basic programming. Take great care in declaring the callback function, its arguments, and its return type. When defining your callback function, use either the ByRef or ByVal keyword with each argument.

And Operator

Category	Operators
Availability	VB:Yes, VBA:Yes, VBScript:Yes
Purpose	Performs a logical or bitwise conjunction operation.
Typical Syntax	*expression1* **And** *expression2*
See Also	Eqv Operator, Imp Operator, Not Operator, Or Operator, Xor Operator.

Use the And operator as needed within your Visual Basic source code. When writing complex statements that involve more than one logical or bitwise operator, use parentheses to indicate the proper precedence and grouping within the calculation.

App Object

Category	Miscellaneous Features
Availability	VB:Yes, VBA:No, VBScript:No
Purpose	Object that supplies information about the application.
Typical Syntax	**App**
Variations	Global.App Object
See Also	Debug Object, Global Object, Screen Object

Use the App object as needed within your Visual Basic source code. Do not use the Global.App variation of this object; refer to the App object directly.

When using Visual Basic for Applications, there may be an object available that is contextually similar to the Visual Basic App object.

AppActivate Statement

Category   Miscellaneous Features
Availability   VB:Yes, VBA:Yes, VBScript:No
Purpose   Activates an application's window.
Typical Syntax   **AppActivate** *title*[, *wait*]
See Also   SendKeys Statement, Shell Function

Use the AppActivate statement as needed within your Visual Basic source code. When specifying the application window title to activate, verify that there is no ambiguity between multiple windows with the same name. If an exact title match is not found, the AppActivate statement matches the beginning of a window title with the supplied title. If possible, use the return value from the Shell function as the *title* argument to the AppActivate statement.

The AppActivate statement accesses information that resides outside of the control of the Visual Basic application. Therefore, you must always use proper error handling in any procedure that uses the AppActivate statement. Make use of the On Error statement to capture any file handling errors, and take the appropriate corrective action.

Array Function

Category   Conversion Functions
Availability   VB:Yes, VBA:Yes, VBScript:Yes
Purpose   Builds and returns a Variant array.
Typical Syntax   **Array(***arglist***)**
See Also   IsArray Function, Option Base Statement

Use the Array function as needed within your Visual Basic source code. If possible, use standard arrays instead of Variant arrays in your source code. Because Variant arrays are not as self-documenting as true arrays (although, how self-documenting is a true array), describe the purpose and structure of each Variant array in your source code comments. The Option Base statement affects the use of the Array statement.

Asc Function

Category   Conversion Functions
Availability   VB:Yes, VBA:Yes, VBScript:Yes
Purpose   Returns the ANSI character code of a character.
Typical Syntax   **Asc(***string***)**
Variations   AscB Function, AscW Function
See Also   Chr Function

Use the Asc function as needed within your Visual Basic source code. If you need to work with the underlying bytes contained within a string, use the AscB function. If you need to work with Unicode characters, use the AscW function. When using the AscW function, verify that your application is running on a platform that supports Unicode.

Atn Function

Category	Math Features
Availability	VB:Yes, VBA:Yes, VBScript:Yes
Purpose	Calculates the arctangent of a number.
Typical Syntax	**Atn(***number***)**
See Also	Cos Function, Sin Function, Tan Function

Use the Atn function as needed within your Visual Basic source code. This function returns a Double value, and accepts a Double value for its parameter. Double floating point values are subject to minor rounding errors. Take care to check the accuracy of the return values when using the Visual Basic intrinsic math functions.

Beep Statement

Category	Miscellaneous Features
Availability	VB:Yes, VBA:Yes, VBScript:No
Purpose	Produces a "beep" sound.
Typical Syntax	**Beep**
See Also	MsgBox Function

Use the Beep statement as needed within your Visual Basic source code. However, an overuse of the statement will irritate your users. Be frugal in the use of the Beep statement.

Be aware that this statement will be useless on some systems as either sound is disabled, or the user is unable to hear the sound. If you need to communicate important conditions to the user, do not use the Beep statement as the primary method. Use visual cues to communicate such conditions.

ByRef Keyword

Category	Declaration Features
Availability	VB:Yes, VBA:Yes, VBScript:Yes
Purpose	Identifies a procedure argument as being passed by reference.
Typical Syntax	**ByRef** *argument* [**As** *type*]
See Also	AddressOf Operator, ByVal Keyword, Declare Statement, Function Statement, Property Get Statement, Property Let Statement, Property Set Statement, Sub Statement

Use the ByRef keyword as needed within your Visual Basic source code. By default, all procedure arguments are passed by reference. Use of the ByRef keyword in Visual Basic procedure arguments is optional. However, when including pass-by-reference arguments in a Declare statement, you must use the ByRef keyword. Also, when defining a procedure that will be used as an argument to the AddressOf operator, use the ByRef or ByVal keyword with every argument.

For more information on the use of the ByRef keyword, and the statements in which it appears, see Chapter 2, *Using Declaration*, and Chapter 9, *Declaration Standards*.

ByVal Keyword

Category	Declaration Features
Availability	VB:Yes, VBA:Yes, VBScript:Yes
Purpose	Identifies a procedure argument as being passed by value.
Typical Syntax	**ByVal** *argument* [**As** *type*]
See Also	ByRef Keyword, Declare Statement, Function Statement, Property Get Statement, Property Let Statement, Property Set Statement, Sub Statement

Use the ByVal keyword as needed within your Visual Basic source code. By default, all procedure arguments are passed by reference. Use of the ByVal keyword in Visual Basic procedure arguments is required to have an argument always passed by value. Also, when including pass-by-value arguments in a Declare statement, you must use the ByVal keyword.

For more information on the use of the ByVal keyword, and the statements in which it appears, see Chapter 2, *Using Declaration*, and Chapter 9, *Declaration Standards*.

Call Statement

Category	Declaration Features
Availability	VB:Yes, VBA:Yes, VBScript:Yes
Purpose	Calls a function or subroutine, either locally or through an API call.
Typical Syntax	[**Call**] *name* [([*argumentlist*])]
See Also	Declare Statement, Function Statement, Procedure Get Statement, Procedure Let Statement, Procedure Set Statement

The Call keyword is implied every time you call a subroutine within Visual Basic. In general, you should omit the Call keyword in procedure calls. However, there are two exceptions. First, if you need to call a function, but wish to ignore its return value, use the Call keyword.

```
Call MyFunction(sArg1, nArg2)
```

The second exception occurs when you call a subroutine that has no parameters, and you wish to include additional statements on the same physical source code line by using the ":" statement separator. The Visual Basic development environment will visibly display such lines as though the subroutine call was a line label. Use the Call keyword to defeat this interpretation.

```
Call MySubroutine: lblResult.Caption = "Done"
```

For more information on the use of procedures within Visual Basic, see Chapter 2, *Using Declaration*, and Chapter 9, *Declaration Standards*.

CallByName Function

Category	Declaration Features
Availability	VB:Yes, VBA:Yes, VBScript:No
Purpose	Calls a procedure indirectly.
Typical Syntax	**CallByName(***object, procedurename, calltype[, arguments()]***)**
See Also	Declare Statement, Function Statement, Procedure Get Statement, Procedure Let Statement, Procedure Set Statement

Use the CallByName function as needed within your Visual Basic source code. However, its use should be restricted to special cases where no other language construct will suffice. When using this statement, include a reasonable defense of your use of the statement in the adjacent source code comments.

The *calltype* argument to the CallByName function accepts an Integer value, or one of a set of intrinsic Visual Basic constants. When available, always use the supplied constants instead of numeric literals.

The CallByName function accesses Visual Basic features in a non-standard way. Therefore, you must always use proper error handling in any procedure that uses the CallByName function. Make use of the On Error statement to capture any errors, and take the appropriate corrective action.

CBool Function

Category	Conversion Functions
Availability	VB:Yes, VBA:Yes, VBScript:Yes
Purpose	Converts an expression to the Boolean data type.
Typical Syntax	**CBool(***expression***)**
See Also	CByte Function, CCur Function, CDate Function, CDbl Function, CDec Function, CInt Function, CLng Function, CSng Function, CStr Function, CVar Function, CVErr Function, False Keyword, True Keyword

Use the CBool function as needed within your Visual Basic source code. All non-zero numeric expressions are converted to True, while zero becomes False. All dates and all times other than midnight are True, while a value of midnight without a date is False. The CBool function considers an Empty expression to be False.

CByte Function

Category	Conversion Functions
Availability	VB:Yes, VBA:Yes, VBScript:Yes
Purpose	Converts an expression to the Byte data type.
Typical Syntax	**CByte(***expression***)**
See Also	CBool Function, CCur Function, CDate Function, CDbl Function, CDec Function, CInt Function, CLng Function, CSng Function, CStr Function, CVar Function, CVErr Function, IsNumeric Function

Use the CByte function as needed within your Visual Basic source code. If the user is supplying the expression, or if you think the expression might fall outside the valid range for the Byte data type, include appropriate code to test the expression, and take corrective action when needed.

CCur Function

Category	Conversion Functions
Availability	VB:Yes, VBA:Yes, VBScript:Yes
Purpose	Converts an expression to the Currency data type.
Typical Syntax	**CCur(***expression***)**
Variations	@ Type Declaration Character
See Also	CBool Function, CByte Function, CDate Function, CDbl Function, CDec Function, CInt Function, CLng Function, CSng Function, CStr Function, CVar Function, CVErr Function, IsNumeric Function

Use the CCur function as needed within your Visual Basic source code. If the user is supplying the expression, or if you think the expression might fall outside the valid range for the Currency data type, include appropriate code to test the expression, and take corrective action when needed.

Never use the CCur function to convert a numeric literal to the Currency data type. Use the @ type declaration character instead.

Incorrect

```
fcStartAmount = CCur(125.5)
```

Correct

```
fcStartAmount = 125.5@
```

CDate Function

Category	Conversion Functions, Date and Time Features
Availability	VB:Yes, VBA:Yes, VBScript:Yes
Purpose	Converts an expression to the Date data type.
Typical Syntax	**CDate(***expression***)**
Variations	CVDate Function
See Also	CBool Function, CByte Function, CCur Function, CDbl Function, CDec Function, CInt Function, CLng Function, CSng Function, CStr Function, CVar Function, CVErr Function, IsDate Function

Use the CDate function as needed within your Visual Basic source code. If the user is supplying the expression, or if you think the expression might contain an invalid date or time, include appropriate code to test the expression, and take corrective action when needed. The IsDate function is useful for testing a potential date or time expression.

Visual Basic also includes the CVDate conversion function for compatibility with previous versions of the language. Do not use the CVDate function, as it does not generate a true Date value. Always use the CDate function for date conversions.

CDbl Function

Category	Conversion Functions
Availability	VB:Yes, VBA:Yes, VBScript:Yes
Purpose	Converts an expression to the Double data type.
Typical Syntax	**CDbl(***expression***)**
Variations	# Type Declaration Character
See Also	CBool Function, CByte Function, CCur Function, CDate Function, CDec Function, CInt Function, CLng Function, CSng Function, CStr Function, CVar Function, CVErr Function, IsNumeric Function

Use the CDbl function as needed within your Visual Basic source code. If the user is supplying the expression, or if you think the expression might fall outside the valid range for the Double data type, include appropriate code to test the expression, and take corrective action when needed.

Never use the CDbl function to convert a numeric literal to the Double data type. Use the # type declaration character instead.

Incorrect

```
fdOffset = CDbl(15)
```

Correct

```
fdOffset = 15#
```

CDec Function

Category	Conversion Functions
Availability	VB:Yes, VBA:Yes, VBScript:No
Purpose	Converts an expression to the Variant (Decimal) data type.
Typical Syntax	**CDec(***expression***)**
See Also	CBool Function, CByte Function, CCur Function, CDate Function, CDbl Function, CInt Function, CLng Function, CSng Function, CStr Function, CVar Function, CVErr Function, IsNumeric Function

Use the CDec function as needed within your Visual Basic source code. Note that the Decimal data type is not a true data type. It exists only as a subtype to the Variant data type.

If the user is supplying the expression, or if you think the expression might fall outside the valid range for the Decimal data type, include appropriate code to test the expression, and take corrective action when needed.

ChDir Statement

Category	File System Features
Availability	VB:Yes, VBA:Yes, VBScript:No
Purpose	Changes the current directory to a new location.
Typical Syntax	**ChDir** *path*
See Also	ChDrive Statement, CurDir Function, Dir Function, MkDir Function, RmDir Function

Use the ChDir statement as needed within your Visual Basic source code. While the syntax of the ChDir statement permits the drive letter to be absent from the path string, always include the drive letter for clarity.

Incorrect

```
ChDir "\temp"
```

Correct

```
ChDir "c:\temp"
```

The ChDir statement only works with paths that reside on a local drive or a mapped drive letter. Do not pass a UNC (Universal Naming Convention) path—one that begins with "\\" characters—to the ChDir statement. If the user supplies the path name, make sure that the path exists on a valid local drive or mapped drive.

The ChDir statement (and all other File System features) accesses information that resides outside of the control of the Visual Basic application. Therefore, you must always use proper error handling in any procedure that uses the ChDir statement. Make use of the On Error statement to capture any file handling errors, and take the appropriate corrective action.

ChDrive Statement

Category	File System Features
Availability	VB:Yes, VBA:Yes, VBScript:No
Purpose	Changes the current drive to a new drive.
Typical Syntax	**ChDrive** *drive*
See Also	ChDir Statement, CurDir Function, Dir Function, MkDir Function, RmDir Function

Use the ChDrive statement as needed within your Visual Basic source code. It is permissible to pass an entire path as an argument to the ChDrive statement; only the first letter of the argument is used by the ChDrive statement.

The ChDrive statement only works with paths that reside on a local drive or a mapped drive letter. Do not pass a UNC (Universal Naming Convention) path—one that begins with "\\" characters—to the ChDrive statement. If the user supplies the path name, make sure that the path exists on a valid local drive or mapped drive.

The ChDrive statement (and all other File System features) accesses information that resides outside of the control of the Visual Basic application. Therefore, you must always use proper error handling in any procedure that uses the ChDrive statement. Make use of the On Error statement to capture any file handling errors, and take the appropriate corrective action.

Choose Function

Category	Flow Control Features
Availability	VB:Yes, VBA:Yes, VBScript:No
Purpose	Returns one of a set of values based on an index.
Typical Syntax	**Choose(***index*, *choice-1*[, *choice-2*, ...[, *choice-n*]]**)**
See Also	IIf Function, Select Case Statement, Switch Function

Use the Choose function as needed within your Visual Basic source code. Always include source code comments that describe the purpose and results of this statement. Always supply an integer value as the *index* argument. While the Choose function will round the value you supply, it is better to deal with the fractional value yourself.

If you supply a value less than 1, or greater than the number of choice elements, the Choose function returns a Null value. Be sure to check the return value for a legitimate result if there is any chance that an invalid index may be supplied. Although only one element will be returned based on the index, all choice elements are evaluated. Make sure that the choices do not contain any code that will fail on invalid conditions, or that should execute with only certain index values.

Chr Function

Category	Conversion Functions
Availability	VB:Yes, VBA:Yes, VBScript:Yes
Purpose	Returns a character based on an ANSI character code.
Typical Syntax	**Chr(***charcode***)**
Variations	Chr$ Function, ChrB Function, ChrB$ Function, ChrW Function, ChrW$ Function.
See Also	Chr Function

Use the Chr function as needed within your Visual Basic source code. Visual Basic, Scripting Edition does not permit the use of the string version of this function. Within a VBScript code section, you must use the syntax

```
Chr(argument)
```

In all other versions of Visual Basic, if you do not require a Variant result, use the string version of this function instead of the Variant version.

```
Chr$(argument)
```

If you need to work with the underlying bytes contained within a string, use the ChrB function, or the ChrB$ function. If you need to work with Unicode characters, use the ChrW function, or the ChrW$ function. When using the ChrW function or the ChrW$ function, verify that your application is running on a platform that supports Unicode.

Visual Basic contains several intrinsic constants that, if they were not present, would require the use of the Chr function to create those values. For example, the "vbNullChar" constant is equivalent to "Chr(0)." The "vbCrLf" function is equivalent to "Chr(13) & Chr(10)." When available, always use the intrinsic constants instead of building the values with the Chr function.

CInt Function

Category	Conversion Functions
Availability	VB:Yes, VBA:Yes, VBScript:Yes
Purpose	Converts an expression to the Integer data type.
Typical Syntax	**CInt(***expression***)**
Variations	% Type Declaration Character
See Also	CBool Function, CByte Function, CCur Function, CDate Function, CDbl Function, CDec Function, CLng Function, CSng Function, CStr Function, CVar Function, CVErr Function, Int Function, IsNumeric Function

Use the CInt function as needed within your Visual Basic source code. If the user is supplying the expression, or if you think the expression might fall outside the valid range for the Integer data type, include appropriate code to test the expression, and take corrective action when needed.

Never use the CInt function to convert a non-decimal numeric literal to the Integer data type. While you could use the % type declaration character to coerce the literal to an integer, all numeric literals in Visual Basic that fall within the range of the Integer data type are automatically cast as Integer.

The Int function cannot be used to convert a value to the Integer data type. Use the Int function to truncate the decimal portion of a numeric expression. Use the CInt function to convert values in the Integer range to the Integer data type.

CLng Function

Category	Conversion Functions
Availability	VB:Yes, VBA:Yes, VBScript:Yes
Purpose	Converts an expression to the Long data type.
Typical Syntax	**CLng(***expression***)**
Variations	& Type Declaration Character
See Also	CBool Function, CByte Function, CCur Function, CDate Function, CDbl Function, CDec Function, CInt Function, CSng Function, CStr Function, CVar Function, CVErr Function, IsNumeric Function

Use the CLng function as needed within your Visual Basic source code. If the user is supplying the expression, or if you think the expression might fall outside the valid range for the Long data type, include appropriate code to test the expression, and take corrective action when needed.

Never use the CLng function to convert a numeric literal to the Long data type. Use the & type declaration character instead.

Incorrect

```
lInitialLimit = CLng(1500)
```

Correct

```
lInitialLimit = 1500&
```

By default, all non-decimal numeric literals that fall outside the range of the Integer data type, but inside the range of the Long data type, are cast as Long.

Close Statement

Category	File System Features
Availability	VB:Yes, VBA:Yes, VBScript:No
Purpose	Closes the specified open file.

Typical Syntax	**Close** [*#*]*filenumber*
See Also	Open Statement, Reset Statement

Use the Close statement as needed within your Visual Basic source code. Always use a file number returned from the FreeFile function as an argument to the Close statement. Although the "#" prefix of the *filenumber* argument is optional, always include it in the syntax of the statement.

The syntax of the Close statement allows multiple comma-separated file numbers to be closed at once with a single statement. For increased clarity, only close a single file with each Close statement in your source code.

The Close statement (and all other File System features) accesses information that resides outside of the control of the Visual Basic application. Therefore, you must always use proper error handling in any procedure that uses the Close statement. Make use of the On Error statement to capture any file handling errors, and take the appropriate corrective action.

Command Function

Category	Miscellaneous Features
Availability	VB:Yes, VBA:Yes, VBScript:No
Purpose	Returns the command-line arguments of the application session.
Typical Syntax	**Command**
Variations	Command$ Function
See Also	App Object

Use the Command function as needed within your Visual Basic source code. Do not use the Command version of this function in your source code. Instead, use the Command$ function.

Incorrect

```
sParse = Command
```

Correct

```
sParse = Command$
```

By convention, Windows command-line options begin with a slash ("/") character. You may also, in addition to the Windows standard, wish to support the UNIX standard, beginning options with a hyphen ("-").

Do not assume that the user supplied valid options through the application command line. Always verify the arguments supplied by the user to confirm that they are valid.

Const Statement

Category	Declaration Features
Availability	VB:Yes, VBA:Yes, VBScript:Yes
Purpose	Defines a named constant for local or global use.
Typical Syntax	[**Public** | **Private**] **Const** *constname* [**As** *type*] **=** *expression*
See Also	#Const Directive, Dim Statement, Global Statement, Private Statement, Public Statement, Static Statement

Use the Const statement as needed within the Declarations section of your Visual Basic source code. While Visual Basic allows you to define a constant anywhere within your application, restrict the use of the Const statement to the Declarations section. Never use this statement within a routine. In VBScript, use the Const statement at the beginning of your script page, but not inside any procedure.

Always precede the Const statement with either the Public or Private keyword, attempting to limit the scope where possible. Include only a single constant declaration on each source code line.

Use constant names that include only upper-case letters, digits, and underscore characters. If you have several constants that work together as a set of constants, prefix them with the same first few letters.

```
Private Const BASE_NONE = -1
Private Const BASE_FIRST = 1
Private Const BASE_SECOND = 2
Private Const BASE_THIRD = 3
Private Const BASE_HOME = 4
```

To make your constant declaration more specific within your source code, use the As clause to define the type of a constant. Type declaration characters can also be used to identify the data type of a constant. For more information about constants and type declaration characters, see Chapter 2, *Using Declaration*, and Chapter 9, *Declaration Standards*.

Control Keyword

Category	Declaration Features
Availability	VB:Yes, VBA:Yes, VBScript:No
Purpose	Provides a generic object type for controls.
Typical Syntax	**Dim** *varname* **As Control**
See Also	Dim Statement, Private Statement, Public Statement

Use the Control keyword as needed within your Visual Basic source code. However, its use should be greatly restricted to only those instances where a more specific solution cannot be clearly or efficiently provided. Supply adequate documentation in the source code comments as to any assumptions about the types of controls that will be assigned to the generic object.

Cos Function

Category	Math Features
Availability	VB:Yes, VBA:Yes, VBScript:Yes
Purpose	Calculates the cosine of an angle.
Typical Syntax	**Cos(***number***)**
See Also	Atn Function, Sin Function, Tan Function

Use the Cos function as needed within your Visual Basic source code. This function returns a Double value, and accepts a Double value for its parameter. Double floating point values are subject to minor rounding errors. Take care to check the accuracy of the return values when using the Visual Basic intrinsic math functions.

CreateObject Function

Category	Declaration Features
Availability	VB:Yes, VBA:Yes, VBScript:Yes
Purpose	Creates a reference to an ActiveX object.
Typical Syntax	**CreateObject(***class*[, *servername*]**)**
See Also	GetObject Function, Set Statement

Use the CreateObject function as needed within your Visual Basic source code. The CreateObject function accesses information that resides outside of the control of the Visual Basic application. Therefore, you must always use proper error handling in any procedure that uses the CreateObject function. Make use of the On Error statement to capture any errors, and take the appropriate corrective action.

CSng Function

Category	Conversion Functions
Availability	VB:Yes, VBA:Yes, VBScript:Yes
Purpose	Converts an expression to the Single data type.
Typical Syntax	**CSng(***expression***)**
Variations	! Type Declaration Character
See Also	CBool Function, CByte Function, CCur Function, CDate Function, CDbl Function, CDec Function, CInt Function, CLng Function, CStr Function, CVar Function, CVErr Function, IsNumeric Function

Use the CSng function as needed within your Visual Basic source code. If the user is supplying the expression, or if you think the expression might fall outside the valid range for the Single data type, include appropriate code to test the expression, and take corrective action when needed.

Never use the CSng function to convert a numeric literal to the Single data type. Use the ! type declaration character instead.

Incorrect

```
fdScale = CSng(39.39)
```

Correct

```
fdScale = 39.39!
```

CStr Function

Category	Conversion Functions
Availability	VB:Yes, VBA:Yes, VBScript:Yes
Purpose	Converts an expression to the String data type.
Typical Syntax	**CStr(***expression***)**
See Also	CBool Function, CByte Function, CCur Function, CDate Function, CDbl Function, CDec Function, CInt Function, CLng Function, CSng Function, CVar Function, CVErr Function, Str Function, StrConv Function

Use the CStr function as needed within your Visual Basic source code. Avoid the Str function when converting numbers to strings. Use the CStr function instead.

CurDir Function

Category	File System Features
Availability	VB:Yes, VBA:Yes, VBScript:No
Purpose	Returns the current directory on the default or specified drive.
Typical Syntax	**CurDir[(***drive***)]**
Variations	CurDir$ Function
See Also	ChDir Statement, ChDrive Statement, Dir Function, MkDir Function, RmDir Function

Use the CurDir function as needed within your Visual Basic source code. If you do not require a Variant result, use the CurDir$ function instead of the CurDir function.

```
vntActiveDir = CurDir
sActiveDir = CurDir$
```

The CurDir function (and all other File System features) accesses information that resides outside of the control of the Visual Basic application. Therefore, you must always use proper error handling in any procedure that uses the CurDir function. Make use of the On Error statement to capture any file handling errors, and take the appropriate corrective action.

CVar Function

Category	Conversion Functions
Availability	VB:Yes, VBA:Yes, VBScript:No
Purpose	Converts an expression to the Variant data type.
Typical Syntax	**CVar(***expression***)**
See Also	CBool Function, CByte Function, CCur Function, CDate Function, CDbl Function, CDec Function, CInt Function, CLng Function, CSng Function, CStr Function, CVErr Function, TypeName Function, VarType Function

Use the CVar function as needed within your Visual Basic source code.

CVErr Function

Category	Conversion Functions
Availability	VB:Yes, VBA:Yes, VBScript:No
Purpose	Converts an expression to the Variant (Error) data type.
Typical Syntax	**CVErr(***expression***)**
See Also	CBool Function, CByte Function, CCur Function, CDate Function, CDbl Function, CDec Function, CInt Function, CLng Function, CSng Function, CStr Function, CVar Function, IsError Function

Use the CVErr function as needed within your Visual Basic source code. Note that the Error data type is not a true data type. It exists only as a subtype to the Variant data type.

Date Function

Category	Date and Time Features
Availability	VB:Yes, VBA:Yes, VBScript:Yes (with restrictions)
Purpose	Returns the current system date.
Typical Syntax	**Date**
Variations	Date$ Function
See Also	Date Statement, Now Function, Time Function, Time Statement

Use the Date function as needed within your Visual Basic source code. A string version of this function, Date$, returns the same information as the standard Date function, but as a true String value. (The Date$ function is not available in VBScript.) In general, you should use the Date version of this function. If you need a date stored or displayed as a string, use the Format function or the FormatDateTime function to properly format the date before use.

Date Statement

Category	Date and Time Features
Availability	VB:Yes, VBA:Yes, VBScript:No
Purpose	Sets the current system date.
Typical Syntax	**Date =** *date*
See Also	Date Function, Now Function, Time Function, Time Statement

Use the Date statement as needed within your Visual Basic source code. However, you must make it clear to the user, either in the documentation or through application notification, that you will be modifying the system clock. On some secure Windows systems, you may be restricted from modifying the system clock.

DateAdd Function

Category	Date and Time Features
Availability	VB:Yes, VBA:Yes, VBScript:Yes
Purpose	Returns a new date value based on an adjustment of another date.
Typical Syntax	**DateAdd(***interval, number, date***)**
See Also	CDate Function, DateSerial Function

Use the DateAdd function as needed within your Visual Basic source code. Although Visual Basic permits it, do not use standard math operators to modify a date value. For example, Visual Basic allows you to add a day to an existing date using the following syntax:

```
dtTomorrow = Date + 1
```

Always use the DateAdd function to perform such date calculations.

```
dtTomorrow = DateAdd("d", 1, Date)
```

DateDiff Function

Category	Date and Time Features
Availability	VB:Yes, VBA:Yes, VBScript:Yes
Purpose	Returns a specified time interval between two dates or times.
Typical Syntax	**DateDiff(***interval, date1, date2[, firstdayofweek[, firstweekofyear]]***)**
See Also	DatePart Function, Day Function, Hour Function, Minute Function, Month Function, Second Function, Year Function

Use the DateDiff function as needed within your Visual Basic source code. Do not use standard arithmetic operators to calculate the difference between two date values. Use the DateDiff function instead.

The *firstdayofweek* and *firstweekofyear* arguments to the DateDiff function accept Integer values, or one of a set of intrinsic Visual Basic constants. When available, always use the supplied constants instead of numeric literals.

DatePart Function

Category	Date and Time Features
Availability	VB:Yes, VBA:Yes, VBScript:Yes
Purpose	Returns a value indicating a portion of a given date or time.
Typical Syntax	**DatePart(***interval*, *date*[, *firstdayofweek*[, *firstweekofyear*]]**)**
See Also	DateDiff Function, Day Function, Hour Function, Minute Function, Month Function, Second Function, Weekday Function, Year Function

Use the DatePart function to return the quarter, day of year, or week of year for a given date. The DatePart function allows other date components to be retrieved. However, those values should be retrieved using their respective functions as listed in Table 10.1.

Table 10.1	Date Component Functions
To Return	**Use the Function**
Day	**Day(***date***)**
Hour	**Hour(***date***)**
Minute	**Minute(***date***)**
Month	**Month(***date***)**
Second	**Second(***date***)**
Weekday	**Weekday(***date*[, *firstdayofweek*]**)**
Year	**Year(***date***)**

The *firstdayofweek* and *firstweekofyear* arguments to the DatePart function accept Integer values, or one of a set of intrinsic Visual Basic constants. When available, always use the supplied constants instead of numeric literals.

If you are using either Visual Basic or Visual Basic for Applications, and you will be using the value returned from this function as a string (for example, to concatenate the date component onto an existing string), consider using the Format$ function instead.

```
sInfo = "This is quarter " & Format$(Date, "q")
```

DateSerial Function

Category	Date and Time Features
Availability	VB:Yes, VBA:Yes, VBScript:Yes
Purpose	Returns a date based on individual year, month, and day values.
Typical Syntax	**DateSerial**(*year, month, day*)
See Also	DateAdd Function, DatePart Function, Day Function, Month Function, TimeSerial Function, Year Function

Use the DateSerial function as needed within your Visual Basic source code. Be aware that if you supply a month or day value that is too large for a valid date, the DateSerial function will increment the value appropriately to compensate for the extra months or days.

```
dtAction = DateSerial(1999, 12, 31)   ' --> 12/31/1999
dtAction = DateSerial(1999, 12, 32)   ' --> 1/1/2000
```

You can also supply negative values for the year, month, or day, and the resulting date will decrement as needed. If you supply values that are either negative or too large for a date element, provide a suitable explanation in the source code comments.

DateValue Function

Category	Date and Time Features
Availability	VB:Yes, VBA:Yes, VBScript:Yes
Purpose	Converts a date expression to a Variant (Date) value.
Typical Syntax	**DateValue**(*date*)
See Also	CDate Function, Date Function, DateSerial Function, Time Function

To convert a date, time, or date/time expression to a Variant (Date) or true Date value, use the CDate function. Avoid the DateValue function for general date conversions. However, if you have an expression that contains both a date and a time, and you wish to retrieve only the date portion of the expression, use the DateValue function. Passing a date and time expression to the CDate function will retain both the date and time portions of the expression. The DateValue function discards the time portion of the original expression. If you are using the DateValue function to remove the time portion of a date/time expression, make it clear in your source code comments that the time portion will be lost.

If you supply a date that contains only digits and valid date separators, ambiguity may occur. For example, the date "12/10/1999" can be interpreted as December 10, 1999, or October 12, 1999, depending on the regional settings of the local system. To interpret such a value, Visual Basic uses the order specified by the Short Date format as set in the Control Panel of the local system. If you will be storing string date expressions in an ambiguous format, or if the user will be permitted to enter values in an ambiguous format, make it clear in both the technical documentation and the user's printed and on-line documentation how you will handle such ambiguous dates in your application.

Day Function

Category	Date and Time Features
Availability	VB:Yes, VBA:Yes, VBScript:Yes
Purpose	Returns a value indicating the day for a given date.
Typical Syntax	**Day(***date***)**
See Also	DatePart Function, Hour Function, Minute Function, Month Function, Second Function, Year Function

Use the Day function as needed within your Visual Basic source code. If you are using either Visual Basic or Visual Basic for Applications, and you will be using the day returned from this function as a string (for example, to concatenate the day onto an existing string), consider using the Format$ function instead.

```
sInfo = "Day number " & Format$(dtAction, "d")
```

DDB Function

Category	Financial Features
Availability	VB:Yes, VBA:Yes, VBScript:No
Purpose	Calculates the depreciation of an asset for a specific time period.
Typical Syntax	**DDB(***cost, salvage, life, period[, factor]***)**
See Also	FV Function, IPmt Function, IRR Function, MIRR Function, NPer Function, NPV Function, Pmt Function, PPmt Function, PV Function, Rate Function, SLN Function, SYD Function

Use the DDB function as needed within your Visual Basic source code. This function returns a Double value, and accepts several Double values for parameters. While values based on the Currency data type are accurate to four decimal places, Double floating point values are subject to minor rounding errors. While you can convert the return value of the DDB function from Double to Currency using the CCur function, this result will be bound to the same rounding conditions of the value returned by the DDB function. Take care to check the accuracy of the return values when using the Visual Basic intrinsic financial functions.

Debug Object

Category   Error Handling and Debugging Features
Availability   VB:Yes, VBA:Yes, VBScript:Yes (with restrictions)
Purpose   Object that supplies debugging features.
Typical Syntax **Debug**
See Also   App Object, Global Object, Screen Object

Use the Debug object as needed within your Visual Basic source code. This object supplies two primary methods: Assert and Print. The Print method is not available in VBScript.

Declare Statement

Category   Declaration Features
Availability   VB:Yes, VBA:Yes, VBScript:No
Purpose   References a procedure stored in a dynamic link library (DLL) for use in your source code.
Typical Syntax **[Private | Public] Declare Function** *name* **Lib** "*lib-name*" **[Alias** "*aliasname*"**]** **[(**[*arglist*]**)]** **[As** *type*]
                    [Private | Public] Declare Sub *name* **Lib** "*libname*" **[Alias** "*aliasname*"**]** **[(**[*arglist*]**)]**
See Also   ByRef Keyword, ByVal Keyword, Function Statement, Optional Keyword, ParamArray Keyword, Property Get Statement, Property Let Statement, Property Set Statement, Sub Statement

Use the Declare statement as needed within your Visual Basic source code. In general, all Declare statements should appear in a single module, although there are times when you may wish to encapsulate functionality within a single module by using private Declare statements. Always start the declaration with the Public or Private keyword. If no arguments are used with the function or subroutine, still follow the procedure name with an empty set of parentheses. When arguments are included, supply the appropriate data type with the As clause on each argument. Also, when declaring functions, end the declaration with the data type of the return value, using the final As clause.

Every argument must include the appropriate ByRef or ByVal keyword. Each argument must also include the appropriate data type, which may be the generic Any data type.

Procedure names appear in mixed case with an initial capital letter. Digits may be included, but underscores should be limited to event procedure names.

For more information about declaring procedures in your Visual Basic source code, see Chapter 2, *Using Declaration*, and Chapter 9, *Declaration Standards*.

DefType Statements

Category	Declaration Features
Availability	VB:Yes, VBA:Yes, VBScript:No
Purpose	Assigns a default data type to declared objects that begin with a specific letter.
Typical Syntax	**DefBool** *letterrange*[, *letterrange*]...
	DefByte *letterrange*[, *letterrange*]...
	DefInt *letterrange*[, *letterrange*]...
	DefLng *letterrange*[, *letterrange*]...
	DefCur *letterrange*[, *letterrange*]...
	DefSng *letterrange*[, *letterrange*]...
	DefDbl *letterrange*[, *letterrange*]...
	DefDec *letterrange*[, *letterrange*]...
	DefDate *letterrange*[, *letterrange*]...
	DefStr *letterrange*[, *letterrange*]...
	DefObj *letterrange*[, *letterrange*]...
	DefVar *letterrange*[, *letterrange*]...
See Also	Dim Statement, Function Statement, Private Statement, Property Get Statement, Public Statement

Do not use the DefType statements within your Visual Basic source code. Every declared variable needs its own As clause to define its data type. Also, return values from functions and Property Get procedures must have the data type of their return values indicated with an appropriate As clause.

DeleteSetting Statement

Category	Miscellaneous Features
Availability	VB:Yes, VBA:Yes, VBScript:No
Purpose	Removes application information from the Windows registry.
Typical Syntax	**DeleteSetting** *appname*, *section*[, *key*]
See Also	GetAllSettings Function, GetSetting Function, SaveSetting Function

Use the DeleteSetting statement as needed within your Visual Basic source code. Document all registry settings used by your application in the technical documentation or user documentation, as appropriate.

The DeleteSetting statement accesses information that resides outside of the control of the Visual Basic application. Therefore, you must always use proper error handling in any procedure that uses the DeleteSetting statement. Make use of the On Error statement to capture any errors, and take the appropriate corrective action.

Dim Statement

Category	Declaration Features
Availability	VB:Yes, VBA:Yes, VBScript:Yes (with restrictions)
Purpose	Declares a variable that is local in scope.
Typical Syntax	**Dim [WithEvents]** *varname*[([*subscripts*])] [**As [New]** *type*]
See Also	Global Statement, Private Statement, Public Statement, ReDim Statement, Static Statement

Use the Dim statement as needed within the routines of your Visual Basic application. Always include the appropriate As clause in the declaration. Do not place more than one variable declaration within a single Dim statement. Place each variable declaration on a separate source code line. In VBScript, it is permissible to place more than one variable with the same Hungarian prefix within the same Dim statement.

Local variables use the Hungarian naming conventions. Local variables do not begin with a Hungarian scope prefix, but start immediately with the Hungarian type identifier.

For more information about local variables and the Hungarian naming conventions, see Chapter 2, *Using Declaration*, and Chapter 9, *Declaration Standards*.

Beginning with Visual Basic 4, the Private statement replaced the Dim statement within the Declarations section of a Visual Basic module. Do not use the Dim statement to declare module-level variables; use the Private statement to make a variable visible in scope to the module. Continue to use the Dim statement to declare local variables within routines.

Dir Function

Category	File System Features
Availability	VB:Yes, VBA:Yes, VBScript:No
Purpose	Returns a file name that matches a pattern.
Typical Syntax	**Dir**[(*pathname*[, *attributes*])]
Variations	Dir$ Function
See Also	ChDir Statement, ChDrive Statement, CurDir Function

Use the Dir function as needed within your Visual Basic source code. If you do not require a Variant result, use the Dir$ function instead of the Dir function.

```
vntFileMatch = Dir("*.*")
sFileMatch = Dir$("*.*")
```

The *pathname* argument supplied to the Dir function may be a local or mapped drive path, a UNC (Universal Naming Convention) path, or a path relative to the current drive and directory. The *attributes* argument accepts an Integer value, or one or more of a set of intrinsic Visual Basic constants. When available, always use the supplied constants instead of numeric literals.

The Dir function (and all other File System features) accesses information that resides outside of the control of the Visual Basic application. Therefore, you must always use proper error handling in any procedure that uses the Dir function. Make use of the On Error statement to capture any file handling errors, and take the appropriate corrective action.

Do...Loop Statement

Category	Flow Control Features
Availability	VB:Yes, VBA:Yes, VBScript:Yes
Purpose	Repeats a block of code until a specified condition is met.
Typical Syntax	**Do** [{**While** | **Until**} *condition*]
	[*statements*]
	Loop
	Do
	[*statements*]
	Loop [{**While** | **Until**} *condition*]
See Also	Exit Block Statement, For Each...Next Statement, For...Next Statement, While...Wend Statement

Use the Do...Loop statement as needed within your Visual Basic source code. When forming the *condition* of your statement, make it as clear as possible, using parentheses to group values when ambiguity (for the reader) is possible. Enclosing the condition in a set of parentheses also improves readability.

```
Do While (condition)
```

The condition can appear at the beginning of the loop (with the Do keyword) or at the end of the loop (with the Loop keyword). Visual Basic allows you to leave the condition off entirely to create an infinite loop. However, you should always include a condition. If you wish to create an infinite loop, use While True as the condition.

```
Do While True
    ' ----- Statements appear here
Loop
```

If you need to exit such an infinite loop, use the Exit Do statement. However, it is better to use a valid condition with the loop's While or Until keyword.

Never jump to a line label in the middle of a loop using a GoTo statement found outside of the loop. Also, do not jump out of a loop using a GoTo statement; use the Exit Do statement instead. If you have nested Do...Loop statements, the Exit Do statement only exits the loop immediately containing the Exit Do statement.

DoEvents Function

Category	Flow Control Features
Availability	VB:Yes, VBA:Yes (with limitations), VBScript:No
Purpose	Yields execution to the operating system so that other application events can be processed.
Typical Syntax	**DoEvents**

Although most programmers treat the DoEvents function like a statement, it is actually a function that returns the number of open forms when running within a true Visual Basic application (but not within a Visual Basic for Applications program).

The use of the DoEvents function can lead to subtle errors within your application. When you give up processing time to the operating system, it may allow the user of your application to perform additional user interface activities *within your application*, circumventing the natural flow of your event-driven source code. Consider a printing form with a **Print** command button on it, and the following event code.

```
Private Sub cmdPrint_Click()
    ' ----- Print the data, then close the form
    Call PreparePrintJob
    DoEvents
    Call PrintThePrintJob
    Unload Me
End Sub
```

If the user attempts to click the Print button twice, it is possible for the printing code to run twice, because the DoEvents temporarily suspends control of the cmdPrint_Click event so that other events (including a new call to cmdPrint_Click) can occur. If you need to prevent a second print from occurring in this instance, you should avoid the use of the DoEvents function. You may also wish to disable the Print button, and other relevant controls, so that the user cannot disrupt the printing process.

If you need to perform periodic processing within your application, consider the use of a timer. While a timer may also interrupt a routine to perform its processing, you can control the interval at which the timer operates.

Never use the DoEvents function simply to allow the forms or controls of your application to redraw themselves. If you need a form or a control to be visually refreshed, use the form or control's Refresh method instead.

Empty Keyword

Category	Declaration Features
Availability	VB:Yes, VBA:Yes, VBScript:Yes
Purpose	Indicates that a variable or value is uninitialized.

Typical Syntax   **Nothing**
See Also   IsEmpty Function, Nothing Keyword, Null Keyword

Use the Empty keyword as needed within your Visual Basic source code. Never test an expression by comparing it with the Empty keyword. Always use the IsEmpty function instead.

Incorrect

```
If (vntBuild = Empty) Then
```

Correct

```
If (IsEmpty(vntBuild)) Then
```

End Statement

Category   Flow Control Features
Availability   VB:Yes, VBA:Yes, VBScript:No
Purpose   Halts program execution immediately.
Typical Syntax   **End**
See Also   End Block Statement, Stop Statement

Your application should include no more than one or two End statements, each located within a centralized cleanup or termination routine. Never use the End statement to abort an application in response to an error. If you encounter a "fatal" error within your application, save as much of the user's data and state information as possible, close all acquired resources, and then use the End statement through a centralized procedure.

In a compiled application, use the End statement instead of the Stop statement to halt application execution.

End Block Statement

Category   Flow Control Features
Availability   VB:Yes, VBA:Yes, VBScript:Yes (with restrictions)
Purpose   Ends a subordinate block of code.
Typical Syntax   **End Function**
                      End If
                      End Property
                      End Select
                      End Sub
                      End Type
                      End With
See Also   End Statement, Function Statement, If...Then...Else Statement, Property Get Statement, Property Let Statement,

Property Set Statement, Select Statement, Sub Statement, Type Statement, With Statement

Use the End Block statements as needed within your Visual Basic source code. Note that the End Type statement is not available within Visual Basic, Scripting Edition. Also, the End If statement is not needed when an If statement and all of its subordinate statements are fully defined on a single source code line.

Enum Statement

Category	Declaration Features
Availability	VB:Yes, VBA:Yes, VBScript:No
Purpose	Defines an enumerated data type.
Typical Syntax	**[Private	Public] Enum** *enumname*
	membername [**=** *constantexpression*]
	. . .
	End Enum
See Also	Const Statement, Type Statement

Use the Enum statement as needed within your Visual Basic source code. Always begin the statement with either the Private or Public keyword, Include a mixed-case *enumname* ending in the word "Enum." Each element within the enumeration should be mixed case, beginning with a common lower-case enumeration prefix.

For more information about enumerated data types, see Chapter 2, *Using Declaration*, and Chapter 9, *Declaration Standards*.

Environ Function

Category	String Features
Availability	VB:Yes, VBA:Yes, VBScript:No
Purpose	Return the value of a system environment variable.
Typical Syntax	**Environ(***envstring* | *number***)**
Variations	Environ$ Function

Use the Environ function as needed within your Visual Basic source code. If you do not require a Variant result, use the Environ$ function instead of the Environ function.

```
vntTempDir = Environ("TEMP")
sTempDir = Environ$("TEMP")
```

EOF Function

Category	File System Features
Availability	VB:Yes, VBA:Yes, VBScript:No

Purpose	Indicates whether or not the end of the specified file has been reached.
Typical Syntax	**EOF**(*filenumber*)
See Also	Loc Function, LOF Function, Open Statement, Seek Function, Seek Statement

Use the EOF function as needed within your Visual Basic source code. Always use a file number returned from the FreeFile function as an argument to the EOF function.

If you open a file for Binary access, and then use the Input function to retrieve values, the EOF function will not be a sufficient indicator of when the end of file has been reached. When using the Input function, use the LOF function and the Loc function together to determine when the end of file has been reached. If you instead retrieve records from a Binary file using the Get Statement, the EOF function is a valid method for determining the end of file status. The EOF function is useless when used on files opened for Output.

The EOF function (and all other File System features) accesses information that resides outside of the control of the Visual Basic application. Therefore, you must always use proper error handling in any procedure that uses the EOF function. Make use of the On Error statement to capture any file handling errors, and take the appropriate corrective action.

Eqv Operator

Category	Operators
Availability	VB:Yes, VBA:Yes, VBScript:Yes
Purpose	Performs a logical or bitwise equivalence operation.
Typical Syntax	*expression1* **Eqv** *expression2*
See Also	And Operator, Imp Operator, Not Operator, Or Operator, Xor Operator

Use the Eqv operator as needed within your Visual Basic source code. When writing complex statements that involve more than one logical or bitwise operator, use parentheses to indicate the proper precedence and grouping within the calculation.

Erase Statement

Category	Declaration Features
Availability	VB:Yes, VBA:Yes, VBScript:Yes
Purpose	Clears the elements of an array, freeing memory if the array is dynamic.
Typical Syntax	**Erase** *arraylist*
See Also	Array Statement, Dim Statement, Private Statement, Public Statement, ReDim Statement, Static Statement

Use the Erase statement as needed within your Visual Basic source code. The syntax of the Erase statement allows more than one array variable to be specified in the same statement. In order to improve the clarity of your code, do not use this syntax. Always issue a separate Erase statement for each array to be erased.

When erasing dynamic arrays (those resized with the ReDim statement), take care not to reuse the array until you have issued another ReDim statement on the array.

Erl Function

Category	Error Handling and Debugging Features
Availability	VB:Yes, VBA:Yes, VBScript:No
Purpose	Identifies the approximate line number where an error occurred.
Typical Syntax	**Erl**
See Also	Debug Object, Err Object, Err Function, Error Function, Error Statement

The Erl function is only valid when you employ numeric line numbers within your source code. In general, alphanumeric line labels should be used instead of numeric line numbers for clarity. Without these numeric line numbers, the Erl function is useless. However, it may be useful to temporary add numeric line numbers to a routine in which an elusive error appears. When you have successfully located and removed the source of the problem, you can also remove the numeric line numbers, and the Erl function, from the code.

The Erl function returns the line number that is approximately near to the location of the error. Its use does not guarantee that you will detect the closest line number. Therefore, you may wish to employ additional conditions to help you narrow down the source of an error.

Err Object

Category	Error Handling and Debugging Features
Availability	VB:Yes, VBA:Yes, VBScript:Yes
Purpose	Object that contains properties and methods for error processing.
Typical Syntax	**Err**
See Also	Debug Object, Error Function, Error Statement

Use the Err object as needed within your Visual Basic source code. The default property of the Err object is the Number property. To obtain the error number of the most recent error, use either the "Err" syntax or the "Err.Number" syntax.

Error Function

Category	Error Handling and Debugging Features
Availability	VB:Yes, VBA:Yes, VBScript:No
Purpose	Returns the message of an error for a given error code.
Typical Syntax	**Error**[(*errornumber*)]
Variations	Error$ Function
See Also	Debug Object, Err Object, Error Statement

Use the Error function as needed within your Visual Basic source code. If you do not require a Variant result, use the Error$ function instead of the Error function.

```
vntErrorText = Error(nRecentError)
MsgBox Error$, vbOKOnly + vbExclamation, "Error"
```

When presenting errors to the user, consider the Err.Description property as well.

Error Statement

Category	Error Handling and Debugging Features
Availability	VB:Yes, VBA:Yes, VBScript:No
Purpose	Simulates the generation of an error.
Typical Syntax	**Error** *errornumber*
See Also	Debug Object, Err Object, Error Function

Do not use the Error statement within your Visual Basic source code. Use the Err object's Raise method instead.

Eval Function

Category	Miscellaneous Features
Availability	VB:No, VBA:No, VBScript:Yes
Purpose	Evaluates a VBScript expression that is stored in a string.
Typical Syntax	**Eval(***expression***)**
See Also	Execute Statement, ExecuteGlobal Statement

Avoid the use of the Eval function in your VBScript source code unless no other solution can be clearly or efficiently provided. If you will be ignoring the return value of the Eval function, consider the Execute statement or the ExecuteGlobal Statement instead.

Event Statement

Category	Declaration Features
Availability	VB:Yes, VBA:Yes, VBScript:No
Purpose	Declares an event.

Typical Syntax	[**Public**] **Event** *name* [(*arglist*)]
See Also	RaiseEvent Statement

Use the Event statement as needed within your Visual Basic source code. Always start the declaration with the Public keyword. If no arguments are used with the function, still follow the event name with an empty set of parentheses. When arguments are included, supply the appropriate data type with the As clause on each argument. Also, identify the passing method of each argument by supplying either the ByRef or ByVal keyword.

Event names appear in mixed case with an initial capital letter. Digits may be included, but underscores are not allowed. An underscore will be automatically added in an event name when an event procedure is written.

Execute Statement

Category	Miscellaneous Features
Availability	VB:No, VBA:No, VBScript:Yes
Purpose	Executes one or more statements stored in a string.
Typical Syntax	**Execute** *statement*
See Also	Eval Function, ExecuteGlobal Statement

Avoid the use of the Execute function in your VBScript source code unless no other solution can be clearly or efficiently provided. If you need to evaluate the return value from the statement, consider the Eval function instead.

ExecuteGlobal Statement

Category	Miscellaneous Features
Availability	VB:No, VBA:No, VBScript:Yes
Purpose	Executes one or more statements stored in a string.
Typical Syntax	**ExecuteGlobal** *statement*
See Also	Eval Function, Execute Statement

Avoid the use of the ExecuteGlobal function in your VBScript source code unless no other solution can be clearly or efficiently provided. If you need to evaluate the return value from the statement, consider the Eval function instead.

Exit Statement

Category	Flow Control Features
Availability	VB:Yes, VBA:Yes, VBScript:Yes
Purpose	Exits a loop or routine immediately.
Typical Syntax	**Exit Do**
	Exit For
	Exit Function

Exit Property
Exit Sub

See Also   Do...Loop Statement, End Block Statement, For...Next Statement, Function Statement, Property Get Statement, Property Let Statement, Property Set Statement, Sub Statement

Use the Exit statements as needed within your Visual Basic source code. If you find yourself using an abundance of these statements, it may indicate a poorly designed procedure or loop construct. For example, if you have several Exit For statements within a single For...Next loop, it may be better to convert the loop to a Do...Loop statement, and test for the exit conditions at the top or bottom of the loop construct. Consider the following For...Next statement:

```
For nCounter = 1 To 10
    If (OutOfSpace() = True) Then Exit For
    ' ----- Perform regular processing here
Next nCounter
```

You can convert this series of statements into a Do...Loop construct, removing the need for the Exit For statement altogether.

```
nCounter = 1
Do While (nCounter <= 10) And _
        (OutOfSpace() = False)
    ' ----- Perform regular processing here
    nCounter = nCounter + 1
Loop
```

If a procedure contains GoSub and On Error statements, all of the destinations should appear at the end of the routine. The last statement in the main body of the routine before the GoSub and On Error destinations should be an Exit Function, Exit Property, or Exit Sub statement.

When handling an error trapped with an On Error statement, you must choose either to exit the procedure using Exit Function, Exit Property, or Exit Sub, or return to the main body of the routine with a Resume statement. If you choose to exit the routine immediately with one of the Exit statements, make sure that you release all resources opened within the routine. Perform as orderly a cleanup as possible before returning to the calling procedure, even if an error prevents you from doing a perfect and complete cleanup.

Exp Function

Category   Math Features
Availability   VB:Yes, VBA:Yes, VBScript:Yes
Purpose   Calculates *e* (the base of natural logarithms) raised to a power.

Typical Syntax   **Exp(***number***)**
See Also   Log Function, Sqr Function

Use the Exp function as needed within your Visual Basic source code. This function returns a Double value, and accepts a Double value for its parameter. Double floating point values are subject to minor rounding errors. Take care to check the accuracy of the return values when using the Visual Basic intrinsic math functions.

The argument to the Exp function can be no greater than 709.78212893. If the expression you pass to the Exp function is supplied by the user, and if that expression is out of the valid range for the Exp function, either correctly handle the error raised by the Exp function, or reject the value entered by the user.

False Keyword

Category   Miscellaneous Features
Availability   VB:Yes, VBA:Yes, VBScript:Yes
Purpose   Provides an intrinsic constant for the False Boolean value.
Typical Syntax **False**
See Also   True Keyword

Use the False keyword as needed within your Visual Basic source code. Although the False keyword has a value equal to 0 (zero), it is not always interpreted as 0 when coerced into other data types. Consider the following statements:

```
Dim sWork As String
Dim nWork As Integer

nWork = False
sWork = nWork & " = " & False
MsgBox sWork
```

Processing this code within a Visual Basic application will display a message box with the text "0 = False" instead of the expected "0 = 0." The False keyword, and all true Boolean values that equate to False, result in the text "False" when converted to a String.

Never use 0 when you mean False. Also, never use False when you mean 0 (zero). When you are testing the value of a Boolean variable, or the result of a Boolean expression, always compare the variable or expression to True or False, never to -1 or 0.

FileAttr Function

Category   File System Features
Availability   VB:Yes, VBA:Yes, VBScript:No
Purpose   Returns the attributes of an open file.

Typical Syntax   **FileAttr(***filenumber, returntype***)**
See Also   FreeFile Statement, GetAttr Function, SetAttr Statement, Open Statement

Use the FileAttr function as needed within your Visual Basic source code. Always use a file number returned from the FreeFile function as the first argument to the FileAttr function.

The FileAttr function (and all other File System features) accesses information that resides outside of the control of the Visual Basic application. Therefore, you must always use proper error handling in any procedure that uses the FileAttr function. Make use of the On Error statement to capture any file handling errors, and take the appropriate corrective action.

FileCopy Statement

Category   File System Features
Availability   VB:Yes, VBA:Yes, VBScript:No
Purpose   Copies a file from one location to another.
Typical Syntax   **FileCopy** *source, destination*
See Also   Kill Statement, Name Statement

Use the FileCopy statement as needed within your Visual Basic source code. The arguments supplied to the FileCopy statement may be local or mapped drive paths, UNC (Universal Naming Convention) paths, or paths relative to the current drive and directory.

Be aware that the FileCopy statement will replace any existing file at the destination with a copy of the source file. If the destination is a user file, make sure you sufficiently inform the user that the file will be overwritten, either through documentation or through application notification.

The FileCopy statement (and all other File System features) accesses information that resides outside of the control of the Visual Basic application. Therefore, you must always use proper error handling in any procedure that uses the FileCopy statement. Make use of the On Error statement to capture any file handling errors, and take the appropriate corrective action.

FileDateTime Function

Category   File System Features
Availability   VB:Yes, VBA:Yes, VBScript:No
Purpose   Returns the modification date and time of a file.
Typical Syntax   **FileDateTime(***pathname***)**
See Also   FileLen Function, GetAttr Function, SetAttr Statement

Use the FileDateTime function as needed within your Visual Basic source code. The argument supplied to the FileDateTime statement may be a local or mapped drive path, a UNC (Universal Naming Convention) path, or a path relative to the current drive and directory.

The FileDateTime function (and all other File System features) accesses information that resides outside of the control of the Visual Basic application. Therefore, you must always use proper error handling in any procedure that uses the FileDateTime function. Make use of the On Error statement to capture any file handling errors, and take the appropriate corrective action.

FileLen Function

Category	File System Features
Availability	VB:Yes, VBA:Yes, VBScript:No
Purpose	Returns the number of bytes in a file.
Typical Syntax	**FileLen(***pathname***)**
See Also	FileDateTime Function, GetAttr Function, LOF Function, SetAttr Statement

Use the FileLen function as needed within your Visual Basic source code. The argument supplied to the FileLen function may be a local or mapped drive path, a UNC (Universal Naming Convention) path, or a path relative to the current drive and directory.

While you can use the FileLen function on an open file, the number of bytes returned is the file size at the time the file was opened. To more accurately determine the size of an open file, use the LOF function.

The FileLen function (and all other File System features) accesses information that resides outside of the control of the Visual Basic application. Therefore, you must always use proper error handling in any procedure that uses the FileLen function. Make use of the On Error statement to capture any file handling errors, and take the appropriate corrective action.

Filter Function

Category	String Features
Availability	VB:Yes, VBA:Yes, VBScript:Yes
Purpose	Returns an array of strings that match or do not match a substring.
Typical Syntax	**Filter(***inputstrings, value*[, *include*[, *compare*]]**)**
See Also	InStr Function, InStrRev Function, Option Compare Statement, Replace Function

Use the Filter function as needed within your Visual Basic source code. The *compare* argument of the Filter function accepts Integer values, or one of a set of intrinsic Visual Basic constants. When available, always use the supplied constants instead of numeric literals. The use of the Option Compare statement can affect the results of the Filter function.

Fix Function

Category	Math Features
Availability	VB:Yes, VBA:Yes, VBScript:Yes
Purpose	Truncates the fractional portion of an expression.
Typical Syntax	**Fix(***expression***)**
See Also	Abs Function, Int Function, Round Function, Sgn Function

Use the Fix function as needed within your Visual Basic source code. For positive numbers, the Fix and Int functions are identical. For negative values, the Fix function truncates the fractional portion of the number, leaving the whole number intact. The Int function returns the next larger negative value when a fractional component is non-zero. If you are sure that you will pass positive values only as arguments, use the Int function instead of the Fix function.

For Each...Next Statement

Category	Flow Control Features
Availability	VB:Yes, VBA:Yes, VBScript:Yes (with restrictions)
Purpose	Repeats a block of code for each element in a collection or array.
Typical Syntax	**For Each** *element* **In** *group*
	[*statements*]
	Next [*element*]
See Also	Do...Loop Statement, Exit Block Statement, For...Next Statement, While...Wend Statement

Use the For Each...Next statement as needed within your Visual Basic source code. Never resize the *group* of elements within the loop. Although Visual Basic does not require *element* in the Next clause, always include it for clarity. In VBScript, you cannot include *element* in the Next clause.

Visual Basic and Visual Basic for Applications allow you to combine multiple *element* variables into a single Next clause. Never use this syntax, as it reduces readability and increases the chance for errors.

Incorrect

```
For Each vntOuter In nOutArray
    For Each vntInner In nInArray
        Debug.Print vntOuter, vntInner
Next vntInner, vntOuter
```

Correct

```
For Each vntOuter In nOutArray
    For Each vntInner In nInArray
        Debug.Print vntOuter, vntInner
```

```
    Next vntInner
Next vntOuter
```

Never jump to a line label in the middle of a loop using a GoTo statement found outside of the loop. Also, do not jump out of a loop using a GoTo statement; use the Exit For statement instead. If you have nested For Each...Next statements, the Exit For statement exits only the loop immediately containing the Exit For statement.

For...Next Statement

Category	Flow Control Features
Availability	VB:Yes, VBA:Yes, VBScript:Yes (with restrictions)
Purpose	Repeats a block of code a specified number of times.
Typical Syntax	**For** *counter* **=** *start* **To** *end* [**Step** *step*]
	[*statements*]
	Next [*counter*]
See Also	Do...Loop Statement, Exit Block Statement, For Each...Next Statement, While...Wend Statement

Use the For...Next statement as needed within your Visual Basic source code. Never change the value of *counter* within the loop. Consider *counter* to be a read-only variable between the For and Next clauses. If you need to change the *counter* value inside of the loop, convert the loop to a Do...Loop statement instead.

Although Visual Basic does not require *counter* in the Next clause, always include it for clarity. In VBScript, you cannot include *counter* in the Next clause.

The *start*, *end*, and *step* values are calculated only once upon entry into the loop. Modifying these values in the middle of the loop has no effect on the loop itself. Consider the following block of code:

```
nUpper = 5
For nCounter = 1 To nUpper
    MsgBox nCounter
    nUpper = nUpper - 1
Next nCounter
```

Although the *end* value (nUpper) is modified in the loop, this loop still executes five times.

Visual Basic and Visual Basic for Applications allow you to combine multiple *counter* variables into a single Next clause. Never use this syntax, as it reduces readability and increases the chance for errors.

Incorrect

```
For nOuter = 1 To 5
    For nInner = 1 To 5
```

```
        MsgBox nOuter, nInner
Next nInner, nOuter
```

Correct

```
For nOuter = 1 To 5
    For nInner = 1 To 5
        MsgBox nOuter, nInner
    Next nInner
Next nOuter
```

Never jump to a line label in the middle of a loop using a GoTo statement found outside of the loop. Also, do not jump out of a loop using a GoTo statement; use the Exit For statement instead. If you have nested For...Next statements, the Exit For statement only exits the loop immediately containing the Exit For statement.

Format Function

Category	String Features
Availability	VB:Yes, VBA:Yes, VBScript:No
Purpose	Formats an expression based on a description.
Typical Syntax	**Format(***expression*[, *format*[, *firstdayofweek*[, *firstweekofyear*]]]**)**
Variations	Format$ Function
See Also	FormatCurrency Function, FormatDateTime Function, FormatNumber Function, FormatPercent Function

Use the Format function as needed within your Visual Basic source code. Always include the *format* argument, even if you will be using the default formatting method for an expression. If you do not require a Variant result, use the Format$ function instead of the Format function.

```
vntDisplay = Format(fcCost, "$#,##0.00")
sDisplay = Format$(fcCost, "$#,##0.00")
```

The *firstdayofweek* and *firstweekofyear* arguments to the Format function accept Integer values, or one of a set of intrinsic Visual Basic constants. When available, always use the supplied constants instead of numeric literals.

FormatCurrency Function

Category	String Features
Availability	VB:Yes, VBA:Yes, VBScript:Yes
Purpose	Formats an expression to look like a currency amount.
Typical Syntax	**FormatCurrency(***expression*[, *decimaldigits*[, *leadingdigit*[, *negativeparens*[, *groupdigits*]]]]**)**

See Also	Format Function, FormatDateTime Function, FormatNumber Function, FormatPercent Function

Use the FormatCurrency function as needed within your Visual Basic source code. The *leadingdigit*, *negativeparens*, and *groupdigits* arguments to the FormatCurrency function each accept an Integer value, or one of a set of intrinsic Visual Basic constants. When available, always use the supplied constants instead of numeric literals. These arguments also accept the values True and False, although the intrinsic literals are preferred.

In VBScript, the FormatCurrency function is one of a family of functions that replaces the Format function. These functions exist in standard Visual Basic, and are quite useful. The FormatCurrency function was designed to provide a common method of formatting currency values in a Visual Basic application or script. However, you may find that the FormatCurrency function has too many restrictions to meet your formatting needs. If you need more flexibility, and you are working with either Visual Basic or Visual Basic for Applications, use the Format function.

FormatDateTime Function

Category	String Features
Availability	VB:Yes, VBA:Yes, VBScript:Yes
Purpose	Formats an expression to look like a date or time.
Typical Syntax	**FormatDateTime(***expression*[, *format*]**)**
See Also	Format Function, FormatCurrency Function, FormatNumber Function, FormatPercent Function

Use the FormatDateTime function as needed within your Visual Basic source code. The *format* argument to the FormatDateTime function accepts an Integer value, or one of a set of intrinsic Visual Basic constants. When available, always use the supplied constants instead of numeric literals.

In VBScript, the FormatDateTime function is one of a family of functions that replaces the Format function. These functions exist in standard Visual Basic, and are quite useful. The FormatDateTime function was designed to provide a common method of formatting date values in a Visual Basic application or script. However, you may find that the FormatDateTime function has too many restrictions to meet your formatting needs. If you need more flexibility, and you are working with either Visual Basic or Visual Basic for Applications, use the Format function.

FormatNumber Function

Category	String Features
Availability	VB:Yes, VBA:Yes, VBScript:Yes
Purpose	Formats an expression to look like a number.

Typical Syntax   **FormatNumber(***expression*[, *decimaldigits*[, *leadingdigit*[, *negativeparens*[, *groupdigits*]]]]**)**

See Also   Format Function, FormatCurrency Function, FormatDate-Time Function, FormatPercent Function

Use the FormatNumber function as needed within your Visual Basic source code. The *leadingdigit, negativeparens,* and *groupdigits* arguments to the FormatNumber function each accept an Integer value, or one of a set of intrinsic Visual Basic constants. When available, always use the supplied constants instead of numeric literals. These arguments also accept the values True and False, although the intrinsic literals are preferred.

In VBScript, the FormatNumber function is one of a family of functions that replaces the Format function. These functions exist in standard Visual Basic, and are quite useful. The FormatNumber function was designed to provide a common method of formatting numeric values in a Visual Basic application or script. However, you may find that the FormatNumber function has too many restrictions to meet your formatting needs. If you need more flexibility, and you are working with either Visual Basic or Visual Basic for Applications, use the Format function.

FormatPercent Function

Category   String Features
Availability   VB:Yes, VBA:Yes, VBScript:Yes
Purpose   Formats an expression to look like a percent.
Typical Syntax   **FormatPercent(***expression*[, *decimaldigits*[, *leadingdigit*[, *negativeparens*[, *groupdigits*]]]]**)**
See Also   Format Function, FormatCurrency Function, FormatDate-Time Function, FormatNumber Function

Use the FormatPercent function as needed within your Visual Basic source code. The *leadingdigit, negativeparens,* and *groupdigits* arguments to the FormatPercent function each accept an Integer value, or one of a set of intrinsic Visual Basic constants. When available, always use the supplied constants instead of numeric literals. These arguments also accept the values True and False, although the intrinsic literals are preferred.

The FormatPercent function multiplies the original value by 100 before formatting the final output. Consider the following statement:

```
MsgBox FormatPercent(25)
```

This statement displays a message box with the following text:

```
2,500.00%
```

In VBScript, the FormatPercent function is one of a family of functions that replaces the Format function. These functions exist in standard Visual Basic, and are quite useful. The FormatPercent function was designed to provide a common method of formatting percent values in a Visual Basic application or script. However, you may find that the FormatPercent function has too many restrictions to meet your formatting needs. If you need more flexibility, and you are working with either Visual Basic or Visual Basic for Applications, use the Format function.

FreeFile Function

Category	File System Features
Availability	VB:Yes, VBA:Yes, VBScript:No
Purpose	Returns an available number for use by the Open statement.
Typical Syntax	**FreeFile[(*rangenumber*)]**
See Also	Open Statement

Use the FreeFile function as needed within your Visual Basic source code. In general, you should not need to supply the optional *rangenumber* argument. However, if your application will use file numbers in the 256–511 range (accessed by using 1 as the *rangenumber* argument), then supply the *rangenumber* argument on every call to FreeFile within your application.

The Open statement allows you to use any valid unused file number as a file identifier. Visual Basic permits you to supply these numbers yourself. However, conflicts may result in large applications if central control of the available numbers is not enforced. Therefore, always obtain a valid file number using the FreeFile statement. Never use numeric literals for the file number.

Incorrect

```
' ----- Open the source file
Open sSourceFile For Input As #1
```

Instead, use the FreeFile function to ensure a valid and available file number.

Correct

```
' ----- Open the source file
nSourceFileID = FreeFile
Open sSourceFile For Input As #nSourceFileID
```

The FreeFile function returns the next available number. If you call the function two times in a row without opening or closing a file, you will receive the same value. Consider the following statements:

```
' ----- Open the source and destination files
nSourceFileID = FreeFile
nDestFileID = FreeFile
Open sSourceFile For Input As #nSourceFileID
Open sDestFile For Output As #nDestFileID
```

This block of code will fail when the destination file is opened because the file number (nDestFileID) is already in use by the source file (through nSourceFileID). To make this code work properly, rewrite it in this manner:

```
' ----- Open the source and destination files
nSourceFileID = FreeFile
Open sSourceFile For Input As #nSourceFileID
nDestFileID = FreeFile
Open sDestFile For Output As #nDestFileID
```

Function Statement

Category	Declaration Features
Availability	VB:Yes, VBA:Yes, VBScript:Yes (with restrictions)
Purpose	Declares a function procedure.
Typical Syntax	[**Private** | **Public** | **Friend**] [**Static**] **Function** *name* [(*arglist*)] [**As** *type*]
	[*statements*]
	End Function
See Also	ByRef Keyword, ByVal Keyword, Optional Keyword, ParamArray Keyword, Property Get Statement, Property Let Statement, Property Set Statement, Sub Statement

Use the Function statement as needed within your Visual Basic source code. Always start the declaration with the Friend, Public, or Private keyword. If no arguments are used with the function, still follow the function name with an empty set of parentheses. When arguments are included, supply the appropriate data type with the As clause on each argument. Also, end the function declaration with the data type of the return value, using the final As clause. (These last two rules do not apply to VBScript functions.)

Procedure names appear in mixed case with an initial capital letter. Digits may be included, but underscores should be limited to event procedure names.

Never include the Static keyword in the Function statement. If you want to include static local variables within your function, declare each variable using the Static statement. The Static keyword is not available in VBScript.

For more information about declaring procedures in your Visual Basic source code, see Chapter 2, *Using Declaration*, and Chapter 9, *Declaration Standards*.

FV Function

Category	Financial Features
Availability	VB:Yes, VBA:Yes, VBScript:No
Purpose	Calculates the future value of an annuity.
Typical Syntax	**FV(***rate, nper, pmt*[, *pv*[, *type*]]**)**
See Also	DDB Function, IPmt Function, IRR Function, MIRR Function, NPer Function, NPV Function, Pmt Function, PPmt Function, PV Function, Rate Function, SLN Function, SYD Function

Use the FV function as needed within your Visual Basic source code. This function returns a Double value, and accepts several Double values for parameters. While values based on the Currency data type are accurate to four decimal places, Double floating point values are subject to minor rounding errors. While you can convert the return value of the FV function from Double to Currency using the CCur function, this result will be bound to the same rounding conditions of the value returned by the FV function. Take care to check the accuracy of the return values when using the Visual Basic intrinsic financial functions.

Get Statement

Category	File System Features
Availability	VB:Yes, VBA:Yes, VBScript:No
Purpose	Reads data from a file and assigns the result to a variable.
Typical Syntax	**Get [#]***filenumber*, [*recnumber*], *varname*
See Also	Open Statement, Put Statement, Seek Statement

Use the Get statement as needed within your Visual Basic source code. Always use a file number returned from the FreeFile function as an argument to the Get statement. Although the "#" prefix of the *filenumber* argument is optional, always include it in the syntax of the statement.

Data written with the Put statement is read with the Get statement. In general, the structure of the data written with the Put statement must be known to the code that will read the file with the Get statement. You may wish to include, at the beginning of your file data, identification values (sometimes called "magic numbers") that prove the file was written with the expected application, and with the appropriate version of that application.

The Get statement (and all other File System features) accesses information that resides outside of the control of the Visual Basic application. Therefore, you must always use proper error handling in any procedure that uses the Get statement. Make use of the On Error statement to capture any file handling errors, and take the appropriate corrective action.

GetAllSettings Function

Category   Miscellaneous Features
Availability   VB:Yes, VBA:Yes, VBScript:No
Purpose   Returns an array of application settings from the Windows registry.
Typical Syntax **GetAllSettings(***appname, section***)**
See Also   DeleteSetting Statement, GetSetting Function, SaveSetting Statement

Use the GetAllSettings function as needed within your Visual Basic source code. Document all registry settings used by your application in the technical documentation or user documentation, as appropriate.

The GetAllSettings function accesses information that resides outside of the control of the Visual Basic application. Therefore, you must always use proper error handling in any procedure that uses the GetAllSettings function. Make use of the On Error statement to capture any errors, and take the appropriate corrective action.

GetAttr Function

Category   File System Features
Availability   VB:Yes, VBA:Yes, VBScript:No
Purpose   Returns the attributes of a file.
Typical Syntax **GetAttr(***pathname***)**
See Also   FileAttr Function, SetAttr Statement

Use the GetAttr function as needed within your Visual Basic source code. The argument supplied to the GetAttr function may be a local or mapped drive path, a UNC (Universal Naming Convention) path, or a path relative to the current drive and directory.

The return value of the GetAttr function is an integer value, represented by a set of intrinsic Visual Basic constants. When available, always use the supplied constants instead of numeric literals.

The GetAttr function (and all other File System features) accesses information that resides outside of the control of the Visual Basic application. Therefore, you must always use proper error handling in any procedure that uses the GetAttr function. Make use of the On Error statement to capture any file handling errors, and take the appropriate corrective action.

GetLocale Function

Category   Miscellaneous Features
Availability   VB:No, VBA:No, VBScript:Yes
Purpose   Identifies the current locale.

Typical Syntax   GetLocale()
See Also   SetLocale Function

Use the GetLocale function as needed within your Visual Basic source code. Visual Basic does not define a set of constants for the Locale ID, which is returned by this function. However, you may wish to declare a constant for the Locale IDs that you use within your application.

GetObject Function

Category   Declaration Features
Availability   VB:Yes, VBA:Yes, VBScript:Yes
Purpose   Retrieves a reference to an ActiveX object.
Typical Syntax   GetObject([*pathname*] [, *class*])
See Also   CreateObject Function

Use the GetObject function as needed within your Visual Basic source code. The GetObject function accesses information that resides outside of the control of the Visual Basic application. Therefore, you must always use proper error handling in any procedure that uses the GetObject function. Make use of the On Error statement to capture any errors, and take the appropriate corrective action.

GetRef Function

Category   Miscellaneous Features
Availability   VB:No, VBA:No, VBScript:Yes
Purpose   Gets a procedure reference for use with DHTML events.
Typical Syntax   GetRef(*procname*)
See Also   AddressOf Operator

Use the GetRef function as needed within your Visual Basic source code.

GetSetting Function

Category   Miscellaneous Features
Availability   VB:Yes, VBA:Yes, VBScript:No
Purpose   Returns an application value from the Windows registry.
Typical Syntax   GetSetting(*appname, section, key*[, *default*])
See Also   DeleteSetting Statement, GetAllSettings Function, SaveSetting Statement

Use the GetSetting function as needed within your Visual Basic source code. Document all registry settings used by your application in the technical documentation or user documentation, as appropriate.

The GetSetting function accesses information that resides outside of the control of the Visual Basic application. Therefore, you must always use proper error handling in any procedure that uses the GetSetting function. Make use of the On Error statement to capture any errors, and take the appropriate corrective action.

Global Statement

Category	Declaration Features
Availability	VB:Yes, VBA:Yes, VBScript:No
Purpose	Declares a variable that is global in scope.
Typical Syntax	**Global** *varname* [**As** *type*]
See Also	Dim Statement, Private Statement, Public Statement, Static Statement

Beginning with Visual Basic 4, the Public statement replaced the Global statement. Do not use the Global statement to declare global variables; use the Public statement to make a variable global to the application.

Global Object

Category	Miscellaneous Features
Availability	VB:Yes, VBA:No, VBScript:No
Purpose	Object that supplies global methods and properties.
Typical Syntax	**Global**
See Also	App Object, Debug Object, Screen Object

Use the Global object as needed within your Visual Basic source code. When using Visual Basic for Applications or Visual Basic, Scripting Edition, there may be an object available that is contextually similar to the Visual Basic Global object.

It is not necessary to prefix the properties and methods of the Global object with the Global keyword, unless other objects made available within your application make such references ambiguous.

Incorrect

```
Global.Printer.EndDoc
```

Correct

```
Printer.EndDoc
```

GoSub...Return Statement

Category	Flow Control Features
Availability	VB:Yes, VBA:Yes, VBScript:No
Purpose	Continues execution at a specified line number or label, then returns to resume the original path of execution.

Typical Syntax	**GoSub** *line*
	• • •
	line:
	• • •
	Return
See Also	GoTo Statement, On Error Statement, On...GoSub Statement, On...GoTo Statement

Use the GoSub...Return statement as needed within your Visual Basic source code. While GoSub statements are useful, their overuse can indicate a problem in the logic of a procedure. Most procedures in your source code should be free of GoSub statements, and if one routine contains more than about four such statements, the procedure should be rewritten in a more structured or procedure-driven manner. For larger blocks of code found within a GoSub destination, you may wish to consider moving them to separate procedures.

Chapter 2, *Using Declaration*, and Chapter 9, *Declaration Standards*, discuss line labels and their use within Visual Basic procedures.

GoTo Statement

Category	Flow Control Features
Availability	VB:Yes, VBA:Yes, VBScript:No
Purpose	Continues execution at a specified line number or label.
Typical Syntax	**GoTo** *line*
See Also	GoSub...Return Statement, On Error Statement, On...GoSub Statement, On...GoTo Statement

Use the GoTo statement as needed within your Visual Basic source code. While GoTo statements are useful, their overuse can indicate a problem in the logic of a procedure. Most procedures in your source code should be free of GoTo statements, and if one routine contains more than about four such statements, the procedure should probably be rewritten in a more structured or procedure-driven manner.

Chapter 2, *Using Declaration*, and Chapter 9, *Declaration Standards*, discuss line labels and their use within Visual Basic procedures.

Hex Function

Category	Conversion Functions, String Features
Availability	VB:Yes, VBA:Yes, VBScript:Yes (with restrictions)
Purpose	Returns a hexadecimal representation of an expression, in string format.
Typical Syntax	**Hex(** *expression* **)**
Variations	Hex$ Function
See Also	Oct Function

Use the Hex function as needed within your Visual Basic source code. Visual Basic, Scripting Edition does not permit the use of the string version of this function. Within a VBScript code section, you must use the syntax

```
Hex(argument)
```

In all other versions of Visual Basic, if you do not require a Variant result, use the string version of this function instead of the Variant version.

```
Hex$(argument)
```

When using the Hex$ version of this function, the argument cannot be Null. If you think that your code will allow a Null value to be passed to the Hex$ function, force the argument to a string first. A quick way to convert a Null to a string is to concatenate an empty string onto the Null value.

```
sDisplayKey = Hex$(rsInfo!EncryptKey & "")
```

It is permissible to use the Empty value as an argument to either the Hex function or the Hex$ function.

Hour Function

Category	Date and Time Features
Availability	VB:Yes, VBA:Yes, VBScript:Yes
Purpose	Returns a value indicating the hour for a given date or time.
Typical Syntax	**Hour(***time***)**
See Also	DatePart Function, Day Function, Minute Function, Month Function, Second Function, Year Function

Use the Hour function as needed within your Visual Basic source code. If you are using either Visual Basic or Visual Basic for Applications, and you will be using the hour returned from this function as a string (for example, to concatenate the hour onto an existing string), consider using the Format$ function instead.

```
sInfo = "Hour number " & Format$(dtAction, "h")
```

If...Then...Else Statement

Category	Flow Control Features
Availability	VB:Yes, VBA:Yes, VBScript:Yes
Purpose	Executes blocks of code based on a condition.
Typical Syntax	**If** *condition* **Then** [*statements*] [**Else** *statements*]
	If *condition* **Then**
	[*statements*]
	[**ElseIf** *condition-n* **Then**

           [*statements*]]...
      [Else
           [*statements*]]
      End If

See Also   #If...Then...#Else Directive, IIf Function, Select Case State-
                ment

Use the If...Then...Else statement as needed within your Visual Basic source
code. When forming the *condition* sections of your statement, make them as
clear as possible, using parentheses to group values when ambiguity (for the
reader) is possible. Enclosing each condition in a set of parentheses also
improves readability.

```
If (condition) Then
```

Although Visual Basic allows you to leave the Then section of statements blank, do not use this syntax. If you find that you need only the Else
section, reverse the condition so that the Else condition becomes a Then section.

Incorrect

```
If (nResult < RESULT_LIMIT) Then
Else
    MsgBox "You went over the limit.", _
        vbOKOnly + vbExclamation, "Notice"
End If
```

Correct

```
If (nResult >= RESULT_LIMIT) Then
    MsgBox "You went over the limit.", _
        vbOKOnly + vbExclamation, "Notice"
End If
```

If your Else section contains only an If statement (even when that If
statement contains subordinate statements), change it to an ElseIf section
instead.

Incorrect

```
If (bGoodCredit) Then
    ' ----- Process order
Else
    If (bLongTimeCustomer) Then
        ' ----- Process with warnings
    End If
End If
```

Correct

```
If (bGoodCredit) Then
    ' ----- Process order
ElseIf (bLongTimeCustomer) Then
    ' ----- Process with warnings
End If
```

Limit your If statement to three ElseIf sections. If you need more ElseIf sections, consider using the Select Case statement instead.

IIf Function

Category	Flow Control Features
Availability	VB:Yes, VBA:Yes, VBScript:No
Purpose	Returns one of a set of values based on a Boolean expression.
Typical Syntax	**IIf**(*expression*, *truepart*, *falsepart*)
See Also	Choose Function, If...Then...Else Statement, Switch Function

Use the IIf function as needed within your Visual Basic source code. Although only one of the result arguments will be returned based on the expression, both result arguments are evaluated. Make sure that the arguments do not contain any code that will fail on invalid conditions, or that should execute only with certain Boolean results.

IMEStatus Function

Category	Miscellaneous Features
Availability	VB:Yes, VBA:Yes, VBScript:No
Purpose	Identifies the current Input Method Editor (IME) mode.
Typical Syntax	**IMEStatus**

Use the IMEStatus function as needed within your Visual Basic source code. This function is available only in the Far East versions of Visual Basic. If you use a common source code base for multiple language versions of your application, use #Const statements and #If...Then...#Else statements to separate Far East source code from non-Far East source code. Also, make it clear in your source code comments, and your technical documentation, how the different language versions of the application differ from the source code point of view.

Imp Operator

Category	Operators
Availability	VB:Yes, VBA:Yes, VBScript:Yes
Purpose	Performs a logical or bitwise implication operation.

Typical Syntax	*expression1* **Imp** *expression2*
See Also	And Operator, Eqv Operator, Not Operator, Or Operator, Xor Operator.

Use the Imp operator as needed within your Visual Basic source code. When writing complex statements that involve more than one logical or bitwise operator, use parentheses to indicate the proper precedence and grouping within the calculation.

Implements Statement

Category	Declaration Features
Availability	VB:Yes, VBA:Yes, VBScript:No
Purpose	Indicates that a specific interface or class will be implemented in a class module.
Typical Syntax	**Implements** [*interface*	*class*]
See Also	Class Statement

Use the Implements statement as needed within your Visual Basic source code. Include in your technical documentation a description of the interface or class to be implemented. Also note in your source code comments for the Implements statement the location in your technical documentation where the interface or class is documented.

Input # Statement

Category	File System Features
Availability	VB:Yes, VBA:Yes, VBScript:No
Purpose	Reads data from a file and assigns the results to variables.
Typical Syntax	**Input #***filenumber, varlist*
See Also	Input Function, Line Input # Statement, Open Statement, Print # Statement, Write # Statement

Use the Input # statement as needed within your Visual Basic source code. Always use a file number returned from the FreeFile function as an argument to the Input # statement. If you wish to retrieve text written with the Print # statement, consider the Line Input # statement instead.

Data written with the Write # statement is read with the Input # statement. In general, the structure of the data written with the Write # statement must be known to the code that will read the file with the Input # statement. You may wish to include, at the beginning of your file data, identification values (sometimes called "magic numbers") that prove the file was written with the expected application, and with the appropriate version of that application.

The Input # statement (and all other File System features) accesses information that resides outside of the control of the Visual Basic application. Therefore, you must always use proper error handling in any procedure that uses the Input # statement. Make use of the On Error statement to capture any file handling errors, and take the appropriate corrective action.

Input Function

Category	File System Features
Availability	VB:Yes, VBA:Yes, VBScript:No
Purpose	Reads characters from an open file.
Typical Syntax	**Input(***number*, [**#**]*filenumber***)**
Variations	Input$ Function, InputB Function, InputB$ Function
See Also	Get Statement, Input # Statement, Line Input # Statement, Open Statement, Print # Statement, Put Statement, Write # Statement

Use the Input function as needed within your Visual Basic source code. Always use a file number returned from the FreeFile function as the second argument to the Input function. Although the "#" prefix of the *filenumber* argument is optional, always include it in the syntax of the statement.

If you do not require a Variant result, use the Input$ function instead of the Input function.

```
vntSampleText = Input(50, #nSourceFile)
sSampleText = Input$(50, #nSourceFile)
```

If you need to work with the underlying bytes contained within the file, use either the InputB function or the InputB$ function.

The Input function (and all other File System features) accesses information that resides outside of the control of the Visual Basic application. Therefore, you must always use proper error handling in any procedure that uses the Input function. Make use of the On Error statement to capture any file handling errors, and take the appropriate corrective action.

InputBox Function

Category	Miscellaneous Features
Availability	VB:Yes, VBA:Yes, VBScript:Yes (with restrictions)
Purpose	Prompts the user for data input.
Typical Syntax	**InputBox(***prompt*[, *title*] [, *default*] [, *xpos*] [, *ypos*] [, *helpfile*, *context*]**)**
Variations	InputBox$ Function
See Also	MsgBox Function

The InputBox function is useful for simple input of minor user data. However, its use should be restricted due to the limited amount of data it can collect. A user-initiated event (such as a command button click) should never result in more than two uses of the InputBox function. If you need to prompt the user for more than two pieces of information, create a new form that contains all of the input fields. Even when you need only a single text field's worth of input, creating a new form is often better than the InputBox function. With a true form, you can verify the user's input on the OK button's Click event without hiding the form. The InputBox form must be removed from the screen before the data can be verified, giving your application a rough feel. Still, for the simplest input needs, the InputBox function is useful.

The user cannot enter an empty string as a valid response through the InputBox function. InputBox returns an empty string when the user clicks the Cancel button. If you need to allow the user to enter an empty string as valid input, create a new form instead of using the InputBox function.

When calling the InputBox function, always supply both the *prompt* and *title* arguments. If possible, supply a reasonable *default* argument as well.

Because the InputBox function contains no error checking, make sure you validate the return value of the function. This is especially true if you are prompting the user for numeric or date information.

Visual Basic, Scripting Edition does not permit the use of the string version of this function. Within a VBScript code section, you must use the syntax

```
InputBox(arguments)
```

In all other versions of Visual Basic, if you do not require a Variant result, use the string version of this function instead of the Variant version.

```
InputBox$(arguments)
```

InStr Function

Category	String Features
Availability	VB:Yes, VBA:Yes, VBScript:Yes
Purpose	Returns the location of a sub-string within a larger string.
Typical Syntax	**InStr(**[*start*,]*string1*, *string2*[, *compare*]**)**
Variations	InStrB Function
See Also	Filter Function, InStrRev Function, Join Function, Option Compare Statement, Replace Function, Split Function

Use the InStr function as needed within your Visual Basic source code. If you need to work with the underlying bytes contained within the original string, use the InStrB function.

It is permissible to omit the *start* argument of the InStr function when searching from the beginning of the string. You can also include this argument, and set it to a value of 1. Both of the following statements are valid, and produce the same result.

```
nPos = InStr(sLargeString, sSubString)
nPos = InStr(1, sLargeString, sSubString)
```

The *compare* argument of the InStr function accepts Integer values, or one of a set of intrinsic Visual Basic constants. When available, always use the supplied constants instead of numeric literals. The use of the Option Compare statement can affect the results of the InStr function.

InStrRev Function

Category	String Features
Availability	VB:Yes, VBA:Yes, VBScript:Yes
Purpose	Returns the location of a sub-string within a larger string, searching from the end of the larger string.
Typical Syntax	**InStrRev(***string1, string2*[, *start*[, *compare*]**)**
See Also	Filter Function, InStr Function, Join Function, Option Compare Statement, Replace Function, Split Function

Use the InStrRev function as needed within your Visual Basic source code. The *compare* argument of the InStrRev function accepts Integer values, or one of a set of intrinsic Visual Basic constants. When available, always use the supplied constants instead of numeric literals. The use of the Option Compare statement can affect the results of the InStrRev function.

Int Function

Category	Math Features
Availability	VB:Yes, VBA:Yes, VBScript:Yes
Purpose	Truncates the fractional portion of an expression.
Typical Syntax	**Int(***expression***)**
See Also	Abs Function, Fix Function, Round Function, Sgn Function

Use the Int function as needed within your Visual Basic source code. For positive numbers, the Int and Fix functions are identical. For negative values, the Fix function truncates the fractional portion of the number, leaving the whole number intact. The Int function returns the next larger negative value when a fractional component is non-zero. If you are sure that you will pass only positive values as arguments, use the Int function instead of the Fix function.

IPmt Function

Category	Financial Features
Availability	VB:Yes, VBA:Yes, VBScript:No
Purpose	Calculates the interest payment for a given period of an annuity.
Typical Syntax	**IPmt(***rate, per, nper, pv*[, *fv*[, *type*]]**)**
See Also	DDB Function, FV Function, IRR Function, MIRR Function, NPer Function, NPV Function, Pmt Function, PPmt Function, PV Function, Rate Function, SLN Function, SYD Function

Use the IPmt function as needed within your Visual Basic source code. This function returns a Double value, and accepts several Double values for parameters. While values based on the Currency data type are accurate to four decimal places, Double floating point values are subject to minor rounding errors. While you can convert the return value of the IPmt function from Double to Currency using the CCur function, this result will be bound to the same rounding conditions of the value returned by the IPmt function. Take care to check the accuracy of the return values when using the Visual Basic intrinsic financial functions.

IRR Function

Category	Financial Features
Availability	VB:Yes, VBA:Yes, VBScript:No
Purpose	Calculates the internal rate of return for a series of periodic cash flows.
Typical Syntax	**IRR**(*values*()[, *guess*])
See Also	DDB Function, FV Function, IPmt Function, MIRR Function, NPer Function, NPV Function, Pmt Function, PPmt Function, PV Function, Rate Function, SLN Function, SYD Function

Use the IRR function as needed within your Visual Basic source code. This function returns a Double value, and accepts an array of Double values for one of its parameters. While values based on the Currency data type are accurate to four decimal places, Double floating point values are subject to minor rounding errors. While you can convert the return value of the IRR function from Double to Currency using the CCur function, this result will be bound to the same rounding conditions of the value returned by the IRR function. Take care to check the accuracy of the return values when using the Visual Basic intrinsic financial functions.

Is Operator

Category	Operators
Availability	VB:Yes, VBA:Yes, VBScript:Yes
Purpose	Determines if two object variables refer to the same underlying object.
Typical Syntax	*object1* **Is** *object2*
See Also	< Operator, <= Operator, <> Operator (Comparison), = Operator (Comparison), > Operator, >= Operator, Like Operator, Not Operator, Nothing Keyword

Use the Is operator as needed within your Visual Basic source code. Note that *object2* can be replaced with the Nothing keyword to test if an object is undefined.

IsArray Function

Category	Declaration Features
Availability	VB:Yes, VBA:Yes, VBScript:Yes
Purpose	Indicates whether a variable is an array.
Typical Syntax	**IsArray(***varname***)**
See Also	Array Function, Dim Statement, IsDate Function, IsEmpty Function, IsError Function, IsMissing Function, IsNull Function, IsNumeric Function, IsObject Function, ReDim Statement, TypeName Function, VarType Function

Use the IsArray function as needed within your Visual Basic source code. In general, you should not have to use this function on variables that were specifically created as arrays, or those that will never be arrays. This function is most useful when testing Variant variables that may be storing values created with the Array function.

IsDate Function

Category	Date and Time Features
Availability	VB:Yes, VBA:Yes, VBScript:Yes
Purpose	Indicates whether an expression is a valid date or time.
Typical Syntax	**IsDate(***expression***)**
See Also	CDate Function, IsArray Function, IsEmpty Function, IsError Function, IsMissing Function, IsNull Function, IsNumeric Function, IsObject Function, TypeName Function, VarType Function

Use the IsDate function as needed within your Visual Basic source code. The IsDate function does not check a date value for Year 2000 compliance.

IsEmpty Function

Category	Declaration Features
Availability	VB:Yes, VBA:Yes, VBScript:Yes
Purpose	Indicates whether a variable or expression is not yet initialized.
Typical Syntax	**IsEmpty(***expression***)**
See Also	Empty Keyword, IsArray Function, IsDate Function, IsError Function, IsMissing Function, IsNull Function, IsNumeric Function, IsObject Function, TypeName Function, VarType Function

Use the IsEmpty function as needed within your Visual Basic source code. Never test a variable by comparing it with the Empty keyword. Always use the IsEmpty function instead.

Incorrect

```
If (vntUserData = Empty) Then
```

Correct

```
If (IsEmpty(vntUserData)) Then
```

IsError Function

Category	Error Handling and Debugging Features
Availability	VB:Yes, VBA:Yes, VBScript:No
Purpose	Indicates whether an expression is an error value.
Typical Syntax	**IsError(***expression***)**
See Also	CVErr Function, Err Object, IsArray Function, IsDate Function, IsEmpty Function, IsMissing Function, IsNull Function, IsNumeric Function, IsObject Function, TypeName Function, VarType Function

Use the IsError function as needed within your Visual Basic source code.

IsMissing Function

Category	Declaration Features
Availability	VB:Yes, VBA:Yes, VBScript:No
Purpose	Indicates whether an optional argument was passed to the procedure.
Typical Syntax	**IsMissing(***argument***)**
See Also	IsArray Function, IsDate Function, IsEmpty Function, IsError Function, IsNull Function, IsNumeric Function, IsObject Function, Optional Keyword, TypeName Function, VarType Function

Use the IsMissing function as needed within your Visual Basic source code. In order for the IsMissing argument to work correctly, the argument must be defined as a Variant. If your only purpose for testing an argument is to supply it with a default value, include the default value in the declaration of the procedure instead.

Incorrect

```
Private Sub DoWork(Optional vntWithEffort As Variant)
    ' ----- Do a lot of work, or just a little
    Dim bWithEffort As Boolean

    ' ----- Start by checking the effort value
    If (IsMissing(vntWithEffort)) Then
        bWithEffort = False
```

```
    Else
        bWithEffort = CBool(vntWithEffort)
    End If
```

Correct

```
Private Sub DoWork(Optional bWithEffort _
        As Boolean = False)
    ' ----- Do a lot of work, or just a little
```

IsNull Function

Category	Declaration Features
Availability	VB:Yes, VBA:Yes, VBScript:Yes
Purpose	Indicates whether an expression is Null.
Typical Syntax	**IsNull(***expression***)**
See Also	IsArray Function, IsDate Function, IsEmpty Function, IsError Function, IsMissing Function, IsNumeric Function, IsObject Function, TypeName Function, VarType Function

Use the IsNull function as needed within your Visual Basic source code. Never test an expression by comparing it with the Null keyword. Always use the IsNull function instead.

Incorrect

```
If (rsInfo!OptionalInformation = Null) Then
```

Correct

```
If (IsNull(rsInfo!OptionalInformation)) Then
```

IsNumeric Function

Category	Math Features
Availability	VB:Yes, VBA:Yes, VBScript:Yes
Purpose	Indicates whether an expression is a valid number.
Typical Syntax	**IsNumeric(***expression***)**
See Also	CCur Function, CDbl Function, CDec Function, CInt Function, CLng Function, CSng Function, IsArray Function, IsDate Function, IsEmpty Function, IsError Function, IsMissing Function, IsNull Function, IsObject Function, TypeName Function, VarType Function

Use the IsNumeric function as needed within your Visual Basic source code. The IsNumeric function considers Empty expressions to be numeric. It also recognizes as numeric strings containing hexadecimal and octal values in the Visual Basic format, as in the "&H1B" hexadecimal expression.

IsObject Function

Category	Declaration Features
Availability	VB:Yes, VBA:Yes, VBScript:Yes
Purpose	Indicates whether a variable is an object.
Typical Syntax	**IsObject(***varname***)**
See Also	CreateObject Function, GetObject Function, IsArray Function, IsDate Function, IsEmpty Function, IsError Function, IsMissing Function, IsNull Function, IsNumeric Function, TypeName Function, VarType Function

Use the IsObject function as needed within your Visual Basic source code. The IsObject function considers Variant variables set to Nothing to be objects.

Join Function

Category	String Features
Availability	VB:Yes, VBA:Yes, VBScript:Yes
Purpose	Joins an array of strings together to form a single string.
Typical Syntax	**Join(***list*[*, delimiter*]**)**
Variations	Join$ Function
See Also	& Operator, Replace Function, Split Function

Use the Join function as needed within your Visual Basic source code. Visual Basic, Scripting Edition does not permit the use of the string version of this function. Within a VBScript code section, you must use the syntax

```
Join(arguments)
```

In all other versions of Visual Basic, if you do not require a Variant result, use the string version of this function instead of the Variant version.

```
Join$(arguments)
```

Kill Statement

Category	File System Features
Availability	VB:Yes, VBA:Yes, VBScript:No
Purpose	Deletes a file.
Typical Syntax	**Kill** *pathname*
See Also	Dir Function, FileCopy Statement, Name Statement

Use the Kill statement as needed within your Visual Basic source code. The argument supplied to the Kill statement may be a local or mapped drive path, a UNC (Universal Naming Convention) path, or a path relative to the current drive and directory.

The pathname supplied to the Kill statement may contain wildcard characters ("*" and "?"). If you need to delete several files that match a pattern, and you are sure that no other user files will be removed in the process, include the wildcard characters as needed. You may also find it useful to determine the name of each file matching the wildcard pattern using the Dir function, then delete each file individually with the Kill statement.

If the file to be removed is a user file, make sure you sufficiently inform the user that the file will be deleted, either through documentation or through application notification.

The Kill statement (and all other File System features) accesses information that resides outside of the control of the Visual Basic application. Therefore, you must always use proper error handling in any procedure that uses the Kill statement. Make use of the On Error statement to capture any file handling errors, and take the appropriate corrective action.

LBound Function

Category	Declaration Features
Availability	VB:Yes, VBA:Yes, VBScript:Yes
Purpose	Returns the lower numeric bound of an array dimension.
Typical Syntax	**LBound(***arrayname*[, *dimension*]**)**
See Also	Erase Statement, ReDim Statement, UBound Function

Use the LBound function as needed within your Visual Basic source code. You cannot use the LBound function on an array that has not yet been dimensioned, or on a redimensioned array that has been cleared with the Erase statement. In VBScript, the lower bound of every array dimension is 0 (zero).

If you are attempting to ascertain the lower bound of a one-dimensional array, do not include the *dimension* argument of the LBound function. If you are using the LBound function on a multi-dimensional array, even if you are testing the first dimension, always include the *dimension* argument.

LCase Function

Category	String Features
Availability	VB:Yes, VBA:Yes, VBScript:Yes (with restrictions)
Purpose	Returns a string converted to lower case.
Typical Syntax	**LCase(***string***)**
Variations	LCase$ Function
See Also	UCase Function

Use the LCase function as needed within your Visual Basic source code. Visual Basic, Scripting Edition does not permit the use of the string version of this function. Within a VBScript code section, you must use the syntax

```
LCase(argument)
```

In all other versions of Visual Basic, if you do not require a Variant result, use the string version of this function instead of the Variant version.

```
LCase$(argument)
```

When using the LCase$ version of this function, the argument cannot be Null. If you think that your code will allow a Null value to be passed to the LCase$ function, force the argument to a string first. A quick way to convert a Null to a string is to concatenate an empty string onto the Null value.

```
sPanel = LCase$(rsInfo!Panel & "")
```

Left Function

Category	String Features
Availability	VB:Yes, VBA:Yes, VBScript:Yes (with restrictions)
Purpose	Returns the left portion of a string.
Typical Syntax	**Left**(*string, length*)
Variations	Left$ Function, LeftB Function, LeftB$ Function
See Also	Mid Function, Right Function

Use the Left function as needed within your Visual Basic source code. Visual Basic, Scripting Edition does not permit the use of the string version of this function. Within a VBScript code section, you must use the syntax

```
Left(arguments)
```

In all other versions of Visual Basic, if you do not require a Variant result, use the string version of this function instead of the Variant version.

```
Left$(arguments)
```

If you need to work with the underlying bytes contained within the original string, use the LeftB function or the LeftB$ function.

When using the Left$ and LeftB$ versions of this function, the first argument cannot be Null. If you think that your code will allow a Null value to be passed to the Left$ or LeftB$ functions, force the argument to a string first. A quick way to convert a Null to a string is to concatenate an empty string onto the Null value.

```
' ----- Extract area code from xxx-xxx-xxxx
sAreaCode = Left$(rsInfo!Phone & "", 3)
```

Len Function

Category	String Features
Availability	VB:Yes, VBA:Yes, VBScript:Yes

Purpose	Returns the length of a string or string variable.
Typical Syntax	**Len(***string* | *varname***)**
Variations	LenB Function

Use the Len function as needed within your Visual Basic source code. If you need to count the underlying bytes of a variable or string expression, use the LenB function.

The argument to the Len function can be Null, but a Null value will be returned as the result. If you think that your code will allow a Null value to be passed to the Len function, and you require a numeric return value, force the argument to a string first. A quick way to convert a Null to a string is to concatenate an empty string onto the Null value.

```
' ----- Determine the name size requirements
nNameLength = Len(rsInfo!CustomerName & "")
```

Let Statement

Category	Miscellaneous Features
Availability	VB:Yes, VBA:Yes, VBScript:Yes
Purpose	Assigns an expression to a variable.
Typical Syntax	**[Let]** *variable* **=** *expression*
See Also	= Operator (Assignment), Property Get Statement, Property Let Statement, Property Set Statement, Set Statement

Use assignment as needed within your Visual Basic source code. However, do not include the Let keyword in the assignment statement. It exists as a holdover from older versions of the BASIC language.

Like Operator

Category	Operators
Availability	VB:Yes, VBA:Yes, VBScript:No
Purpose	Determines if one string matches a pattern.
Typical Syntax	*string* **Like** *pattern*
See Also	< Operator, <= Operator, <> Operator (Comparison), = Operator (Comparison), > Operator, >= Operator, Is Operator, Not Operator, Option Compare Statement

Use the Like operator as needed within your Visual Basic source code. The use of the Option Compare statement can affect comparisons performed with the Like operator.

Line Input # Statement

Category	File System Features
Availability	VB:Yes, VBA:Yes, VBScript:No

Purpose	Reads a single line from an open sequential file.
Typical Syntax	**Line Input #***filenumber, varname*
See Also	Input # Statement, Open Statement, Print # Statement, Write # Statement

Use the Line Input # statement as needed within your Visual Basic source code. Always use a file number returned from the FreeFile function as an argument to the Line Input # statement. If you wish to retrieve values written with the Write # statement, use the Input # statement instead.

The Line Input # statement (and all other File System features) accesses information that resides outside of the control of the Visual Basic application. Therefore, you must always use proper error handling in any procedure that uses the Line Input # statement. Make use of the On Error statement to capture any file handling errors, and take the appropriate corrective action.

Load Statement

Category	Declaration Features
Availability	VB:Yes, VBA:Yes, VBScript:No
Purpose	Creates an instance of a form or control.
Typical Syntax	**Load** *object*
See Also	Unload Statement

Use the Load statement as needed within your Visual Basic source code.

LoadPicture Function

Category	Miscellaneous Features
Availability	VB:Yes, VBA:Yes, VBScript:Yes (with restrictions)
Purpose	Loads a graphic into a picture-bearing object.
Typical Syntax	**LoadPicture(**[*filename*], [*size*], [*colordepth*], [*x, y*]**)**
See Also	LoadResData Function, LoadResPicture Function, LoadResString Function, SavePicture Statement

Use the LoadPicture function as needed within your Visual Basic source code. The *size* and *colordepth* arguments of the LoadPicture function accept Integer values, or one of a set of intrinsic Visual Basic constants. When available, always use the supplied constants instead of numeric literals. Visual Basic, Scripting Edition uses only the *filename* argument.

The LoadPicture function accesses information that resides outside of the control of the Visual Basic application. Therefore, you must always use proper error handling in any procedure that uses the LoadPicture function. Make use of the On Error statement to capture any errors, and take the appropriate corrective action.

LoadResData Function

Category   Miscellaneous Features
Availability   VB:Yes, VBA:Yes, VBScript:No
Purpose   Loads data from a resource file.
Typical Syntax   **LoadResData(***index, format***)**
See Also   LoadPicture Function, LoadResPicture Function, LoadResString Function, SavePicture Statement

Use the LoadResData function as needed within your Visual Basic source code. If you need to load a cursor, bitmap, or icon, and you do not need the loaded resource stored as a Byte array, use the LoadResPicture function instead. If you need to load a string, and you do not need the loaded resource stored as a Byte array, use the LoadResString function instead.

If you know in advance the arrangement of the resource file, define a set of constants, one constant for each indexed item in the file that you will load into the application.

The *format* argument of the LoadResData function accepts an Integer value. Visual Basic does not include a set of constants for use with this argument. When using this function, define your own constants for use with the *format* argument, or sufficiently define the use of the second argument in the source code comments that accompany the use of the LoadResData function.

LoadResPicture Function

Category   Miscellaneous Features
Availability   VB:Yes, VBA:Yes, VBScript:No
Purpose   Loads a bitmap, icon, or cursor from a resource file.
Typical Syntax   **LoadResPicture(***index, format***)**
See Also   LoadPicture Function, LoadResData Function, LoadResString Function, SavePicture Statement

Use the LoadResPicture function as needed within your Visual Basic source code. If you know in advance the arrangement of the resource file, define a set of constants, one constant for each indexed item in the file that you will load into the application.

The *format* argument of the LoadResPicture function accepts Integer values, or one of a set of intrinsic Visual Basic constants. When available, always use the supplied constants instead of numeric literals.

LoadResString Function

Category   Miscellaneous Features, String Features
Availability   VB:Yes, VBA:Yes, VBScript:No
Purpose   Loads a string from a resource file.

Typical Syntax	**LoadResString(***index***)**
See Also	LoadPicture Function, LoadResData Function, LoadResPicture Function, SavePicture Statement

Use the LoadResString function as needed within your Visual Basic source code. If you know in advance the arrangement of the resource file, define a set of constants, one constant for each indexed item in the file that you will load into the application.

Loc Function

Category	File System Features
Availability	VB:Yes, VBA:Yes, VBScript:No
Purpose	Returns the current position in an open file.
Typical Syntax	**Loc(***filenumber***)**
See Also	EOF Function, LOF Function, Open Statement, Seek Function, Seek Statement

Use the Loc function as needed within your Visual Basic source code. Always use a file number returned from the FreeFile function as an argument to the Loc function.

The Loc function is primarily used with files opened in Random or Binary mode. Using the Loc function on a file opened in Input mode, or another sequential mode, will not return expected results. For such files, use the Seek function instead.

The Loc function (and all other File System features) accesses information that resides outside of the control of the Visual Basic application. Therefore, you must always use proper error handling in any procedure that uses the Loc function. Make use of the On Error statement to capture any file handling errors, and take the appropriate corrective action.

Lock # Statement

Category	File System Features
Availability	VB:Yes, VBA:Yes, VBScript:No
Purpose	Locks a portion or all of an open file.
Typical Syntax	**Lock** [**#**]*filenumber*[, *recordrange*]
See Also	Open Statement, Unlock # Statement

Use the Lock # statement as needed within your Visual Basic source code. Always use a file number returned from the FreeFile function as an argument to the Lock # statement. Although the "#" prefix of the *filenumber* argument is optional, always include it in the syntax of the statement.

The Lock # statement (and all other File System features) accesses information that resides outside of the control of the Visual Basic application. Therefore, you must always use proper error handling in any procedure that uses the Lock # statement. Make use of the On Error statement to capture any file handling errors, and take the appropriate corrective action.

LOF Function

Category	File System Features
Availability	VB:Yes, VBA:Yes, VBScript:No
Purpose	Returns the length in bytes of an open file.
Typical Syntax	**LOF(**_filenumber_**)**
See Also	EOF Function, FileLen Function, Loc Function, Open Statement, Seek Function, Seek Statement

Use the LOF function as needed within your Visual Basic source code. Always use a file number returned from the FreeFile function as an argument to the LOF function. To determine the length of a file that has not yet been opened, use the FileLen function.

The LOF function (and all other File System features) accesses information that resides outside of the control of the Visual Basic application. Therefore, you must always use proper error handling in any procedure that uses the LOF function. Make use of the On Error statement to capture any file handling errors, and take the appropriate corrective action.

Log Function

Category	Math Features
Availability	VB:Yes, VBA:Yes, VBScript:Yes
Purpose	Calculates the natural logarithm of a number.
Typical Syntax	**Log(**_number_**)**
See Also	Exp Function, Sqr Function

Use the Log function as needed within your Visual Basic source code. This function returns a Double value, and accepts a Double value for its parameter. Double floating point values are subject to minor rounding errors. Take care to check the accuracy of the return values when using the Visual Basic intrinsic math functions.

The argument to the Log function must be greater than 0 (zero). If the value you pass to the Log function is supplied by the user, and the user enters a value outside of the valid range, either correctly handle the error raised by the Log function, or reject the value entered by the user.

LSet Statement

Category	String Features
Availability	VB:Yes, VBA:Yes, VBScript:No
Purpose	Left aligns a string within a string variable. Another syntax copies the bytes of one user-defined type variable into another user-defined type variable.

Typical Syntax	**LSet** *stringvar* **=** *string*
	LSet *varname1* **=** *varname2*
See Also	Left Function, RSet Statement, Space Function

Use the LSet function as needed within your Visual Basic source code. If you use the second syntax of the LSet statement to copy one user-defined type variable to another, and the variables are not based on the same Type statement, fully document the purpose and impact of the copy in the source code comments.

LTrim Function

Category	String Features
Availability	VB:Yes, VBA:Yes, VBScript:Yes (with restrictions)
Purpose	Returns a string with leading spaces removed.
Typical Syntax	**LTrim(***string***)**
Variations	LTrim$ Function
See Also	RTrim Function, Trim Function

Use the LTrim function as needed within your Visual Basic source code. Visual Basic, Scripting Edition does not permit the use of the string version of this function. Within a VBScript code section, you must use the syntax

```
LTrim(argument)
```

In all other versions of Visual Basic, if you do not require a Variant result, use the string version of this function instead of the Variant version.

```
LTrim$(argument)
```

Some Visual Basic programmers originally learned programming in languages that included functions equivalent to LTrim and RTrim, but did not have an equivalent to the Trim function. In such languages, you could perform a Trim by combining the LTrim and RTrim statements.

```
sClean = LTrim$(RTrim$(sOriginal))
```

Avoid this usage in Visual Basic; always use the Trim function to remove both leading and trailing spaces.

```
sClean = Trim$(sOriginal)
```

When using the LTrim$ version of this function, the argument cannot be Null. If you think that your code will allow a Null value to be passed to the LTrim$ function, force the argument to a string first. A quick way to convert a Null to a string is to concatenate an empty string onto the Null value.

```
sTitle = LTrim$(rsInfo!Title & "")
```

Me Keyword

Category   Miscellaneous Features
Availability   VB:Yes, VBA:Yes, VBScript:No
Purpose   Refers to the local instance of a class.
Typical Syntax   **Me**

Use the Me keyword as needed within your Visual Basic source code. When you are working with multiple instances of a class, and you need to refer to the instance of the class from which the current code is executing, use Me to remove any instance ambiguity.

When writing code within a class module, such as a Form, use the Me keyword when referring to properties or methods of the class. However, avoid using the Me keyword when referring to subordinate objects or controls of the class.

Correct

```
sFormName = Me.Name
Me.MousePointer = vbHourglass
Me.Show vbModal
txtName.SetFocus
```

Incorrect

```
sFormName = Name
MousePointer = vbHourglass
Show vbModal
Me.txtName.SetFocus
```

Mid Function

Category   String Features
Availability   VB:Yes, VBA:Yes, VBScript:Yes (with restrictions)
Purpose   Returns the middle portion of a string.
Typical Syntax   **Mid(***string, start*[, *length*]**)**
Variations   Mid$ Function, MidB Function, MidB$ Function
See Also   Left Function, Mid Statement, Right Function

Use the Mid function as needed within your Visual Basic source code. Visual Basic, Scripting Edition does not permit the use of the string version of this function. Within a VBScript code section, you must use the syntax

```
Mid(arguments)
```

In all other versions of Visual Basic, if you do not require a Variant result, use the string version of this function instead of the Variant version.

```
Mid$(arguments)
```

If you need to work with the underlying bytes contained within the original string, use the MidB function or the MidB$ function.

When using the Mid$ and MidB$ versions of this function, the first argument cannot be Null. If you think that your code will allow a Null value to be passed to the Mid$ or MidB$ function, force the argument to a string first. A quick way to convert a Null to a string is to concatenate an empty string onto the Null value.

```
' ----- Extract area code from (xxx) xxx-xxxx
sAreaCode = Mid$(rsInfo!Phone & "", 2, 3)
```

Never use the Mid function to obtain the leftmost or rightmost characters in a string. Use the Left function to extract the leftmost characters, or the Right function to extract the rightmost characters.

Incorrect

```
sAreaCode = Mid$(sPhone, 1, 3)
```

Correct

```
sAeaCode = Left$(sPhone, 3)
```

Mid Statement

Category	String Features
Availability	VB:Yes, VBA:Yes, VBScript:No
Purpose	Sets the middle portion of a string.
Typical Syntax	**Mid**(*stringvar, start*[, *length*]) **=** *string*
Variations	Mid$ Statement, MidB Statement, MidB$ Statement
See Also	Left Function, Mid Function, Right Function

In general, avoid the use of the Mid statement and its variants. The movement of the primary expression processing of a statement to the left side of the assignment is distracting at its best, and error-prone at its worst. If you feel that the use of the Mid statement is warranted in a specific coding situation, sufficiently document its use and purpose in the source code comments.

Be aware that the interpretation of the third argument in the Mid statement (the *length* argument) differs slightly from that of the Mid function's third argument. If you omit the third argument in the Mid statement, you are not indicating that the remainder of the string should be replaced (as you would expect from the use of the Mid function). Instead, you are saying, "replace characters with the new string up to the length of the new string, leaving trailing characters intact." The new string will also not be extended to accommodate a longer modification string. Including the third argument states that at most, *length* characters will be replaced.

If you need to work with the underlying bytes contained within the original string, use the MidB and MidB$ statements.

Minute Function

Category	Date and Time Features
Availability	VB:Yes, VBA:Yes, VBScript:Yes
Purpose	Returns a value indicating the minute for a given date or time.
Typical Syntax	**Minute(***time***)**
See Also	DatePart Function, Day Function, Hour Function, Month Function, Second Function, Year Function

Use the Minute function as needed within your Visual Basic source code. If you are using either Visual Basic or Visual Basic for Applications, and you will be using the minute returned from this function as a string (for example, to concatenate the minute onto an existing string), consider using the Format$ function instead.

```
sInfo = "Minute number " & Format$(dtAction, "n")
```

MIRR Function

Category	Financial Features
Availability	VB:Yes, VBA:Yes, VBScript:No
Purpose	Calculates the modified internal rate of return for a series of periodic cash flows.
Typical Syntax	**MIRR(***values***()**, *financerate, reinvestrate***)**
See Also	DDB Function, FV Function, IPmt Function, IRR Function, NPer Function, NPV Function, Pmt Function, PPmt Function, PV Function, Rate Function, SLN Function, SYD Function

Use the MIRR function as needed within your Visual Basic source code. This function returns a Double value, and accepts several Double values for parameters. While values based on the Currency data type are accurate to four decimal places, Double floating point values are subject to minor rounding errors. While you can convert the return value of the MIRR function from Double to Currency using the CCur function, this result will be bound to the same rounding conditions of the value returned by the MIRR function. Take care to check the accuracy of the return values when using the Visual Basic intrinsic financial functions.

MkDir Statement

Category	File System Features
Availability	VB:Yes, VBA:Yes, VBScript:No
Purpose	Creates a new directory.
Typical Syntax	**MkDir** *path*
See Also	ChDir Statement, ChDrive Statement, CurDir Function, Dir Function, RmDir Function

Use the MkDir statement as needed within your Visual Basic source code. The argument supplied to the MkDir statement may be a local or mapped drive path, a UNC (Universal Naming Convention) path, or a path relative to the current drive and directory.

The MkDir statement (and all other File System features) accesses information that resides outside of the control of the Visual Basic application. Therefore, you must always use proper error handling in any procedure that uses the MkDir statement. Make use of the On Error statement to capture any file handling errors, and take the appropriate corrective action.

Mod Operator

Category	Operators
Availability	VB:Yes, VBA:Yes, VBScript:Yes
Purpose	Divides one number into another, and returns the remainder.
Typical Syntax	*expression1* **Mod** *expression2*
See Also	- Operator (Binary), - Operator (Unary), & Operator, * Operator, / Operator, \ Operator, ^ Operator, + Operator (Assignment), = Operator (Assignment)

Use the Mod operator as needed within your Visual Basic source code. The second expression cannot be 0 (zero). If the second expression is supplied by the user, or if you think that the second expression may be zero, include appropriate code to test the second expression, and take corrective action when needed.

The Mod operator rounds the expressions before the division takes place. If you need to use a different system of rounding or fractional truncation, use the Fix function, the Int function, or the Round function on the expressions before passing those expressions to the Mod operator.

Month Function

Category	Date and Time Features
Availability	VB:Yes, VBA:Yes, VBScript:Yes
Purpose	Returns a value indicating the month for a given date.
Typical Syntax	**Month(***date***)**
See Also	DatePart Function, Day Function, Hour Function, Minute Function, Second Function, Year Function

Use the Month function as needed within your Visual Basic source code. If you are using either Visual Basic or Visual Basic for Applications, and you will be using the month returned from this function as a string (for example, to concatenate the month onto an existing string), consider using the Format$ function instead.

```
sInfo = "Month number " & Format$(dtAction, "m")
```

MonthName Function

Category   Date and Time Features
Availability   VB:Yes, VBA:Yes, VBScript:Yes (with restrictions)
Purpose   Returns the name of the month for a given date.
Typical Syntax   **MonthName(***month*[, *abbreviate*]**)**
Variations   MonthName$ Function
See Also   Weekday Function, WeekdayName Function

Use the MonthName function as needed within your Visual Basic source code. Visual Basic, Scripting Edition does not permit the use of the string version of this function. Within a VBScript code section, you must use the syntax

```
MonthName(arguments)
```

In all other versions of Visual Basic, if you do not require a Variant result, use the string version of this function instead of the Variant version.

```
MonthName$(arguments)
```

MsgBox Function

Category   Miscellaneous Features
Availability   VB:Yes, VBA:Yes, VBScript:Yes
Purpose   Displays a message to the user.
Typical Syntax   **MsgBox(***prompt*[, *buttons*] [, *title*] [, *helpfile, context*]**)**
Variations   MsgBox Statement
See Also   Beep Statement, InputBox Function

Use the MsgBox function as needed within your Visual Basic source code. Although the syntax of the MsgBox function allows most of the arguments to be excluded, always include the first three arguments (*prompt, buttons, title*). Use the same *title* text in every MsgBox function call throughout your application. You may wish to create a global constant with a short version of the application name to be used in the title of each message box.

```
Public Const PROGRAM_TITLE = "Info Manager"
```

The *buttons* argument of the MsgBox function accepts Integer values, or combinations of a set of intrinsic Visual Basic constants. The return value also comes from a set of intrinsic constants. When available, always use the supplied constants instead of numeric literals. When combining constants, use the addition operator (+) to add the values together. Do not use the Or operator to combine the constants.

It is permissible to alter the syntax of the MsgBox function so that it becomes a MsgBox statement. The MsgBox statement has no return value, and never uses buttons other than the OK button.

```
nResult = MsgBox("I am the MsgBox function, all right?", _
    vbYesNo + vbQuestion, PROGRAM_TITLE)

MsgBox "I am the MsgBox statement.", _
    vbOKOnly + vbInformation, PROGRAM_TITLE
```

Some of the constants used in the *buttons* argument indicate the names of the buttons that should appear on the message box. Always include at least one of these constants. Also, there are constants to indicate the icon that should display on the message box. One of these constants must also be included. All other constants are optional. In the simplest, least important message box, display the OK button and an informational icon.

```
MsgBox "All fields are up to date.", _
    vbOKOnly + vbInformation, PROGRAM_TITLE
```

Name Statement

Category	File System Features
Availability	VB:Yes, VBA:Yes, VBScript:No
Purpose	Renames a file or directory.
Typical Syntax	**Name** *oldpathname* **As** *newpathname*
See Also	FileCopy Statement, Kill Statement, MkDir Statement, RmDir Statement

Use the Name statement as needed within your Visual Basic source code. The arguments supplied to the Name statement may be local or mapped drive paths, UNC (Universal Naming Convention) paths, or paths relative to the current drive and directory.

The file or directory specified by the *newpathname* argument must not exist. If you think that the destination name may exist, remove it first with the Kill statement or the RmDir statement.

The Name statement (and all other File System features) accesses information that resides outside of the control of the Visual Basic application. Therefore, you must always use proper error handling in any procedure that uses the Name statement. Make use of the On Error statement to capture any file handling errors, and take the appropriate corrective action.

Not Operator

Category	Operators
Availability	VB:Yes, VBA:Yes, VBScript:Yes
Purpose	Performs a logical or bitwise negation operation.
Typical Syntax	**Not** *expression*
See Also	And Operator, Eqv Operator, Imp Operator, Or Operator, Xor Operator.

Use the Not operator as needed within your Visual Basic source code. When writing complex statements that involve more than one logical or bitwise operator, use parentheses to indicate the proper precedence and grouping within the calculation.

When performing simple one-operator comparisons between two expressions, do not negate the result with the Not operator. Instead, use the inverse of the comparison operator to achieve the same result.

Incorrect

```
If Not (nFirst = nSecond) Then
```

Correct

```
If (nFirst <> nSecond) Then
```

Nothing Keyword

Category	Declaration Features
Availability	VB:Yes, VBA:Yes, VBScript:Yes
Purpose	Indicates that an object variable is not associated with an instance of an object.
Typical Syntax	**Nothing**
See Also	Empty Keyword, Is Operator, Null Keyword

Use the Nothing keyword as needed within your Visual Basic source code. Never test an expression by comparing it directly with the Nothing keyword. Always use the Is keyword of the If statement instead.

Incorrect

```
If (objStatus = Nothing) Then
```

Correct

```
If (objStatus Is Nothing) Then
```

Now Function

Category	Date and Time Features
Availability	VB:Yes, VBA:Yes, VBScript:Yes
Purpose	Returns the current system date and time.
Typical Syntax	**Now**
See Also	Date Function, Date Statement, Time Function, Time Statement

Use the Now function as needed within your Visual Basic source code. Always use the Now function if you need to simultaneously retrieve both the date and time. Do not use the alternative method of adding the separate results of the Date function and the Time function.

Incorrect

```
dtCurrentTime = Date + Time
```

Correct

```
dtCurrentTime = Now
```

NPer Function

Category	Financial Features
Availability	VB:Yes, VBA:Yes, VBScript:No
Purpose	Calculates the number of periods for an annuity.
Typical Syntax	**NPer(***rate, pmt, pv*[, *fv*[, *type*]]**)**
See Also	DDB Function, FV Function, IPmt Function, IRR Function, MIRR Function, NPV Function, Pmt Function, PPmt Function, PV Function, Rate Function, SLN Function, SYD Function

Use the NPer function as needed within your Visual Basic source code. This function returns a Double value, and accepts several Double values for parameters. While values based on the Currency data type are accurate to four decimal places, Double floating point values are subject to minor rounding errors. Take care to check the accuracy of the return values when using the Visual Basic intrinsic financial functions.

NPV Function

Category	Financial Features
Availability	VB:Yes, VBA:Yes, VBScript:No
Purpose	Calculates the net present value of an investment.
Typical Syntax	**NPV(***rate, values***())**
See Also	DDB Function, FV Function, IPmt Function, IRR Function, MIRR Function, NPer Function, Pmt Function, PPmt Function, PV Function, Rate Function, SLN Function, SYD Function

Use the NPV function as needed within your Visual Basic source code. This function returns a Double value, and accepts Double values for parameters. While values based on the Currency data type are accurate to four decimal places, Double floating point values are subject to minor rounding errors. While you can convert the return value of the NPV function from Double to Currency using the CCur function, this result will be bound to the same rounding conditions of the value returned by the NPV function. Take care to check the accuracy of the return values when using the Visual Basic intrinsic financial functions.

Null Keyword

Category	Declaration Features
Availability	VB:Yes, VBA:Yes, VBScript:Yes
Purpose	Indicates that a variable or expression contains no valid data.
Typical Syntax	**Null**
See Also	Empty Keyword, IsNull Function, Nothing Keyword

Use the Null keyword as needed within your Visual Basic source code. Never test an expression by comparing it with the Null keyword. Always use the IsNull function instead.

Incorrect

```
If (rsInfo!OptionalInformation = Null) Then
```

Correct

```
If (IsNull(rsInfo!OptionalInformation)) Then
```

Commonly, database fields will contain Null values. However, many Visual Basic features, primarily string functions, do not accept Null values. Before using a potential Null value when a string is expected, concatenate an empty string onto the value.

```
sResponse = rsInfo!Response & ""
```

In Visual Basic and Visual Basic for Applications, you can use the Val function to convert potentially Null numeric values to a true numeric format.

```
nScore = Val(rsInfo!FinalScore & "")
```

Oct Function

Category	Conversion Functions, String Features
Availability	VB:Yes, VBA:Yes, VBScript:Yes (with restrictions)
Purpose	Returns an octal representation of an expression, in string format.
Typical Syntax	**Oct(**_expression_**)**
Variations	Oct$ Function
See Also	Hex Function

Use the Oct function as needed within your Visual Basic source code. Visual Basic, Scripting Edition does not permit the use of the string version of this function. Within a VBScript code section, you must use the syntax

```
Oct(argument)
```

In all other versions of Visual Basic, if you do not require a Variant result, use the string version of this function instead of the Variant version.

```
Oct$(argument)
```

When using the Oct$ version of this function, the argument cannot be Null. If you think that your code will allow a Null value to be passed to the Oct$ function, force the argument to a string first. A quick way to convert a Null to a string is to concatenate an empty string onto the Null value.

```
sAccess = Oct$(rsInfo!AccessBits & "")
```

It is permissible to use the Empty value as an argument to either the Oct function or the Oct$ function.

On Error Statement

Category	Error Handling and Debugging Features
Availability	VB:Yes, VBA:Yes, VBScript:Yes (with restrictions)
Purpose	Enables error handling within a procedure.
Typical Syntax	**On Error GoTo** *line*
	On Error Resume Next
	On Error GoTo 0
See Also	Erl Statement, Err Function, Err Object, Error Function, Error Statement, Resume Statement

Use the On Error statement as needed in your Visual Basic source code. In general, you should place an error handler in any procedure that accesses resources outside of the application itself. This includes access to file system objects, the Windows registry, databases, network connections, printers, and shared resources.

The On Error GoTo *line* version of this statement is not available within VBScript. To test for an error in VBScript, use the On Error Resume Next statement, then test the Err object after a statement that may cause an error.

```
On Error Resume Next

' ----- Query the database
Err.Clear
sSQL = "SELECT * FROM MyTable"
Set rsInfo = conData.Execute(sSQL)
```

```
If (Err <> 0) Then
    ' ----- An error occurred
```

For more information about error handlers, see Chapter 2, *Using Declaration*, and Chapter 9, *Declaration Standards*.

On...GoSub Statement

Category	Flow Control Features
Availability	VB:Yes, VBA:Yes, VBScript:No
Purpose	Branches to one or more code sections based on an expression, then returns.
Typical Syntax	**On** *expression* **GoSub** *destinationlist*
See Also	Choose Function, GoSub Statement, GoTo Statement, IIf Function, On...GoTo Statement, Resume Statement, Select Case Statement

Do not use the On...GoSub statement within your Visual Basic source code. Usage of this statement can result in subtle errors, maintenance difficulties, and debugging nightmares. Use a Select Case statement instead to redirect your procedure based on an expression value.

On...GoTo Statement

Category	Flow Control Features
Availability	VB:Yes, VBA:Yes, VBScript:No
Purpose	Branches to one or more code sections based on an expression.
Typical Syntax	**On** *expression* **GoTo** *destinationlist*
See Also	Choose Function, GoSub Statement, GoTo Statement, IIf Function, On...GoSub Statement, Resume Statement, Select Case Statement

Do not use the On...GoTo statement within your Visual Basic source code. Usage of this statement can result in subtle errors, maintenance difficulties, and debugging nightmares. Use a Select Case statement instead to redirect your procedure based on an expression value.

Open Statement

Category	File System Features
Availability	VB:Yes, VBA:Yes, VBScript:No
Purpose	Opens a file for input or output.
Typical Syntax	**Open** *pathname* **For** *mode* [**Access** *access*] [*lock*] **As** [**#**]*filenumber* [**Len=***reclength*]

See Also   Close Statement, EOF Function, FileAttr Function, FreeFile Statement, Get Statement, Input Function, Input # Statement, Line Input # Statement, Loc Function, Lock # Statement, LOF Function, Print # Statement, Put Statement, Seek Function, Seek Statement, Unlock # Statement, Width # Statement, Write # Statement

Use the Open statement as needed within your Visual Basic source code. Always use a file number returned from the FreeFile function as an argument to the Open statement. If you are opening a file for modification or replacement, make sure you sufficiently inform the user that the file will be changed, either through documentation or through application notification.

The Open statement (and all other File System features) accesses information that resides outside of the control of the Visual Basic application. Therefore, you must always use proper error handling in any procedure that uses the Open statement. Make use of the On Error statement to capture any file handling errors, and take the appropriate corrective action.

Option Base Statement

Category   Declaration Features
Availability   VB:Yes, VBA:Yes, VBScript:No
Purpose   Indicates the default lower bound for all declared arrays.
Typical Syntax **Option Base {0 | 1}**
See Also   Dim Statement, Option Compare Statement, Option Explicit Statement, Option Private Statement, Private Statement, Public Statement, ReDim Statement

Do not use the Option Base statement within your Visual Basic source code. Instead, indicate the lower and upper bound of every declared array using the To clause of the Dim statement, the Private statement, the Public statement, and the ReDim statement. In Visual Basic, Scripting Edition, the lower bound of every array dimension is always 0 (zero).

Option Compare Statement

Category   Declaration Features
Availability   VB:Yes, VBA:Yes, VBScript:No
Purpose   Indicates the type of comparison used within a source code module.
Typical Syntax **Option Compare {Binary | Text | Database}**
See Also   Option Base Statement, Option Explicit Statement, Option Private Statement

Use the Option Compare statement as needed within your Visual Basic source code. If you use this statement in one module, include the statement in all modules within your application, and specify the same option type in every module. If you need to have one module that varies from the other modules in the use of this statement, indicate clearly the reason for the deviation in the source code comments.

Option Explicit Statement

Category   Declaration Features
Availability   VB:Yes, VBA:Yes, VBScript:Yes
Purpose   Requires all variables and constants to be declared before use.
Typical Syntax   **Option Explicit**
See Also   Option Base Statement, Option Compare Statement, Option Private Statement

The Option Explicit statement must appear as the first non-comment statement in every module in your Visual Basic and Visual Basic for Applications source code. It must also appear as the first non-comment line of every Visual Basic script file, unless that file will be included or inserted into a parent VBScript file.

For more information about the Option Explicit statement, and declaration in general, see Chapter 2, *Using Declaration*, and Chapter 9, *Declaration Standards*.

Option Private Statement

Category   Declaration Features
Availability   VB:Yes (with restrictions), VBA:Yes, VBScript:No
Purpose   Limits references to a module's contents from being accessed outside of the project.
Typical Syntax   **Option Private Module**
See Also   Option Base Statement, Option Compare Statement, Option Explicit Statement

Use the Option Private statement as needed within your Visual Basic for Applications source code. Although this statement can be used within standard Visual Basic code, it has no effect on the application. Therefore, use it only within Visual Basic for Applications source code.

Optional Keyword

Category   Declaration Features
Availability   VB:Yes, VBA:Yes, VBScript:No
Purpose   Identifies a procedure argument as optional.
Typical Syntax   **Optional [ByVal | ByRef] [ParamArray]** *varname*[( )] **[As** *type*] [= *defaultvalue*]

See Also   ByRef Keyword, ByVal Keyword, Function Statement, IsMissing Function, ParamArray Keyword, Property Get Statement, Property Let Statement, Property Set Statement, Sub Statement

Use the Optional keyword as needed within your Visual Basic source code. As with non-optional arguments, always supply the data type with the As clause, and include the ByVal keyword if needed. If you wish to use the IsMissing function with an optional argument, the data type of the argument must be declared as Variant.

Or Operator

Category	Operators
Availability	VB:Yes, VBA:Yes, VBScript:Yes
Purpose	Performs a logical or bitwise disjunction operation.
Typical Syntax	*expression1 **Or** expression2*
See Also	And Operator, Eqv Operator, Imp Operator, Not Operator, Xor Operator.

Use the Or operator as needed within your Visual Basic source code. When writing complex statements that involve more than one logical or bitwise operator, use parentheses to indicate the proper precedence and grouping within the calculation.

ParamArray Keyword

Category	Declaration Features
Availability	VB:Yes, VBA:Yes, VBScript:No
Purpose	Provides a mechanism for the caller of a procedure to send a variable number of arguments.
Typical Syntax	**ParamArray** *varname*[( )] [**As** *type*]
See Also	ByRef Keyword, ByVal Keyword, Function Statement, LBound Function, Optional Keyword, Property Get Statement, Property Let Statement, Property Set Statement, Sub Statement, UBound Function

Use the ParamArray keyword as needed within your Visual Basic source code. Only one ParamArray argument can appear in your argument list, and it must be the last argument. Include a description of the expected parameters that the calling routine might send as part of the initial procedure comment.

You cannot use the IsMissing function to test for the absence of any ParamArray arguments. Instead, test the upper and lower bounds of the array. When no parameters are sent for the ParamArray argument, the upper bound of the array will be lower than the lower bound.

Partition Function

Category	Miscellaneous Features
Availability	VB:Yes, VBA:Yes, VBScript:No
Purpose	Identifies the element in a series of ranges in which a value appears.
Typical Syntax	**Partition(***number, start, stop, interval***)**

Use the Partition function as needed within your Visual Basic source code. In general, the Partition function is used to perform grouping within a SQL query destined for the Microsoft Jet engine. When using the Partition function for other purposes, include sufficient documentation in your source code comments to explain your particular usage of the returned ranges.

Pmt Function

Category	Financial Features
Availability	VB:Yes, VBA:Yes, VBScript:No
Purpose	Calculates the payment for an annuity.
Typical Syntax	**Pmt(***rate, nper, pv*[, *fv*[, *type*]]**)**
See Also	DDB Function, FV Function, IPmt Function, IRR Function, MIRR Function, NPer Function, NPV Function, PPmt Function, PV Function, Rate Function, SLN Function, SYD Function

Use the Pmt function as needed within your Visual Basic source code. This function returns a Double value, and accepts several Double values for parameters. While values based on the Currency data type are accurate to four decimal places, Double floating point values are subject to minor rounding errors. While you can convert the return value of the Pmt function from Double to Currency using the CCur function, this result will be bound to the same rounding conditions of the value returned by the Pmt function. Take care to check the accuracy of the return values when using the Visual Basic intrinsic financial functions.

PPmt Function

Category	Financial Features
Availability	VB:Yes, VBA:Yes, VBScript:No
Purpose	Calculates the principal payment for an annuity.
Typical Syntax	**PPmt(***rate, per, nper, pv*[, *fv*[, *type*]]**)**
See Also	DDB Function, FV Function, IPmt Function, IRR Function, MIRR Function, NPer Function, NPV Function, Pmt Function, PV Function, Rate Function, SLN Function, SYD Function

Use the PPmt function as needed within your Visual Basic source code. This function returns a Double value, and accepts several Double values for parameters. While values based on the Currency data type are accurate to four decimal places, Double floating point values are subject to minor rounding errors. While you can convert the return value of the PPmt function from Double to Currency using the CCur function, this result will be bound to the same rounding conditions of the value returned by the PPmt function. Take care to check the accuracy of the return values when using the Visual Basic intrinsic financial functions.

Print # Statement

Category	File System Features
Availability	VB:Yes, VBA:Yes, VBScript:No
Purpose	Outputs text to a sequential file.
Typical Syntax	**Print #**filenumber, [outputlist]
See Also	Input Function, Line Input # Statement, Open Statement, Spc Function, Tab Function, Write # Statement

Use the Print # statement as needed within your Visual Basic source code. Always use a file number returned from the FreeFile function as an argument to the Print # statement. If you wish to output data in a delimited format to be read later by your application, use the Write # statement instead.

Do not forget to include the "#" character in the syntax of the Print statement. Omitting the "#" character is valid when the code appears in a form's code module. The statement will print all values onto the form background.

The Print # statement (and all other File System features) accesses information that resides outside of the control of the Visual Basic application. Therefore, you must always use proper error handling in any procedure that uses the Print # statement. Make use of the On Error statement to capture any file handling errors, and take the appropriate corrective action.

Private Statement

Category	Declaration Features
Availability	VB:Yes, VBA:Yes, VBScript:Yes (with restrictions)
Purpose	Declares a variable that is "module-level" in scope.
Typical Syntax	**Private** [**WithEvents**] varname[([subscripts])] [**As** [**New**] type]
See Also	Dim Statement, Global Statement, Public Statement, Static Statement

Use the Private statement as needed within the Declarations section of your Visual Basic application. Always include the appropriate As clause in the declaration. Do not place more than one variable declaration within a single Private statement. Place each variable declaration on a separate source code line.

In VBScript, it is permissible to place more than one variable with the same Hungarian prefix within the same Private statement.

Beginning with Visual Basic 4, the Private statement replaced the Dim statement within the Declarations section of a Visual Basic module. Do not use the Dim statement to declare module-level variables; use the Private statement to make a variable visible in scope to the module. Continue to use the Dim statement to declare local variables within routines.

Private variables use the Hungarian naming conventions. All private variables begin with the "m" Hungarian prefix to indicate that they are module-level in scope.

For more information about private variables and the Hungarian naming conventions, see Chapter 2, *Using Declaration*, and Chapter 9, *Declaration Standards*.

Property Get Statement

Category	Declaration Features
Availability	VB:Yes, VBA:Yes, VBScript:Yes (with restrictions)
Purpose	Declares a property retrieval procedure.
Typical Syntax	**[Private | Public | Friend] [Static] Property Get** *name* **[(***arglist***)] [As** *type***]**
	[*statements*]
	End Property
See Also	ByRef Keyword, ByVal Keyword, Function Statement, Optional Keyword, ParamArray Keyword, Property Let Statement, Property Set Statement, Sub Statement

Use the Property Get statement as needed within your Visual Basic source code. Always start the declaration with the Friend, Public, or Private keyword. If no arguments are used with the procedure, still follow the property name with an empty set of parentheses. When arguments are included, supply the appropriate data type with the As clause on each argument. Also, end the property declaration with the data type of the return value, using the final As clause. (These last two rules do not apply to VBScript procedures.)

Procedure names appear in mixed case with an initial capital letter. Digits may be included, but underscores should be limited to event procedure names.

Never include the Static keyword in the Property Get statement. If you want to include static local variables within your procedure, declare each variable using the Static statement. The Static keyword is not available in VBScript.

For more information about declaring procedures in your Visual Basic source code, see Chapter 2, *Using Declaration*, and Chapter 9, *Declaration Standards*.

Property Let Statement

Category	Declaration Features
Availability	VB:Yes, VBA:Yes, VBScript:Yes (with restrictions)
Purpose	Declares a property assignment procedure.
Typical Syntax	**[Private	Public	Friend] [Static] Property Let** *name* **(**[*arglist,*] *value***)**
	[*statements*]
	End Property
See Also	ByRef Keyword, ByVal Keyword, Function Statement, Optional Keyword, ParamArray Keyword, Property Get Statement, Property Set Statement, Sub Statement

Use the Property Let statement as needed within your Visual Basic source code. Always start the declaration with the Friend, Public, or Private keyword. Supply the appropriate data type with the As clause on each argument. (This last rule does not apply to VBScript procedures.)

Procedure names appear in mixed case with an initial capital letter. Digits may be included, but underscores should be limited to event procedure names.

Never include the Static keyword in the Property Let statement. If you want to include static local variables within your procedure, declare each variable using the Static statement. The Static keyword is not available in VBScript.

For more information about declaring procedures in your Visual Basic source code, see Chapter 2, *Using Declaration*, and Chapter 9, *Declaration Standards*.

Property Set Statement

Category	Declaration Features
Availability	VB:Yes, VBA:Yes, VBScript:Yes (with restrictions)
Purpose	Declares an object property assignment procedure.
Typical Syntax	**[Private	Public	Friend] [Static] Property Set** *name* **(**[*arglist,*] *reference***)**
	[*statements*]
	End Property
See Also	ByRef Keyword, ByVal Keyword, Function Statement, Optional Keyword, ParamArray Keyword, Property Get Statement, Property Let Statement, Sub Statement

Use the Property Set statement as needed within your Visual Basic source code. Always start the declaration with the Friend, Public, or Private keyword. Supply the appropriate data type with the As clause on each argument in *arglist*. (This last rule does not apply to VBScript procedures.)

Procedure names appear in mixed case with an initial capital letter. Digits may be included, but underscores should be limited to event procedure names.

Never include the Static keyword in the Property Set statement. If you want to include static local variables within your procedure, declare each variable using the Static statement. The Static keyword is not available in VBScript.

For more information about declaring procedures in your Visual Basic source code, see Chapter 2, *Using Declaration*, and Chapter 9, *Declaration Standards*.

Public Statement

Category	Declaration Features
Availability	VB:Yes, VBA:Yes, VBScript:Yes (with restrictions)
Purpose	Declares a variable that is global in scope.
Typical Syntax	**Public** [**WithEvents**] *varname*[([*subscripts*])] [**As** [**New**] *type*]
See Also	Dim Statement, Global Statement, Private Statement, Static Statement

Use the Public statement as needed within the Declarations section of your Visual Basic application. Always include the appropriate As clause in the declaration. Do not place more than one variable declaration within a single Public statement. Place each variable declaration on a separate source code line. In VBScript, it is permissible to place more than one variable with the same Hungarian prefix within the same Public statement. Generally, it will not be necessary to declare a Public variable in VBScript.

Beginning with Visual Basic 4, the Public statement replaced the Global statement. Do not use the Global statement to declare global variables; use the Public statement to make a variable global to the application.

Public variables use the Hungarian naming conventions. All public variables begin with the "g" Hungarian prefix to indicate that they are global in scope.

For more information about public variables and the Hungarian naming conventions, see Chapter 2, *Using Declaration*, and Chapter 9, *Declaration Standards*.

Put Statement

Category	File System Features
Availability	VB:Yes, VBA:Yes, VBScript:No
Purpose	Writes data from a variable to an open file.
Typical Syntax	**Put** [**#**]*filenumber*, [*recnumber*], *varname*
See Also	Get Statement, Open Statement, Seek Statement

Use the Put statement as needed within your Visual Basic source code. Always use a file number returned from the FreeFile function as an argument to the Put statement. Although the "#" prefix of the *filenumber* argument is optional, always include it in the syntax of the statement.

Data written with the Put statement is read with the Get statement. In general, the structure of the data written with the Put statement must be known to the code that will read the file with the Get statement. You may wish to include, at the beginning of your file data, identification values (sometimes called "magic numbers") that prove the file was written with the expected application, and with the appropriate version of that application.

The Put statement (and all other File System features) accesses information that resides outside of the control of the Visual Basic application. Therefore, you must always use proper error handling in any procedure that uses the Put statement. Make use of the On Error statement to capture any file handling errors, and take the appropriate corrective action.

PV Function

Category	Financial Features
Availability	VB:Yes, VBA:Yes, VBScript:No
Purpose	Calculates the present value of an annuity.
Typical Syntax	**PV(***rate, nper, pmt*[, *fv*[, *type*]]**)**
See Also	DDB Function, FV Function, IPmt Function, IRR Function, MIRR Function, NPer Function, NPV Function, Pmt Function, PPmt Function, Rate Function, SLN Function, SYD Function

Use the PV function as needed within your Visual Basic source code. This function returns a Double value, and accepts several Double values for parameters. While values based on the Currency data type are accurate to four decimal places, Double floating point values are subject to minor rounding errors. While you can convert the return value of the PV function from Double to Currency using the CCur function, this result will be bound to the same rounding conditions of the value returned by the PV function. Take care to check the accuracy of the return values when using the Visual Basic intrinsic financial functions.

QBColor Function

Category	Miscellaneous Features
Availability	VB:Yes, VBA:Yes, VBScript:No
Purpose	Returns an RGB color based on a "color number."
Typical Syntax	**QBColor(***color***)**
See Also	RGB Function

Do not use the QBColor function within your Visual Basic source code. Visual Basic now provides intrinsic constants that represent many common colors, plus constants that identify user modifiable system colors. If you need to use one of the colors generated by the QBColor function for which Visual Basic does not provide a suitable constant, generate the color value with the RBG function instead.

RaiseEvent Statement

Category	Declaration Features
Availability	VB:Yes, VBA:Yes, VBScript:No
Purpose	Raises an event declared with the Event statement.
Typical Syntax	**RaiseEvent** *eventname* [(*argumentlist*)]
See Also	Event Statement

Use the RaiseEvent statement as needed within your Visual Basic source code. Document any special concerns or assumptions in the source code comments when using the RaiseEvent statement, especially if multiple event interactions can cause unpredictable results.

Randomize Statement

Category	Math Features
Availability	VB:Yes, VBA:Yes, VBScript:Yes
Purpose	Initializes the random number generator with a seed value.
Typical Syntax	**Randomize** [*number*]
See Also	Rnd Function

Use the Randomize statement as needed within your Visual Basic source code. Only use the *number* argument if you need to record or create a consistent "random" sequence. Without the argument, the default action of the Randomize statement is to use the system timer to provide the seed value. Do not initialize the random number generator with the system clock value.

Incorrect

```
Randomize Timer
```

Correct

```
Randomize
```

If you wish to repeat a specific series of random numbers, you must first use the Rnd function with a negative argument, then call the Randomize statement with a numeric argument that you will use each time. If you do not immediately precede the Randomize call with a call to the Rnd function using a negative argument, a new, unique random sequence will occur.

Correct

```
' ----- In the Declarations section
Public Const STANDARD_SEED = 150
' ----- Later, in a routine
Call Rnd(-1)
Randomize STANDARD_SEED
```

Rate Function

Category	Financial Features
Availability	VB:Yes, VBA:Yes, VBScript:No
Purpose	Calculates the interest rate per period of an annuity.
Typical Syntax	**Rate(***nper, pmt, pv*[, *fv*[, *type*[, *guess*]]]**)**
See Also	DDB Function, FV Function, IPmt Function, IRR Function, MIRR Function, NPer Function, NPV Function, Pmt Function, PPmt Function, PV Function, SLN Function, SYD Function

Use the Rate function as needed within your Visual Basic source code. This function returns a Double value, and accepts several Double values for parameters. While values based on the Currency data type are accurate to four decimal places, Double floating point values are subject to minor rounding errors. While you can convert the return value of the Rate function from Double to Currency using the CCur function, this result will be bound to the same rounding conditions of the value returned by the Rate function. Take care to check the accuracy of the return values when using the Visual Basic intrinsic financial functions.

ReDim Statement

Category	Declaration Features
Availability	VB:Yes, VBA:Yes, VBScript:Yes (with restrictions)
Purpose	Reallocates an array dynamically to increase or decrease storage.
Typical Syntax	**ReDim** [**Preserve**] *varname*(*subscripts*) [**As** *type*]
See Also	Dim Statement, Global Statement, LBound Function, Private Statement, Public Statement, Static Statement, UBound Function

Use the ReDim statement as needed within your Visual Basic source code. Do not place more than one variable declaration within a single ReDim statement. Place each variable declaration on a separate source code line.

When you create a dynamic array variable for use with the ReDim statement, decide how many array dimensions it will have, and never alter that number. If you use an array with two dimensions, never give it one, three, four, or more dimensions.

In Visual Basic and Visual Basic for applications, always use the To keyword when defining the ranges of each dimension in the array. Always specify both the lower and upper bounds for each dimension, both during the initial use of the ReDim statement, and on any subsequent uses. This rule does not apply to VBScript, since the lower bound is always 0 (zero) for every dimension.

Incorrect for VB, VBA; Correct for VBScript

```
ReDim maElements(nNewElement)
```

Correct for VB, VBA

```
ReDim maElements(1 To nNewElement)
```

For more information about array variables and the Hungarian naming conventions, see Chapter 2, *Using Declaration*, and Chapter 9, *Declaration Standards*.

Rem Statement

Category	Miscellaneous Features
Availability	VB:Yes, VBA:Yes, VBScript:Yes
Purpose	Begins a source code comment line or line section.
Typical Syntax	**Rem** *comment*
See Also	' Comment Operator

Do not use the Rem statement in your source code. When adding comments to your source code, always use the comment operator (').

For full information on the use and style of comments within your source code, see Chapter 3, *Commenting and Style*.

Replace Function

Category	String Features
Availability	VB:Yes, VBA:Yes, VBScript:Yes (with restrictions)
Purpose	Replaces one sub-string with another sub-string in a larger string.
Typical Syntax	**Replace(***expression, find, replacewith*[, *start*[, *count*[, *compare*]]]**)**
Variations	Replace$ Function
See Also	Filter Function, InStr Function, InStrRev Function, Join Function, Option Compare Statement, Split Function

Use the Replace function as needed within your Visual Basic source code. Visual Basic, Scripting Edition does not permit the use of the string version of this function. Within a VBScript code section, you must use the syntax

```
Replace(argument)
```

In all other versions of Visual Basic, if you do not require a Variant result, use the string version of this function instead of the Variant version.

```
Replace$(argument)
```

When using the Replace$ version of this function, the first argument cannot be Null. If you think that your code will allow a Null value to be passed to the Replace$ function, force the argument to a string first. A quick way to convert a Null to a string is to concatenate an empty string onto the Null value.

```
sFields = Replace$(rsInfo!FieldTitles & "", ",", vbTab)
```

The *compare* argument of the Replace function accepts Integer values, or one of a set of intrinsic Visual Basic constants. When available, always use the supplied constants instead of numeric literals. The use of the Option Compare statement can affect the results of the Replace function.

Reset Statement

Category	File System Features
Availability	VB:Yes, VBA:Yes, VBScript:No
Purpose	Closes all open files.
Typical Syntax	**Reset**
See Also	Close Statement, Open Statement

Do not use the Reset statement in your Visual Basic source code as a standard method for closing files. Always close each open file with a Close statement. However, if you need to immediately close all files in response to a fatal error in your application, it is permissible to use the Reset statement.

The Reset statement (and all other File System features) accesses information that resides outside of the control of the Visual Basic application. Therefore, you must always use proper error handling in any procedure that uses the Reset statement. Make use of the On Error statement to capture any file handling errors, and take the appropriate corrective action.

Resume Statement

Category	Error Handling and Debugging Features
Availability	VB:Yes, VBA:Yes, VBScript:No

Purpose	Resumes execution of a procedure after error handling in an On Error statement.
Typical Syntax	**Resume [0]**
	Resume Next
	Resume *line*
See Also	Err Object, Exit Statement, On Error Statement

Use the Resume statement as needed within your Visual Basic source code. When using the first syntax to resume execution with the line or procedure call that caused the error, exclude the optional "0" argument.

RGB Function

Category	Miscellaneous Features
Availability	VB:Yes, VBA:Yes, VBScript:Yes
Purpose	Returns a value for a color based on distinct red, green, and blue values.
Typical Syntax	**RGB(***red, green, blue***)**
See Also	QBColor Function

Use the RBG function as needed within your Visual Basic source code. The Long value returned by this function stores each color value in a mathematically distinct section of the number, and each of the original values can be extracted from the new single value. Interestingly, the three color values are reversed in the combined Long value, so that they appear in blue, green, red order. Use the following calculations to extract the original red, green, and blue color values.

```
' ----- Extract red, green, and blue
nRed = lColor Mod &H100
nGreen = (lColor \ &H100) Mod &H100
nBlue = lColor \ &H10000
```

Right Function

Category	String Features
Availability	VB:Yes, VBA:Yes, VBScript:Yes (with restrictions)
Purpose	Returns the right portion of a string.
Typical Syntax	**Right(***string, length***)**
Variations	Right$ Function, RightB Function, RightB$ Function
See Also	Left Function, Mid Function

Use the Right function as needed within your Visual Basic source code. Visual Basic, Scripting Edition does not permit the use of the string version of this function. Within a VBScript code section, you must use the syntax

```
Right(arguments)
```

In all other versions of Visual Basic, if you do not require a Variant result, use the string version of this function instead of the Variant version.

```
Right$(arguments)
```

If you need to work with the underlying bytes contained within the original string, use the RightB and RightB$ functions.

When using the Right$ and RightB$ versions of this function, the first argument cannot be Null. If you think that your code will allow a Null value to be passed to the Right$ or RightB$ function, force the argument to a string first. A quick way to convert a Null to a string is to concatenate an empty string onto the Null value.

```
' ----- Extract state abbreviation from City, ST
sState = Right$(rsInfo!CityState & "", 2)
```

RmDir Statement

Category	File System Features
Availability	VB:Yes, VBA:Yes, VBScript:No
Purpose	Deletes a directory.
Typical Syntax	**RmDir** *path*
See Also	ChDir Statement, ChDrive Statement, CurDir Function, Dir Function, Kill Statement, MkDir Function

Use the RmDir statement as needed within your Visual Basic source code. The argument supplied to the RmDir statement may be a local or mapped drive path, a UNC (Universal Naming Convention) path, or a path relative to the current drive and directory.

The directory to be removed by the RmDir statement must not contain any files or subordinate directories. If the directory to be removed is a user directory, make sure you sufficiently inform the user that the directory will be deleted, either through documentation or through application notification.

The RmDir statement (and all other File System features) accesses information that resides outside of the control of the Visual Basic application. Therefore, you must always use proper error handling in any procedure that uses the RmDir statement. Make use of the On Error statement to capture any file handling errors, and take the appropriate corrective action.

Rnd Function

Category	Math Features
Availability	VB:Yes, VBA:Yes, VBScript:Yes
Purpose	Generates a pseudo-random number.
Typical Syntax	**Rnd**[(*number*)]
See Also	Randomize Statement

Use the Rnd function as needed within your Visual Basic source code. To generate a random number between a specific lower and upper bound, inclusive, use the following formula:

```
Int((nUpper - nLower + 1) * Rnd + nLower)
```

Round Function

Category	Math Features
Availability	VB:Yes, VBA:Yes, VBScript:Yes
Purpose	Rounds a value to a specific number of decimal places.
Typical Syntax	**Round(***expression*[, *numdecimalplaces*]**)**
See Also	Abs Function, Fix Function, Int Function, Sgn Function

Use the Round function as needed within your Visual Basic source code. To round a value to an integer (that is, no decimal places), omit the optional *numdecimalplaces* argument.

When the most significant decimal place to be truncated is a 5, and is followed by only zeros, the Round function rounds up when the next significant digit (the digit to the left) is odd, and rounds down when the next significant digit is even. That is, rounding 34.5 to zero decimal places results in 34, but rounding 35.5 results in 36. Rounding -34.5 similarly results in -34, while rounding -35.5 gives -36.

RSet Statement

Category	String Features
Availability	VB:Yes, VBA:Yes, VBScript:No
Purpose	Right aligns a string within a string variable.
Typical Syntax	**RSet** *stringvar* **=** *string*
See Also	LSet Statement, Right Function, Space Function

Use the RSet function as needed within your Visual Basic source code.

RTrim Function

Category	String Features
Availability	VB:Yes, VBA:Yes, VBScript:Yes (with restrictions)
Purpose	Returns a string with trailing spaces removed.
Typical Syntax	**RTrim(***string***)**
Variations	RTrim$ Function
See Also	LTrim Function, Trim Function

Use the RTrim function as needed within your Visual Basic source code. Visual Basic, Scripting Edition does not permit the use of the string version of this function. Within a VBScript code section, you must use the syntax

```
RTrim(argument)
```

In all other versions of Visual Basic, if you do not require a Variant result, use the string version of this function instead of the Variant version.

```
RTrim$(argument)
```

Some Visual Basic programmers originally learned programming in languages that included functions equivalent to LTrim and RTrim, but did not have an equivalent to the Trim function. In such languages, you could perform a Trim by combining the LTrim and RTrim statements.

```
sClean = LTrim$(RTrim$(sOriginal))
```

Avoid this usage in Visual Basic; always use the Trim function to remove both leading and trailing spaces.

```
sClean = Trim$(sOriginal)
```

When using the RTrim$ version of this function, the argument cannot be Null. If you think that your code will allow a Null value to be passed to the RTrim$ function, force the argument to a string first. A quick way to convert a Null to a string is to concatenate an empty string onto the Null value.

```
sFlushRight = RTrim$(rsInfo!Message & "")
```

SavePicture Statement

Category	Miscellaneous Features
Availability	VB:Yes, VBA:Yes, VBScript:No
Purpose	Saves a graphic to a file.
Typical Syntax	**SavePicture** *picture, pathname*
See Also	LoadPicture Function, LoadResData Function, LoadResPicture Function, LoadResString Function

Use the SavePicture statement as needed within your Visual Basic source code. The SavePicture statement accesses information that resides outside of the control of the Visual Basic application. Therefore, you must always use proper error handling in any procedure that uses the SavePicture statement. Make use of the On Error statement to capture any errors, and take the appropriate corrective action.

SaveSetting Statement

Category	Miscellaneous Features
Availability	VB:Yes, VBA:Yes, VBScript:No
Purpose	Saves application information in the Windows registry.

Typical Syntax   **SaveSetting** *appname, section, key, setting*
See Also   DeleteSetting Statement, GetAllSettings Function, GetSetting Function

Use the SaveSetting statement as needed within your Visual Basic source code. Document all registry settings used by your application in the technical documentation or user documentation, as appropriate.

The SaveSetting statement accesses information that resides outside of the control of the Visual Basic application. Therefore, you must always use proper error handling in any procedure that uses the SaveSetting statement. Make use of the On Error statement to capture any errors, and take the appropriate corrective action.

Screen Object

Category   Miscellaneous Features
Availability   VB:Yes, VBA:No, VBScript:No
Purpose   Object that supplies screen and display related properties.
Typical Syntax   **Screen**
See Also   App Object, Debug Object, Global Object

Use the Screen object as needed within your Visual Basic source code. When using Visual Basic for Applications or Visual Basic, Scripting Edition, there may be an object available that is contextually similar to the Visual Basic Screen object.

ScriptEngine Function

Category   Miscellaneous Features
Availability   VB:No, VBA:No, VBScript:Yes
Purpose   Returns the name of the engine processing the VBScript code.
Typical Syntax   **ScriptEngine**
See Also   ScriptEngineBuildVersion Function, ScriptEngineMajorVersion Function, ScriptEngineMinorVersion Function

Use the ScriptEngine function as needed within your VBScript source code.

ScriptEngineBuildVersion Function

Category   Miscellaneous Features
Availability   VB:No, VBA:No, VBScript:Yes
Purpose   Returns the build version number of the engine processing the VBScript code.
Typical Syntax   **ScriptEngineBuildVersion**
See Also   ScriptEngine Function, ScriptEngineMajorVersion Function, ScriptEngineMinorVersion Function

Use the ScriptEngineBuildVersion function as needed within your VBScript source code.

ScriptEngineMajorVersion Function

Category	Miscellaneous Features
Availability	VB:No, VBA:No, VBScript:Yes
Purpose	Returns the major version number of the engine processing the VBScript code.
Typical Syntax	**ScriptEngineMajorVersion**
See Also	ScriptEngine Function, ScriptEngineBuildVersion Function, ScriptEngineMinorVersion Function

Use the ScriptEngineMajorVersion function as needed within your VBScript source code.

ScriptEngineMinorVersion Function

Category	Miscellaneous Features
Availability	VB:No, VBA:No, VBScript:Yes
Purpose	Returns the minor version number of the engine processing the VBScript code.
Typical Syntax	**ScriptEngineMinorVersion**
See Also	ScriptEngine Function, ScriptEngineBuildVersion Function, ScriptEngineMajorVersion Function

Use the ScriptEngineMinorVersion function as needed within your VBScript source code.

Second Function

Category	Date and Time Features
Availability	VB:Yes, VBA:Yes, VBScript:Yes
Purpose	Returns a value indicating the second for a given date or time.
Typical Syntax	**Second(***time***)**
See Also	DatePart Function, Day Function, Hour Function, Minute Function, Month Function, Year Function

Use the Second function as needed within your Visual Basic source code. If you are using either Visual Basic or Visual Basic for Applications, and you will be using the seconds returned from this function as a string (for example, to concatenate the second onto an existing string), consider using the Format$ function instead.

```
sInfo = "Second number " & Format$(dtAction, "s")
```

Seek Function

Category	File System Features
Availability	VB:Yes, VBA:Yes, VBScript:No
Purpose	Returns the current position in an open file.
Typical Syntax	**Seek(***filenumber***)**
See Also	EOF Function, Loc Function, LOF Function, Open Statement, Seek Statement

Use the Seek function as needed within your Visual Basic source code. Always use a file number returned from the FreeFile function as an argument to the Seek function.

Using the Seek function on a file opened in Append, Binary, Input, or Output mode returns the current byte position. However, the Seek function returns the current record number when used on a file opened in Random mode.

When determining the current location in a file opened in Append, Input, or Output mode, use the Seek function instead of the Loc function.

The Seek function (and all other File System features) accesses information that resides outside of the control of the Visual Basic application. Therefore, you must always use proper error handling in any procedure that uses the Seek function. Make use of the On Error statement to capture any file handling errors, and take the appropriate corrective action.

Seek Statement

Category	File System Features
Availability	VB:Yes, VBA:Yes, VBScript:No
Purpose	Sets the current position in an open file.
Typical Syntax	**Seek [#]***filenumber, position*
See Also	EOF Function, Loc Function, LOF Function, Open Statement, Seek Function

Use the Seek statement as needed within your Visual Basic source code. Always use a file number returned from the FreeFile function as the first argument to the Seek statement. Although the "#" prefix of the *filenumber* argument is optional, always include it in the syntax of the statement.

The minimum file position is 1 (one). If you specify a position that is greater than the current length of a writeable file, the next write operation will extend the file to that length.

The Seek statement (and all other File System features) accesses information that resides outside of the control of the Visual Basic application. Therefore, you must always use proper error handling in any procedure that uses the Seek statement. Make use of the On Error statement to capture any file handling errors, and take the appropriate corrective action.

Select Case Statement

Category	Flow Control Features
Availability	VB:Yes, VBA:Yes, VBScript:Yes (with restrictions)
Purpose	Executes one of several blocks of code based on an expression.
Typical Syntax	**Select Case** *expression*
	[**Case** *expressionlist-n*
	[*statements*]]...
	[**Case Else**
	[*statements*]]
	End Select
See Also	Choose Function, If...Then...Else Statement, Switch Function

Use the Select Case statement as needed within your Visual Basic source code. Note that the VBScript version of the Select Case statement puts restrictions on the types of expressions that can occur in individual Case expression lists.

Do not use a GoTo statement to jump inside of the Select Case statement. Also, do not use a GoTo statement to jump from one Case section to another. If two Case sections need to share a section of code, include them in the same Case section, then use an If...Then...Else statement within the section to differentiate between the different process activities. You might also consider using the GoSub statement, or calling a procedure, to process the common parts of two or more Case sections.

SendKeys Statement

Category	Miscellaneous Features
Availability	VB:Yes, VBA:Yes, VBScript:No
Purpose	Sends keystrokes to the active window.
Typical Syntax	**SendKeys** *string*[, *wait*]
See Also	AppActivate Statement, DoEvents Statement, Shell Function

Do not use the SendKeys statement to perform actions on the forms of your application. Instead, implement the needed features using code logic.

Incorrect

```
' ----- Click on the action button
cmdAction.SetFocus
SendKeys "%A"
```

Correct

```
' ----- Click on the action button
cmdAction_Click
```

Use the SendKeys statement to send keystrokes only to windows in other applications.

The SendKeys statement may access information that resides outside of the control of the Visual Basic application. Therefore, you must always use proper error handling in any procedure that uses the SendKeys statement. Make use of the On Error statement to capture any errors, and take the appropriate corrective action.

Set Statement

Category   Declaration Features
Availability   VB:Yes, VBA:Yes, VBScript:Yes
Purpose   Assigns an object reference to an object variable.
Typical Syntax **Set** *objectvar* **=** {[**New**] *objectexpression* | **Nothing**}
See Also   = Operator (Assignment), Nothing Keyword, Property Set Statement

Use the Set statement as needed within your Visual Basic source code. When you have many object variables referring to the same instance of an object, document any potential conflicts that may result from such multiple references in your source code comments.

SetAttr Statement

Category   File System Features
Availability   VB:Yes, VBA:Yes, VBScript:No
Purpose   Sets the attributes of a file.
Typical Syntax **SetAttr** *pathname, attributes*
See Also   FileAttr Function, GetAttr Function

Use the SetAttr statement as needed within your Visual Basic source code. The first argument supplied to the SetAttr statement may be a local or mapped drive path, a UNC (Universal Naming Convention) path, or a path relative to the current drive and directory.

The *attributes* argument to the SetAttr statement accepts an Integer value, or a combination of a set of intrinsic Visual Basic constants. When available, always use the supplied constants instead of numeric literals. When combining multiple constants, use either the addition operator (+) or the Or operator.

The SetAttr statement (and all other File System features) accesses information that resides outside of the control of the Visual Basic application. Therefore, you must always use proper error handling in any procedure that uses the SetAttr statement. Make use of the On Error statement to capture any file handling errors, and take the appropriate corrective action.

SetLocale Function

Category	Miscellaneous Features
Availability	VB:No, VBA:No, VBScript:Yes
Purpose	Sets a new locale while identifying the previous locale.
Typical Syntax	**SetLocale(***lcid***)**
See Also	GetLocale Function

Use the SetLocale function as needed within your Visual Basic source code. Visual Basic does not define a set of constants for the *lcid* (Locale ID). However, you may wish to declare a constant for the Locale IDs that you use within your application.

Sgn Function

Category	Math Features
Availability	VB:Yes, VBA:Yes, VBScript:Yes
Purpose	Returns -1, 0, or 1, depending on the sign of the passed expression.
Typical Syntax	**Sgn(***expression***)**
See Also	Abs Function, Fix Function, Int Function, Round Function

Use the Sgn function as needed within your Visual Basic source code.

Shell Function

Category	Miscellaneous Features
Availability	VB:Yes, VBA:Yes, VBScript:No
Purpose	Runs another program, and returns the task ID if successful.
Typical Syntax	**Shell(***pathname*[, *windowstyle*]**)**
See Also	AppActivate Statement, SendKeys Statement

Use the Shell function as needed within your Visual Basic source code. The *pathname* argument supplied to the Shell function may be a local or mapped drive path, a UNC (Universal Naming Convention) path, or a path relative to the current drive and directory. You can also include command-line arguments accepted by the new program.

While the *windowstyle* argument is optional, it should always be supplied to avoid the default non-user-friendly "minimized with focus" startup method. The *windowstyle* argument to the Shell function accepts an Integer value, or one of a set of intrinsic Visual Basic constants. When available, always use the supplied constants instead of numeric literals.

The Shell function accesses information that resides outside of the control of the Visual Basic application. Therefore, you must always use proper error handling in any procedure that uses the Shell function. Make use of the On Error statement to capture any errors, and take the appropriate corrective action.

Sin Function

Category	Math Features
Availability	VB:Yes, VBA:Yes, VBScript:Yes
Purpose	Calculates the sine of an angle.
Typical Syntax	**Sin(**number**)**
See Also	Atn Function, Cos Function, Tan Function

Use the Sin function as needed within your Visual Basic source code. This function returns a Double value, and accepts a Double value for its parameter. Double floating point values are subject to minor rounding errors. Take care to check the accuracy of the return values when using the Visual Basic intrinsic math functions.

SLN Function

Category	Financial Features
Availability	VB:Yes, VBA:Yes, VBScript:No
Purpose	Calculates the straight-line depreciation of an asset for one period.
Typical Syntax	**SLN(**cost, salvage, life**)**
See Also	DDB Function, FV Function, IPmt Function, IRR Function, MIRR Function, NPer Function, NPV Function, Pmt Function, PPmt Function, PV Function, Rate Function, SYD Function

Use the SLN function as needed within your Visual Basic source code. This function returns a Double value, and accepts all Double values for parameters. While values based on the Currency data type are accurate to four decimal places, Double floating point values are subject to minor rounding errors. While you can convert the return value of the SLN function from Double to Currency using the CCur function, this result will be bound to the same rounding conditions of the value returned by the SLN function. Take care to check the accuracy of the return values when using the Visual Basic intrinsic financial functions.

Space Function

Category	String Features
Availability	VB:Yes, VBA:Yes, VBScript:Yes (with restrictions)
Purpose	Returns a string of space characters repeated a specified number of times.
Typical Syntax	**Space(**number**)**
Variations	Space$ Function
See Also	Spc Function, String Function

Use the Space function as needed within your Visual Basic source code. Visual Basic, Scripting Edition does not permit the use of the string version of this function. Within a VBScript code section, you must use the syntax

```
Space(argument)
```

In all other versions of Visual Basic, if you do not require a Variant result, use the string version of this function instead of the Variant version.

```
Space$(argument)
```

Do not use the Space function to generate extremely short runs of spaces (say, 1 to 5 characters in length). Use literal strings or constants instead.

Spc Function

Category	File System Features
Availability	VB:Yes, VBA:Yes, VBScript:No
Purpose	Positions output when using the Print # statement.
Typical Syntax	**Spc(***number***)**
See Also	Print # Statement, Space Function, Tab Function

Use the Spc function as needed within your Visual Basic source code. Depending on your usage of the Print # statement (and other similar Print methods), you may achieve better spacing results by using either the Space function or the Tab function.

Split Function

Category	String Features
Availability	VB:Yes, VBA:Yes, VBScript:Yes
Purpose	Returns an array of strings extracted from a larger string based on a delimiter.
Typical Syntax	**Split(***expression*[, *delimiter*[, *count*[, *compare*]]]**)**
See Also	InStr Function, InStrRev Function, Join Function, Option Compare Statement

Use the Split function as needed within your Visual Basic source code. The *compare* argument to the Split function accepts an Integer value, or one of a set of intrinsic Visual Basic constants. When available, always use the supplied constants instead of numeric literals. The use of the Option Compare statement can affect the Split function.

Sqr Function

Category	Math Features
Availability	VB:Yes, VBA:Yes, VBScript:Yes

Purpose	Calculates the square root of a number.
Typical Syntax	**Sqr(***number***)**
See Also	Exp Function, Log Function

Use the Sqr function as needed within your Visual Basic source code. This function returns a Double value, and accepts a Double value for its parameter. Double floating point values are subject to minor rounding errors. Take care to check the accuracy of the return values when using the Visual Basic intrinsic math functions.

The argument to the Sqr function must be greater than or equal to 0 (zero). If the value you pass to the Sqr function is supplied by the user, and the value falls outside of the valid range, either correctly handle the error raised by the Sqr function, or reject the value entered by the user.

Static Statement

Category	Declaration Features
Availability	VB:Yes, VBA:Yes, VBScript:No
Purpose	Declares a variable that is local in scope, but maintains its data throughout the life of the application.
Typical Syntax	**Static** *varname*[([*subscripts*])] [**As** [**New**] *type*]
See Also	Dim Statement, Global Statement, Private Statement, Public Statement

Use the Static statement as needed within the routines of your Visual Basic application. Always include the appropriate As clause in the declaration. Do not place more than one variable declaration within a single Static statement. Place each variable declaration on a separate source code line.

Static variables use the Hungarian naming conventions. All static variables begin with the "x" Hungarian prefix to indicate that they are local in scope and static in persistence.

For more information about static variables and the Hungarian naming conventions, see Chapter 2, *Using Declaration*, and Chapter 9, *Declaration Standards*.

Visual Basic allows you to mark all variables local to a routine as static by including the optional Static keyword in the procedure definition. Do not use this feature to identify static variables. Instead, declare each static variable within a routine using the Static statement.

Stop Statement

Category	Flow Control Features
Availability	VB:Yes, VBA:Yes, VBScript:Yes (with restrictions)
Purpose	Pauses or halts program execution immediately.
Typical Syntax	**Stop**
See Also	End Statement

In a compiled application, use the End statement instead of the Stop statement to halt application execution. In general, the Stop statement should never be used within your Visual Basic application. However, if you are performing some complex debugging, and it is too cumbersome to continually establish breakpoints throughout your source code, it is reasonable to include the Stop statement at key locations within the code.

The Stop statement is available in Visual Basic, Scripting Edition. However, it is only useful with debugging tools such as the Windows Script Debugger.

Always mark your Stop statements with an appropriate *When* comment. (*When* comments are discussed in Chapter 3, *Commenting and Style.*)

```
Stop      ' !!! Remove after debugging
```

Str Function

Category	Conversion Functions, String Features
Availability	VB:Yes, VBA:Yes, VBScript:No
Purpose	Converts a number to the String data type.
Typical Syntax	**Str(***number***)**
Variations	Str$ Function
See Also	CStr Function, StrConv Function, Val Function

Do not use the Str function, or its Str$ variation, within your source code. Use the CStr function instead.

StrComp Function

Category	String Features
Availability	VB:Yes, VBA:Yes, VBScript:Yes
Purpose	Compares two string values.
Typical Syntax	**StrComp(***string1*, *string2*[, *compare*]**)**
See Also	< Operator, <= Operator, <> Operator (Comparison), = Operator (Comparison), > Operator, >= Operator, Is Operator, Like Operator, Not Operator, Option Compare Statement

Use the StrComp function as needed within your Visual Basic source code. The use of the Option Compare statement can affect comparisons performed with the StrComp function. The *compare* argument to the StrComp function accepts an Integer value, or one of a set of intrinsic Visual Basic constants. When available, always use the supplied constants instead of numeric literals.

StrConv Function

Category	Conversion Functions, String Features
Availability	VB:Yes, VBA:Yes, VBScript:No

Purpose	Converts a string to a different format.
Typical Syntax	**StrConv(***string, conversion*[, *lcid*]**)**
See Also	Chr Function, CStr Function, Str Function, Val Function

Use the StrConv function as needed within your Visual Basic source code. However, if you only need to convert a single-byte character string in the local language to upper or lower case, use the UCase function or the LCase function instead.

The *conversion* argument to the StrConv function accepts an Integer value, or a combination of a set of intrinsic Visual Basic constants. When available, always use the supplied constants instead of numeric literals. You may also wish to declare a constant for the *lcid* (Locale ID) argument.

String Function

Category	String Features
Availability	VB:Yes, VBA:Yes, VBScript:Yes (with restrictions)
Purpose	Returns a string with a character repeated a specified number of times.
Typical Syntax	**String(***number, character***)**
Variations	String$ Function
See Also	Space Function

Use the String function as needed within your Visual Basic source code. Visual Basic, Scripting Edition does not permit the use of the string version of this function. Within a VBScript code section, you must use the syntax

```
String(arguments)
```

In all other versions of Visual Basic, if you do not require a Variant result, use the string version of this function instead of the Variant version.

```
String$(arguments)
```

If you need to generate a string of only space characters, use the Space function instead. Do not use the String function to generate extremely short runs of characters (say, 1 to 5 characters in length). Use literal strings or constants instead.

The syntax of the String function permits you to pass an integer ASCII value for the *character* argument. If the character is a printable character, pass an example of the character instead. For non-printable characters, it is preferable to pass the ASCII value.

Incorrect

```
sWork = String$(25, 42)
sWork = String$(15, Chr$(1))   ' Control-A
```

Correct

```
sWork = String$(25, "*")
sWork = String$(15, 1)  ' Control-A
```

StrReverse Function

Category	String Features
Availability	VB:Yes, VBA:Yes, VBScript:Yes (with restrictions)
Purpose	Returns a string with the characters of the original string reversed.
Typical Syntax	**StrReverse(***string***)**
Variations	StrReverse$ Function

Use the StrReverse function as needed within your Visual Basic source code. Visual Basic, Scripting Edition does not permit the use of the string version of this function. Within a VBScript code section, you must use the syntax

```
StrReverse(argument)
```

In all other versions of Visual Basic, if you do not require a Variant result, use the string version of this function instead of the Variant version.

```
StrReverse$(argument)
```

When using the StrReverse$ version of this function, the argument cannot be Null. If you think that your code will allow a Null value to be passed to the StrReverse$ function, force the argument to a string first. A quick way to convert a Null to a string is to concatenate an empty string onto the Null value.

```
sConfuse = StrReverse$(rsInfo!Password & "")
```

Sub Statement

Category	Declaration Features
Availability	VB:Yes, VBA:Yes, VBScript:Yes (with restrictions)
Purpose	Declares a subroutine procedure.
Typical Syntax	**[Private	Public	Friend] [Static] Sub** *name* [(*arglist*)] [*statements*] **End Sub**
See Also	ByRef Keyword, ByVal Keyword, Function Statement, Optional Keyword, ParamArray Keyword, Property Get Statement, Property Let Statement, Property Set Statement

Use the Sub statement as needed within your Visual Basic source code. Always start the declaration with the Friend, Public, or Private keyword. If no arguments are used with the subroutine, still follow the subroutine name with an empty set of parentheses. When arguments are included, supply the appropriate data type with the As clause on each argument. (This rule does not apply to VBScript procedures.)

Procedure names appear in mixed case with an initial capital letter. Digits may be included, but underscores should be limited to event procedure names.

Never include the Static keyword in the Sub statement. If you want to include static local variables within your subroutine, declare each variable using the Static statement. The Static keyword is not available in VBScript.

For more information about declaring procedures in your Visual Basic source code, see Chapter 2, *Using Declaration*, and Chapter 9, *Declaration Standards*.

Switch Function

Category	Flow Control Features
Availability	VB:Yes, VBA:Yes, VBScript:No
Purpose	Returns a value associated with the first True expression in a list of expressions.
Typical Syntax	**Switch(***expr-1, value-1*[, *expr-2, value-2*...[, *expr-n, value-n*]]**)**
See Also	Choose Function, IIf Function, If...Then...Else Statement, Partition Function, Select Case Statement

Use the Switch function as needed within your Visual Basic source code. Always include source code comments that describe the purpose and results of the use of this statement.

If none of the evaluated expressions are True, the Switch function returns a Null value. Be sure to check the return value for a legitimate result if there is any chance one of the expressions will result in a True value. Although only one argument will be returned (or possibly none), and even if the first expression evaluates to True, all expressions and values are evaluated. Make sure that the expressions and values do not contain any code that will fail on invalid conditions, or that should execute only with certain condition values.

SYD Function

Category	Financial Features
Availability	VB:Yes, VBA:Yes, VBScript:No
Purpose	Calculates the sum-of-years' digits depreciation for an asset for one period.
Typical Syntax	**SYD(***cost, salvage, life, period***)**
See Also	DDB Function, FV Function, IPmt Function, IRR Function, MIRR Function, NPer Function, NPV Function, Pmt Function, PPmt Function, PV Function, Rate Function, SLN Function

Use the SYD function as needed within your Visual Basic source code. This function returns a Double value, and accepts all Double values for parameters. While values based on the Currency data type are accurate to four decimal places, Double floating point values are subject to minor rounding errors. While you can convert the return value of the SYD function from Double to Currency using the CCur function, this result will be bound to the same rounding conditions of the value returned by the SYD function. Take care to check the accuracy of the return values when using the Visual Basic intrinsic financial functions.

Tab Function

Category	File System Features
Availability	VB:Yes, VBA:Yes, VBScript:No
Purpose	Positions output when using the Print # statement.
Typical Syntax	**Tab**[(*number*)]
See Also	Print # Statement, Space Function, Spc Function

Use the Tab function as needed within your Visual Basic source code. Depending on your usage of the Print # statement (and other similar Print methods), you may achieve better spacing results by using either the Space function or the Spc function.

Tan Function

Category	Math Features
Availability	VB:Yes, VBA:Yes, VBScript:Yes
Purpose	Calculates the tangent of an angle.
Typical Syntax	**Tan**(*number*)
See Also	Atn Function, Cos Function, Sin Function

Use the Tan function as needed within your Visual Basic source code. This function returns a Double value, and accepts a Double value for its parameter. Double floating point values are subject to minor rounding errors. Take care to check the accuracy of the return values when using the Visual Basic intrinsic math functions.

Time Function

Category	Date and Time Features
Availability	VB:Yes, VBA:Yes, VBScript:Yes (with restrictions)
Purpose	Returns the current system time.
Typical Syntax	**Time**
Variations	Time$ Function
See Also	Date Function, Date Statement, Now Function, Time Statement

Use the Time function as needed within your Visual Basic source code. A string version of this function, Time$, returns the same information as the standard Time function, but as a true String value. (The Time$ function is not available in VBScript.) In general, you should use the Time version of this function. If you need a time stored or displayed as a string, use the Format function or the FormatDateTime function to properly format the time before use.

Time Statement

Category	Date and Time Features
Availability	VB:Yes, VBA:Yes, VBScript:No
Purpose	Sets the current system time.
Typical Syntax	**Time =** *time*
See Also	Date Function, Date Statement, Now Function, Time Function

Use the Time statement as needed within your Visual Basic source code. However, you must make it clear to the user, either in the documentation or through application notification, that you will be modifying the system clock. On some secure Windows systems, you may be restricted from modifying the system clock.

Timer Function

Category	Date and Time Features
Availability	VB:Yes, VBA:Yes, VBScript:Yes
Purpose	Returns the number of seconds since midnight.
Typical Syntax	**Timer**
See Also	DateDiff Function, Time Function, Time Statement

Use the Timer function as needed within your Visual Basic source code. When using the Timer function to compare start and stop times, recall that the return value of the Timer function will revert to 0 (zero) at midnight.

TimeSerial Function

Category	Date and Time Features
Availability	VB:Yes, VBA:Yes, VBScript:Yes
Purpose	Returns a time based on individual hour, minute, and second values.
Typical Syntax	**TimeSerial(***hour, minute, second***)**
See Also	DateAdd Function, DatePart Function, DateSerial Function, Hour Function, Minute Function, Second Function

Use the TimeSerial function as needed within your Visual Basic source code. Be aware that if you supply hour, minute, or second values that are too large for a valid time, the TimeSerial function will increment the value appropriately to compensate for the extra time elements.

```
dtAction = TimeSerial(13, 59, 59)    ' --> 1:59:59pm
dtAction = TimeSerial(13, 59, 60)    ' --> 2:00:00pm
```

You can also supply negative values for the hour, minute, or second, and the resulting time will decrement as needed. However, if you supply values that are either negative or too large for a time element, provide a suitable explanation in the source code comments.

TimeValue Function

Category	Date and Time Features
Availability	VB:Yes, VBA:Yes, VBScript:Yes
Purpose	Converts a time expression to a Variant (Date) value.
Typical Syntax	**TimeValue(***date***)**
See Also	CDate Function, Date Function, DateSerial Function, DateValue Function

To convert a date, time, or date/time expression to a Variant (Date) or true Date value, use the CDate function. Avoid the TimeValue function for general time conversions. However, if you have an expression that contains both a date and a time, and you wish to retrieve only the time portion of the expression, use the TimeValue function. Passing a date and time expression to the CDate function will retain both the date and time portions of the expression. The TimeValue function discards the date portion of the original expression. If you are using the TimeValue function to remove the date portion of a date/time expression, make it clear in your source code comments that the date portion will be lost.

Trim Function

Category	String Features
Availability	VB:Yes, VBA:Yes, VBScript:Yes (with restrictions)
Purpose	Returns a string with leading and trailing spaces removed.
Typical Syntax	**Trim(***string***)**
Variations	Trim$ Function
See Also	LTrim Function, RTrim Function

Use the Trim function as needed within your Visual Basic source code. Visual Basic, Scripting Edition does not permit the use of the string version of this function. Within a VBScript code section, you must use the syntax

```
Trim(argument)
```

In all other versions of Visual Basic, if you do not require a Variant result, use the string version of this function instead of the Variant version.

```
Trim$(argument)
```

Some Visual Basic programmers originally learned programming in languages that included functions equivalent to LTrim and RTrim, but did not have an equivalent to the Trim function. In such languages, you could perform a Trim by combining the LTrim and RTrim statements.

```
sClean = LTrim$(RTrim$(sOriginal))
```

Avoid this usage in Visual Basic; always use the Trim function to remove both leading and trailing spaces.

```
sClean = Trim$(sOriginal)
```

When using the Trim$ version of this function, the argument cannot be Null. If you think that your code will allow a Null value to be passed to the Trim$ function, force the argument to a string first. A quick way to convert a Null to a string is to concatenate an empty string onto the Null value.

```
sFirstName = Trim$(rsInfo!FirstName & "")
```

True Keyword

Category	Miscellaneous Features
Availability	VB:Yes, VBA:Yes, VBScript:Yes
Purpose	Provides an intrinsic constant for the True Boolean value.
Typical Syntax	**True**
See Also	False Keyword

Use the True keyword as needed within your Visual Basic source code. Although the True keyword has a value equal to -1, it is not always interpreted as -1 when coerced into other data types. Consider the following statements:

```
Dim sWork As String
Dim nWork As Integer

nWork = True
sWork = nWork & " = " & True
MsgBox sWork
```

Processing this code within a Visual Basic application will display a message box with the text "-1 = True" instead of the expected "-1 = -1." The True keyword, and all true Boolean values that equate to True, result in the text "True" when converted to a String.

Never use -1 when you mean True. When you are testing the value of a Boolean variable, or the result of a Boolean expression, always compare the variable or expression to True or False, never to -1 or 0.

When converted to a numeric value, True equates to -1. Many Windows applications are written in the C and C++ programming languages, which also include a TRUE value, either as an intrinsic constant, or as a declared constant. Within these programming languages, the numeric value of TRUE is 1, not -1. When you interact with Windows API calls that either accept or return Boolean values, verify whether or not it makes a difference to interpret TRUE as either 1 or -1. False has a numeric value of 0 (zero) in Visual Basic, C, and C++.

Type Statement

Category	Declaration Features
Availability	VB:Yes, VBA:Yes, VBScript:No
Purpose	Defines the structure of a user-defined data type.
Typical Syntax	**[Private	Public] Type** *typename*
	elementname **[([**subscripts**])] As** *type*
	. . .
	End Type
See Also	Const Statement, Dim Statement, Enum Statement, Global Statement, Private Statement, Public Statement, ReDim Statement, Static Statement

Use the Type statement as needed within your Visual Basic source code. Always begin the statement with either the Private or Public keyword, Include a mixed-case *typename* ending in the word "Type." Each element within the type should follow the Hungarian naming standards for local variables, and include the appropriate As clause.

For more information about user-defined data types and the Hungarian naming conventions, see Chapter 2, *Using Declaration*, and Chapter 9, *Declaration Standards*.

TypeName Function

Category	Declaration Features
Availability	VB:Yes, VBA:Yes, VBScript:Yes
Purpose	Returns the name of the type of data contained in a Variant variable or expression.
Typical Syntax	**TypeName(**expression**)**
See Also	VarType Function

Use the TypeName function as needed within your Visual Basic source code. When taking an action based on the type of data contained in a Variant expression, it may be more convenient to use the VarType function.

UBound Function

Category	Declaration Features
Availability	VB:Yes, VBA:Yes, VBScript:Yes
Purpose	Returns the upper numeric bound of an array dimension.
Typical Syntax	**UBound(***arrayname*[, *dimension*]**)**
See Also	Erase Statement, LBound Function, ReDim Statement

Use the UBound function as needed within your Visual Basic source code. You cannot use the UBound function on an array that has not yet been dimensioned, or on a redimensioned array that has been cleared with the Erase statement.

If you are attempting to ascertain the upper bound of a one-dimensional array, do not include the *dimension* argument of the UBound function. If you are using the UBound function on a multi-dimensional array, even if you are testing the first dimension, always include the *dimension* argument.

UCase Function

Category	String Features
Availability	VB:Yes, VBA:Yes, VBScript:Yes (with restrictions)
Purpose	Returns a string converted to upper case.
Typical Syntax	**UCase(***string***)**
Variations	UCase$ Function
See Also	LCase Function

Use the UCase function as needed within your Visual Basic source code. Visual Basic, Scripting Edition does not permit the use of the string version of this function. Within a VBScript code section, you must use the syntax

```
UCase(argument)
```

In all other versions of Visual Basic, if you do not require a Variant result, use the string version of this function instead of the Variant version.

```
UCase$(argument)
```

When using the UCase$ version of this function, the argument cannot be Null. If you think that your code will allow a Null value to be passed to the UCase$ function, force the argument to a string first. A quick way to convert a Null to a string is to concatenate an empty string onto the Null value.

```
sPostalCode = UCase$(rsInfo!PostalCode & "")
```

Unload Statement

Category	Declaration Features
Availability	VB:Yes, VBA:Yes, VBScript:No

Purpose	Removes an instance of a form or control from memory.
Typical Syntax	**Unload** *object*
See Also	Load Statement

Use the Unload statement as needed within your Visual Basic source code.

Unlock # Statement

Category	File System Features
Availability	VB:Yes, VBA:Yes, VBScript:No
Purpose	Unlocks a portion or all of an open file.
Typical Syntax	**Unlock** [*#*]*filenumber*[, *recordrange*]
See Also	Open Statement, Lock # Statement

Use the Unlock # statement as needed within your Visual Basic source code. Always use a file number returned from the FreeFile function as an argument to the Unlock # statement. Although the "#" prefix of the *filenumber* argument is optional, always include it in the syntax of the statement.

The Unlock # statement (and all other File System features) accesses information that resides outside of the control of the Visual Basic application. Therefore, you must always use proper error handling in any procedure that uses the Unlock # statement. Make use of the On Error statement to capture any file handling errors, and take the appropriate corrective action.

Val Function

Category	Conversion Functions
Availability	VB:Yes, VBA:Yes, VBScript:No
Purpose	Converts the first numbers found in a string expression to a number.
Typical Syntax	**Val**(*string*)
See Also	CCur Function, CDbl Function, CDec Function, CInt Function, CLng Function, CSng Function

Use the Val function as needed within your Visual Basic source code. However, it is better to use the other numeric conversion functions (CCur Function, CDbl Function, CDec Function, CInt Function, CLng Function, CSng Function) to change a string representation of a number into a true number.

The Val function is useful for converting strings with invalid or missing numbers to a number, even if that number is zero. The Val function converts all empty strings to the value 0. This is useful when retrieving possibly Null numeric fields from a database result set. Concatenate an empty string onto the end of the potentially Null value to prepare it for use with the Val function.

```
' ----- Retrieve the patient's age
fsAge = Val(rsInfo!Age & "")
```

VarType Function

Category   Declaration Features
Availability   VB:Yes, VBA:Yes, VBScript:Yes
Purpose   Identifies the type of data contained in a Variant variable or expression.
Typical Syntax **VarType(***expression***)**
See Also   TypeName Function

Use the VarType function as needed within your Visual Basic source code. When describing the type of data contained in a Variant expression to the user, it may be more convenient to use the TypeName function.

The return value of the VarType function is an Integer value, or a combination of a set of intrinsic Visual Basic constants. When available, always use the supplied constants instead of numeric literals. Note that the vbArray constant may be combined with another constant in the return value.

Weekday Function

Category   Date and Time Features
Availability   VB:Yes, VBA:Yes, VBScript:Yes
Purpose   Returns a value indicating the weekday for a given date.
Typical Syntax **Weekday(***date*[, *firstdayofweek*]**)**
See Also   MonthName Function, WeekdayName Function

Use the Weekday function as needed within your Visual Basic source code. The *firstdayofweek* argument to the Weekday function accepts an Integer value, or one of a set of intrinsic Visual Basic constants. When available, always use the supplied constants instead of numeric literals.

The return value of the Weekday function returns a whole number indicating the day of the week for the supplied date. The set of return values from this function exists as a set of intrinsic Visual Basic constants. When available, always use the supplied constants instead of numeric literals. If you will use the return value directly in a numeric capacity (for example, as an array subscript), supply a comment to indicate which day of the week equates to which numeric value.

```
' ----- The maDailyInfo array ranges from 0 (Sunday)
'       to 6 (Saturday).
bInUse = maDailyInfo(Weekday(dtAction)).bInUse
```

WeekdayName Function

Category   Date and Time Features
Availability   VB:Yes, VBA:Yes, VBScript:Yes (with restrictions)
Purpose   Return the name of the weekday for a given date.
Typical Syntax **WeekdayName(***weekday*[, *abbreviate*[, *firstdayofweek*]]**)**

Variations	WeekdayName$ Function
See Also	MonthName Function, Weekday Function

Use the WeekdayName function as needed within your Visual Basic source code. Visual Basic, Scripting Edition does not permit the use of the string version of this function. Within a VBScript code section, you must use the syntax

```
WeekdayName(arguments)
```

In all other versions of Visual Basic, if you do not require a Variant result, use the string version of this function instead of the Variant version.

```
WeekdayName$(arguments)
```

The *firstdayofweek* argument to the WeekdayName function accepts an Integer value, or one of a set of intrinsic Visual Basic constants. When available, always use the supplied constants instead of numeric literals.

While...Wend Statement

Category	Flow Control Features
Availability	VB:Yes, VBA:Yes, VBScript:Yes
Purpose	Processes one or more statements repeatedly while a condition remains true.
Typical Syntax	**While** *condition*
	[*statements*]
	Wend
See Also	Do...Loop Statement

The While...Wend statement is provided within all versions of Visual Basic for backward compatibility. While Microsoft has no plans to remove the construct from the language, its use is discouraged. Instead, use the Do...Loop statement with a While clause. For example, if you are considering writing the following While statement:

```
While (bFail = False)
    ' ---- Process one instance of the data set
    nSet = nSet + 1
    bFail = ProcessOneSet(nSet)
Wend
```

Replace it with this syntax instead:

```
Do While (bFail = False)
    ' ---- Process one instance of the data set
    nSet = nSet + 1
    bFail = ProcessOneSet(nSet)
Loop
```

Width # Statement

Category   File System Features
Availability   VB:Yes, VBA:Yes, VBScript:No
Purpose   Identifies an open file as having output lines of a specific
                      width.
Typical Syntax   **Width #***filenumber, width*
See Also   Open Statement, Print # Statement

Use the Width # statement as needed within your Visual Basic source code. Always use a file number returned from the FreeFile function as an argument to the Width # statement.

The Width # statement permits automatic wrapping of characters within an output file. By default the line width is 0 (zero), which indicates an unlimited line length. The largest line length you can specify with the Width # statement is 255 characters. If you need to have lines wrap at a line length larger than 255 characters, you must perform the wrapping yourself before outputting the lines.

The Width # statement (and all other File System features) accesses information that resides outside of the control of the Visual Basic application. Therefore, you must always use proper error handling in any procedure that uses the Width # statement. Make use of the On Error statement to capture any file handling errors, and take the appropriate corrective action.

With Statement

Category   Flow Control Features
Availability   VB:Yes, VBA:Yes, VBScript:Yes
Purpose   Enters a code block with an assumed object prefix.
Typical Syntax   **With** *object*
                          [*statements*]
                      End With

Use the With statement as needed within your Visual Basic source code. Do not use the With statement based on a simple one-level, non-array object.

Incorrect

```
With Me
With objStatus
With frmMain
With txtName
```

Correct

```
With txtName(Index)
With gaCustomer(nActiveCust).aOrder(nActiveOrder)
```

Write # Statement

Category	File System Features
Availability	VB:Yes, VBA:Yes, VBScript:No
Purpose	Outputs delimited data to a sequential file.
Typical Syntax	**Write #***filenumber*, [*outputlist*]
See Also	Input # Statement, Open Statement, Print # Statement

Use the Write # statement as needed within your Visual Basic source code. Always use a file number returned from the FreeFile function as an argument to the Write # statement. If you wish to output text in a format to be read later by people instead of by an application, consider using the Print # statement instead.

Data written with the Write # statement is read with the Input # statement. In general, the structure of the data written with the Write # statement must be known to the code that will read the file with the Input # statement. You may wish to include, at the beginning of your file data, identification values (sometimes called "magic numbers") that prove the file was written with the expected application, and with the appropriate version of that application.

The Write # statement (and all other File System features) accesses information that resides outside of the control of the Visual Basic application. Therefore, you must always use proper error handling in any procedure that uses the Write # statement. Make use of the On Error statement to capture any file handling errors, and take the appropriate corrective action.

Xor Operator

Category	Operators
Availability	VB:Yes, VBA:Yes, VBScript:Yes
Purpose	Performs a logical or bitwise exclusion operation.
Typical Syntax	*expression1* **Xor** *expression2*
See Also	And Operator, Eqv Operator, Imp Operator, Not Operator, Or Operator.

Use the Xor operator as needed within your Visual Basic source code. When writing complex statements that involve more than one logical or bitwise operator, use parentheses to indicate the proper precedence and grouping within the calculation.

Year Function

Category	Date and Time Features
Availability	VB:Yes, VBA:Yes, VBScript:Yes
Purpose	Returns a value indicating the year for a given date.
Typical Syntax	**Year(***date***)**

See Also   DatePart Function, Day Function, Hour Function, Minute Function, Month Function, Second Function

Use the Year function as needed within your Visual Basic source code. If you are using either Visual Basic or Visual Basic for Applications, and you will be using the year returned from this function as a string (for example, to concatenate the year onto an existing string), consider using the Format$ function instead.

```
sInfo = "You were born in " & Format$(dtBirthdate, "yyyy")
```

Summary

While a summary of this chapter would be almost as big as the chapter itself, there are several guidelines that appeared throughout the keyword entries in this chapter.

- Several functions and statements access information that resides outside of the control of the Visual Basic application. Therefore, you must always use proper error handling in any procedure that uses these features. This includes access to file system objects, the Windows registry, databases, network connections, printers, and shared resources. Make use of the On Error statement to capture any errors, and take the appropriate corrective action.
- Visual Basic has several data types that represent floating point values. While some data types (such as Double and Single) can hold extremely large values, they are prone to minor rounding errors. Other data types (like the Currency data type) are more accurate, but have a limited range. When using math and financial features in Visual Basic, make sure you are aware of the rounding and range limitations of each data type.
- Several statements and functions accept and return Integer and Long values for which Visual Basic has defined sets of intrinsic constants (such as the vbOKOnly and vbInformation constants used in the arguments of the MsgBox function). There are also several intrinsic constants for general use that are not tied to any one function or statement (such as the vbNullChar constant). When available, use these constants instead of equivalent literals.
- Several operators and procedure arguments have limited ranges for the incoming data. If the user is supplying data for these operators and procedures, and you think that the user's data may fall outside the valid range of values, check the values before using these operators or procedures. For example, if you are dividing one number into another with the division operator (/) and you think that the second of the two operands may be 0 (zero), check for zero before performing the division. When invalid data is encountered, make the appropriate correction or inform the user of the data issue.

- Several statements and functions in the Visual Basic language have optional arguments, and generally these arguments can be omitted unless the added functionality that they provide is needed. However, some optional arguments should be included, even if they provide no logic benefit, so that source code clarity is retained. For example, the *format* argument (the second argument) of the Format function is optional. However, leaving out this argument makes it unclear to the reader (unless the reader has memorized this function's manual page) how the data will be formatted. In these cases, always supply the optional arguments. Such cases are noted throughout this chapter.
- Several functions do not accept Null values as arguments. A quick way to convert a Null to a string is to concatenate an empty string onto the Null value.
- Several functions offer both a string version and a Variant version, when used in Visual Basic and Visual Basic for Applications. In such cases, use the string version unless you must have a Variant result.
- Finally, use the numerous keywords available in Visual Basic to bring clarity to your source code, both for the reader and for the Visual Basic engine.

Control and User Interface Standards

In the early days of computer programming, the user interface was not an issue. Hollerith cards, toggle switches on a mainframe front panel, punched paper tapes, these were all the interface that a real programmer needed. And why not? The programmers were generally the only ones who ever interacted with the computer. As long as the programmer could understand the input and output, there was really no reason to provide any more convenience or complexity to the application.

Today, programmers are one of the smallest groups of users to approach a computer. Many computer users (possibly most) are practically computer illiterate. The responsibilities placed on the programmer are much higher today because they will not be the primary ones interacting with the computer. In order to simplify the computer experience for the average user, programmers make use of user interface standards to bring a more consistent and familiar experience to each application. Chapter 4, *User Interface Consistency*, provided a high-level overview of user interface programming guidelines. Here in Chapter 11, more details about individual user interface elements complete the picture. While some of the general guidelines presented in this chapter apply to the user interfaces available through Visual Basic, Visual Basic for Applications, and Visual Basic, Scripting Edition, individual implementations of VBA and VBScript may provide user interface controls and features that are similar, but not identical to those available in the standard Visual Basic development environment. This chapter focuses on those elements available in standard Visual Basic.

General Considerations

Some aspects of control use affect all controls equally. These general elements appear in this section.

Communication

The purpose of creating a form within your Visual Basic application is to communicate with the user. Since generally you will not be there to handhold the user through the process of using the application, you must build forms that best communicate the purpose and intent of the application to the user.

The aesthetics of your application plays a large role in how you communicate with the user. Make your forms look professional. Microsoft's official idea of what a professional program looks like appears in its text *Microsoft Windows User Experience*. You should also study the way the most popular off-the-shelf applications perform actions similar to those that will appear in your program. While there are some bad applications out there, if a program is in use by tens of thousands of users over several years, you can be sure that some usability research went into the presentation.

Computers are now powerful enough that you can include active visuals and sounds in your application, through easy-to-use multimedia extensions. Do not make such features the only way in which you communicate with the user (unless you are programming a graphic game or similar multimedia application). Always include standard methods of presenting and obtaining data from the user to increase accessibility to the widest possible audience.

When presenting data in individual fields, format and accept the data in ways that will reduce errors. Present data in a complete, yet simple, format. For example, when displaying a date in a text field for user modification, never show a long date, such as "February 5, 2000," as the user may assume that he or she must use this full form when modifying the date. (Such a date is good for use in a static label.) On the opposite end of the spectrum, do not truncate essential information, such as the century digits of the year. Displaying "2/5/00" in a text field can be misleading, and can result in the problem formerly known as Y2K. Consider values such as "2/5/2000," although even in this case you may need to consider the nationalistic background of your users (some of whom would interpret that date as May 2, 2000). When there is doubt, document your intentions.

The tab order of the controls on a form may seem inconsequential, especially if you tend to use the mouse as your primary mode of input. Some users have an aversion to using the mouse, and reach for the keyboard to perform almost all tasks within the Windows environment. Always define the tab order of all controls, including Label controls, in a way that the users would expect. Following the example of other programs, increase the tab order as fields progress from top to bottom, left to right (or right to left in some foreign language applications). Use the TabStop property of controls as needed to remove from the tab order controls that should not receive the focus.

Control Interaction

Communication between your source code and controls is as important as communication between the controls and the user. Write your source code in a way that maximizes accurate and efficient interaction with a form's controls. For example, when a control contains lists of items (as in the List Box control), never identify individual elements by position alone. Instead, use the features of the control to uniquely identify each element. In the List Box control, each element has an associated ItemData entry, a Long value that can uniquely identify each item in the list.

Use the features of each control as they were intended. You can move a control around the form by modifying its Left and Top settings. However, it may be more visually appealing to the user if you use the control's Move method to affect the Left and Top properties at once. Also, when redrawing controls, use the control's Refresh method instead of the global DoEvents function.

Some properties and methods of a control will generate an error if used improperly. Always confirm, through restricted code or the testing of user data, that your control's attributes will be used in a way that avoids error. For example, if you have a control that will be enabled and disabled throughout the lifetime of the form, make sure that the control's SetFocus method is never used at a time when the control is disabled, as this will generate an error.

Documentation

A discussion of your user interface in your technical documentation, your user documentation, and in the source code comments, is an essential method of communication with all those involved in your application. While most controls are simple and self-documenting (at least from the programmer's point of view), other controls are very complex, and include design-time features not visible through the Properties window of the Visual Basic development environment (consider the Image List control as one example). In these instances, complete and clear documentation is essential.

Document all advanced or obscure features used within your application. For instance, if you employ sub-classing in one or more of your user interface forms, document the purpose of the sub-classes in the appropriate WinProc functions, and in your technical documentation.

Most of the controls available in Visual Basic include intrinsic constants that can be used as property values, and as arguments to the methods and events of the control. When available, always use these constants instead of meaningless numeric literals. For example, remove a Picture Box control's border at run time by setting its BorderStyle property to vbBSNone instead of 0 (zero).

If you include pictures (bitmaps, icons, mouse pointers, or other custom images) at design time in your forms and controls, keep a copy of each graphic in its original file format in your technical documentation or source code directory tree. This will make it easier to update a form in the event that you need to modify the graphics.

Specific Control Information

The remainder of this chapter describes the usage of the commonly used Visual Basic controls. Due to the popularity of Visual Basic and the entrepreneurial spirit that surrounds those who work with Visual Basic, it is not possible to consider all available controls in this chapter. Only the most commonly used controls supplied by Microsoft are listed here. If a control you use is not included in this chapter, amend this chapter through your own documentation, identifying all issues having to do with a consistent use of the control.

ADO Data Control

Purpose	Provides a VCR-style interface for scrolling through a set of ADO data.
Availability	Independent control
Hungarian Prefix	dta
See Also	Data Control, Remote Data Control

Use the ADO Data control within your Visual Basic application to connect one or more data bound controls to a database recordset. However, the ADO Data control itself should not be made visible to the user. Use more user-friendly data manipulation methods instead. See Chapter 12, *Database Standards*, for a discussion of data manipulation methods.

Animation Control

Purpose	Displays a graphic animation.
Availability	Windows Common Controls set 2
Hungarian Prefix	ani
See Also	Multimedia Control

Use the Animation control as needed within your Visual Basic application. While there is no requirement that you close an animation with the Close method when you have finished with the control, it is always a good idea to close previously opened resources in Visual Basic.

If you will supply an animation (AVI) file for use with an Animation control when you distribute your application, document the presence of the AVI file in your technical documentation. While it is good practice to identify AVI files with an "avi" extension, the Animation control will work with any valid animation file, regardless of the extension associated with the file.

The Open method of the Animation control accesses information that resides outside of the control of the Visual Basic application. Therefore, you must always use proper error handling in any procedure that uses the Open method. Make use of the On Error statement to capture any errors, and take the appropriate corrective action.

Calendar Control

Purpose	Displays a calendar or calendar portion.
Availability	Independent control
Hungarian Prefix	cal
See Also	Month View Control, Date Time Picker Control

Use the Calendar control as needed within your Visual Basic application. If you will be using a user-supplied value to initialize the Value property of the Calendar control, verify that it is a valid date. Visual Basic can represent dates as numeric values. If the user supplies a number that you then pass to the Value property, unexpected displays may result. The following routine checks for a valid date, and also checks for a four-digit year.

```
Public Function CheckDate(sOrigDate As String) _
      As Boolean
   ' ----- Return True if the supplied value is a date
   '       with a four-digit year.
   CheckDate = False
   If (Not(IsDate(sOrigDate))) Then Exit Function
   If (InStr(sOrigDate, CStr(Year(sOrigDate))) <> 0) Then
      CheckDate = True
   End If
End Function
```

You can assign a Null value to the Value property of the Calendar control. When a Null value is used, the control will still display the previously active month and year, although no day will be selected. To determine if the calendar control currently has a Null value, you must test the Value property with the IsEmpty function, not the IsNull function.

Incorrect

```
If (IsNull(calStartDate.Value)) Then
```

Correct

```
If (IsEmpty(calStartDate.Value)) Then
```

If you need to elicit only a date from the user, consider the Date Picker control, the Month View control, or a Text Box control instead. Use the Calendar control when the user must interact with a variety of dates over the life of a form.

Chart Control

Purpose	Displays a graphical chart of data.
Availability	Independent control
Hungarian Prefix	cht
See Also	Picture Box Control

Use the Chart control (MSChart) as needed within your Visual Basic application. The Chart control is one of the most complex controls available with Visual Basic, sporting dozens upon dozens of properties, methods, and events. Many of the control properties can be set up at design time through the Property Page supplied with the control. Because of the complexity of the control, document any special design-time configuration issues within the source code comments of the form that contains the control.

Check Box Control

Purpose	Allows entry of bi-state (Boolean) and tri-state flag information.
Availability	Core Visual Basic control
Hungarian Prefix	chk
See Also	Command Button Control, Option Button Control

Use the Check Box control as needed within your Visual Basic application. Avoid the use of the Graphical style of this control unless no other efficient method for presenting or obtaining the associated data is available. Note that when using the Graphical style of this control, there is no visible difference between the unchecked and grayed values.

The Value property of the Check Box control uses one of a set of intrinsic constants. When available, always use these constants within your source code. The three possible constants are vbUnchecked (0), vbChecked (1), and vbGrayed (2). If you need to represent a Boolean value with a Check Box control, the Boolean value must be converted before use. Early versions of Visual Basic allowed True and False values to be assigned to the Value property in place of vbChecked and vbUnchecked. Newer versions of Visual Basic generate an error when True is assigned to the control. The following functions can be used to convert between Boolean and Check Box control values.

```
Public Function BoolToCheck(bValue As Boolean) As Integer
    ' ----- Convert a Boolean value to a value usable by
    '          a check box's Value property.
```

```
      BoolToCheck = IIf(bValue, vbChecked, vbUnchecked)
End Function

Public Function CheckToBool(nValue As Integer) As Boolean
    ' ----- Convert a check box's Value property to a
    '       Boolean.
    CheckToBool = (nValue = vbChecked)
End Function
```

Combo Box Control

Purpose   Displays a list of elements in a "drop-down" format.
Availability   Core Visual Basic control
Hungarian Prefix   cbo
See Also   Data Combo Control, List Box Control, Image Combo
                         Control

Use the Combo Box control as needed within your Visual Basic application. Combo Box controls come in three styles: Dropdown Combo (Style 0), Simple Combo (Style 1), and Dropdown List (Style 2). In general, only the Dropdown List (Style 2) should be used unless you cannot perform some functionality efficiently without resorting to one of the other two styles.

When using a Dropdown Combo (Style 0) or Simple Combo (Style 1) Combo Box control, you should highlight the text in the text field when the control receives the focus. You can use the same routine that a Text Box control uses to highlight the text.

```
' ----- In the global Declarations section...
Public Declare Function GetKeyState Lib "user32" _
    (ByVal nVirtKey As Long) As Integer

Public Sub SelectText(ctrWhich As Control)
    ' ----- Highlight the text of a Text Box or
    '       Combo Box control, but not if the mouse
    '       was used to enter the control.
    If (GetKeyState(vbKeyLButton) >= 0) Then
        ctrWhich.SelStart = 0
        ctrWhich.SelLength = Len(ctrWhich.Text)
    End If
End Sub

' ----- And in the form's code view...
Private Sub cboOrderType_GotFocus()
    ' ----- Highlight the entire text
    SelectText cboOrderType
End Sub
```

When adding items to and referencing items in a Combo Box control, always identify an item by its associated ItemData value, never by its position.

Even if you are adding a known number of items in a known order to the control, always supply and use the ItemData values. When adding new items, use the NewIndex property to correctly interact with the new item.

Incorrect

```
cboLocation.Clear
cboLocation.AddItem "In-house"
cboLocation.ItemData(0) = LOC_IN_HOUSE
```

Correct

```
cboLocation.Clear
cboLocation.AddItem "In-house"
cboLocation.ItemData(cboLocation.NewIndex) = LOC_IN_HOUSE
```

Once you have added your items to the Combo Box control, you can access them by their ItemData value. The following function is useful for accessing the index of an item by its ItemData value. It returns -1 when no matching item is found.

```
Public Function ListByItem(ctrWhich As Control, _
      lItemData As Long) As Long
    ' ----- Locate an item in a List Box or Combo Box
    '       control.  Return the position, or -1 if
    '       the item is not found.
    Dim lCounter As Long

    On Error Resume Next
    ListByItem = -1

    ' ----- Compare each item in the list.
    For lCounter = 0 to ctrWhich.ListCount - 1
        If (ctrWhich.ItemData(lCounter) = lItemData) Then
            ' ----- Found a match.
            ListByItem = lCounter
            Exit For
        End If
    Next lCounter
End Function
```

Never present a Dropdown List (Style 2) Combo Box control that has no list items to the user. If no items are available to add to the list, add a single item with a meaningful "no item available" name, displayed in angle brackets. You may wish to disable the control as well until a valid list item can be added to the control.

Correct

```
If (cboToys.ListCount = 0) Then
    ' ----- Indicate a lack of toys
```

```
      cboToys.Enabled = False
      cboToys.AddItem "<No Toys Available>"
      cboToys.ItemData(cboToys.NewIndex) = -1
      cboToys.ListIndex = cboToys.NewIndex
End If
```

Adding a list item with a "no item selected" value, and an ItemData value of -1, is also a useful way to provide the user with a method to "unselect" any item in the list.

Be careful not to confuse the Change and Click events. When using a Dropdown List (Style 2) Combo Box control, you will rely on the Click event for item selection by the user. When using other styles of Combo Box controls, both the Click and Change events may be useful. Regardless of the style type selected, do not use the Scroll event for major display or data processing. Use the Scroll event to make minor display or data adjustments only. Use the Click or Change event for complete display and data processing.

Never assume that a user selected a list item, especially if you are using a Dropdown List (Style 2) Combo Box control. Always test the ListIndex property to verify that a list item was selected before you work with the control's ItemData, List, or Selected arrays.

Often, when adding items to a Combo Box control, the width of some list items will exceed the width of the control itself. Windows provides features that allow the dropped-down portion of a Dropdown Combo (Style 0) or Dropdown List (Style 2) Combo Box control to be wider than the control, wide enough to display the entire text. The following code sections can be used to implement such a feature.

```
Public Const SM_CXVSCROLL = 2
Public Const CB_SETDROPPEDWIDTH = &H160
Public Declare Function GetSystemMetrics Lib "user32" _
      (ByVal nIndex As Long) As Long
Public Declare Function SendMessage Lib "user32" _
      Alias "SendMessageA" (ByVal hwnd As Long, _
      ByVal wMsg As Long, ByVal wParam As Long, _
      lParam As Any) As Long

Public Sub SetComboWidth(cboWhich As ComboBox, _
          frmWhich As Form)
      ' ----- This function sets the width of the drop-down
      '          portion of a combo box to be wide enough to
      '          hold the widest text item in the list.  This
      '          function assumes that the form's font matches
      '          the combo box's font.
      Dim nCounter As Integer
      Dim lMaxWidth As Long
      Dim lNewWidth As Long
      Dim nSaveMode As Integer
```

```
' ----- Process each combo box item.  Do all work in
'        twips because some containers (such as
'        frames) do not have a pixels mode.
nSaveMode = frmWhich.ScaleMode
frmWhich.ScaleMode = vbTwips
lMaxWidth = 0
For nCounter = 0 To cboWhich.ListCount - 1
    ' ----- Figure out the width of this item.
    lNewWidth = frmWhich.TextWidth( _
        cboWhich.List(nCounter))
    If (lNewWidth > lMaxWidth) Then _
        lMaxWidth = lNewWidth
Next nCounter

' ----- Add about 8 pixels just for good measure.
'        Also, add in the width of a scroll bar if
'        needed.
lMaxWidth = lMaxWidth + ((8 + _
    GetSystemMetrics(SM_CXVSCROLL)) * _
    Screen.TwipsPerPixelX)

' ----- Set the combo width if it is wider than
'        the combo itself.
If (lMaxWidth > cboWhich.Width) Then
    ' ----- Send the message in pixels
    lMaxWidth = lMaxWidth \ Screen.TwipsPerPixelX
    SendMessage cboWhich.hwnd, CB_SETDROPPEDWIDTH, _
        lMaxWidth, 0&
End If
frmWhich.ScaleMode = nSaveMode
End Sub
```

The SetComboWidth routine is easy to use. Just call it after all of the initial list items have been added to the Combo Box control. Be sure to call the routine again when adding a new item to the Combo Box due to a user action.

```
SetComboWidth cboCities, Me
```

By default, the Dropdown List (Style 2) Combo Box control moves to the next item that begins with the letter typed by the user when the control has the focus. For example, if you have a Combo Box control with a list of state names in the United States, pressing the letter "N" twice will first select "Nebraska" and then "Nevada." Another method of accessing list elements by name is to track the letters typed by the user and compare them to the first few letters of each list item until a match is found. The following code, found in the global code module, presents one method for implementing such a feature.

```
' ----- Constants used in the ListTyping routine
Public Const TYPING_GOTFOCUS = 1
```

```
Public Const TYPING_KEYDOWN = 2
Public Const TYPING_KEYPRESS = 3
Public Const CB_ERR = (-1)
Public Const CB_FINDSTRING = &H14C
Public Const LB_ERR = (-1)
Public Const LB_FINDSTRING = &H18F
Public Declare Function SendMessage Lib "user32" _
    Alias "SendMessageA" (ByVal hwnd As Long, _
    ByVal wMsg As Long, ByVal wParam As Long, _
    lParam As Any) As Long

Public Function ListTyping(ctrWhich As Control, _
    nMsgType As Integer, nMsgValue As Integer) As Integer
    ' ----- Allow the user to type the name of an item in
    '       a list box or combo box and have the list
    '       jump to that item in the list. This routine
    '       should be called during the GotFocus,
    '       KeyDown, and KeyPress events of the control.
    '       nMsgType is either TYPING_GOTFOCUS,
    '       TYPING_KEYDOWN, or TYPING_KEYPRESS.  If
    '       TYPING_KEYDOWN is used, nMsgValue is KeyCode.
    '       If TYPING_KEYPRESS is used, nMsgValue is
    '       KeyAscii.  WARNING: This function will alter
    '       the Tag property of the control.  The new
    '       KeyCode or KeyAscii is returned.
    Dim sSearch As String
    Dim lPos As Long

    ListTyping = nMsgValue

    Select Case (nMsgType)
        Case TYPING_GOTFOCUS
            ' ----- Start all over
            ctrWhich.Tag = ""
        Case TYPING_KEYDOWN
            ' ----- If movement keys are used, start over
            Select Case (nMsgValue)
                Case vbKeyUp, vbKeyDown, vbKeyLeft, _
                        vbKeyRight, vbKeyHome, vbKeyEnd, _
                        vbKeyPageUp, vbKeyPageDown
                    ctrWhich.Tag = ""
            End Select
        Case TYPING_KEYPRESS
            ' ----- Add this text to the on-going list of
            '       characters and search for a matching
            '       string.  We only care about characters
            '       in the range of printable letters.
            If (nMsgValue >= Asc(" ")) Then
                ctrWhich.Tag = ctrWhich.Tag & _
                    UCase$(Chr$(nMsgValue))
```

```
                    If (ctrWhich.ListIndex <> -1) Then
                        If (Left$(UCase$(ctrWhich.List( _
                                ctrWhich.ListIndex)), _
                                Len(ctrWhich.Tag)) = _
                                ctrWhich.Tag) Then
                            ' ----- We're already on a
                            '         matching item
                            ListTyping = 0
                            Exit Function
                        End If
                    End If
                    sSearch = ctrWhich.Tag & Chr$(0)
                    If (TypeOf ctrWhich Is ComboBox) Then
                        ' ----- Combo box
                        lPos = SendMessage(ctrWhich.hwnd, _
                            CB_FINDSTRING, _
                            ctrWhich.ListIndex, ByVal sSearch)
                    Else
                        ' ----- List box
                        lPos = SendMessage(ctrWhich.hwnd, _
                            LB_FINDSTRING, _
                            ctrWhich.ListIndex, ByVal sSearch)
                    End If
                    If (lPos = CB_ERR) Or (lPos = LB_ERR) Then
                        ' ----- String not found
                        ctrWhich.Tag = ""
                    Else
                        ' ----- Fount it.  Move there.
                        ctrWhich.ListIndex = lPos
                    End If
                    ListTyping = 0
                End If
    End Select
End Function
```

To use this code, call it from the GotFocus, KeyDown, and KeyPress
events of the Combo Box control.

```
Private Sub cboCities_GotFocus()
    ' ----- Handle the list-typing feature
    Call ListTyping(cboCities, TYPING_GOTFOCUS, 0)
End Sub

Private Sub cboCities_KeyDown(KeyCode As Integer, _
        Shift As Integer)
    ' ----- Handle the list-typing feature
    KeyCode = ListTyping(cboCities, TYPING_KEYDOWN, _
        KeyCode)
End Sub
```

```
Private Sub cboCities_KeyPress(KeyAscii As Integer)
    ' ----- Handle the list-typing feature
    KeyAscii = ListTyping(cboCities, TYPING_KEYPRESS, _
        KeyAscii)
End Sub
```

Command Button Control

Purpose   Provides a standard push button action control.
Availability   Core Visual Basic control
Hungarian Prefix   cmd
See Also   Check Box Control

Use the Command Button control as needed within your Visual Basic application. If possible, make all command buttons on each form, and throughout your application, the same width and height.

If you have a need for a very small button, you may find that the text of the button becomes distorted when the button receives the focus. In such a case, consider setting the Style property to Graphical. When using this setting, the text will distort to a lesser extent.

When applicable, include one Command Button control with the Default property set to True, and one Command Button control with the Cancel property set to True on every form. When placing the default and cancel buttons on a form, consider the placement of such buttons as done in other applications. Also consider the user interface guidelines supplied by Microsoft in the *Microsoft Windows User Experience* manual.

If your form contains an **OK** button and a **Cancel** button, and it is possible for the user to save data without closing the form, change the name of the **Cancel** button to "Close" when any data is saved. Consider the form in Figure 11–1.

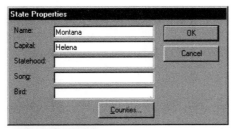

Figure 11–1   *Command Button example.*

The **Counties** button on the State Properties form brings up another form through which each of the state's counties can be maintained. If a user clicks on this button and makes changes to a county, the **Cancel** button on the State Properties form must be changed to "Close" to indicate that changes were made that cannot be canceled. If your form contains **OK**, **Cancel**, and **Apply** buttons, the **Cancel** button should also change to a **Close** button when the **Apply** button is used.

Common Dialog Box Control

Purpose	Provides access to several useful and commonly used dialog boxes.
Availability	Independent control
Hungarian Prefix	dlg

Use the Common Dialog Box control as needed within your Visual Basic application. When instructing the control to display one of its many dialog boxes, do not use the Action property. Instead, use the ShowColor, Show-Font, ShowHelp, ShowOpen, ShowPrinter, or ShowSave method.

Incorrect

```
dlgCommon.Action = 1
```

Correct

```
dlgCommon.ShowOpen
```

If you use the same Common Dialog control for more than one purpose, do not assume that the flags are correct from call to call. Always reset all values to confirm that the flags and other properties of the control are set as expected for each use of the control.

Several of the features of the Common Dialog control access information that resides outside of the control of the Visual Basic application (especially the ShowOpen and ShowSave methods). Therefore, you must always use proper error handling in any procedure that uses these features. Make use of the On Error statement to capture any errors, and take the appropriate corrective action.

The common dialogs encapsulated within the Common Dialog control can be accessed through Windows API calls as well as through this control. For example, there is a WinHelp API function that displays pre-HTMLHelp on-line help.

```
Public Declare Function WinHelp Lib "user32" _
    Alias "WinHelpA" (ByVal hwnd As Long, _
    ByVal lpHelpFile As String, ByVal wCommand As Long, _
    ByVal dwData As Any) As Long
```

Table 11.1 describes some of the API calls that can be used to replace the use of the Common Dialog control.

	Table 11.1	Common Dialogs via API Calls		
Feature	API Function	Location	Microsoft Knowledge Base Article
HTML Help	HTMLHelp	hhctrl.ocx	Q183434
Win Help	WinHelp	user32.dll	Q202563
File Open	GetOpenFileName	comdlg32.dll	Q161286
File Save	GetSaveFileName	comdlg32.dll	N/A
Choose Font	ChooseFont	comdlg32.dll	N/A
Choose Color	ChooseColor	comdlg32.dll	N/A

The declarations for each of the API calls in Table 11.1 can be found in the API viewer program that ships with Visual Basic.

Communication Control

Purpose   Provides access to the system's serial port(s).
Availability   Independent control
Hungarian Prefix   comm
See Also   Internet Transfer Control, Winsock Control

Use the Communication control (MSComm) as needed within your Visual Basic application. Several of the features of the Communication control access information that resides outside of the control of the Visual Basic application. Therefore, you must always use proper error handling in any procedure that uses these features. Make use of the On Error statement to capture any errors, and take the appropriate corrective action.

Once you establish a connection via a serial port, there is no guarantee that the connection will remain until you no longer need it. Handle unexpected termination of serial communication gracefully. Alert the user to the situation, and either retry the connection, cleanly exit the application, or degrade performance where appropriate.

Cool Bar Control

Purpose   Provides a multi-band set of subordinate controls.
Availability   Windows Common Controls set 3
Hungarian Prefix   clb
See Also   Toolbar Control

Use the Cool Bar control as needed within your Visual Basic application. While the Align property can be set to "None," never use this setting. Set the alignment to one of the four sides of the window.

Data Control

Purpose	Provides a VCR-style interface for scrolling through a set of data.
Availability	Core Visual Basic control
Hungarian Prefix	dta
See Also	ADO Data Control, Remote Data Control

Use the Data control within your Visual Basic application to connect one or more data bound controls to a database recordset. However, the Data control itself should not be made visible to the user. Use more user-friendly data manipulation methods instead. See Chapter 12, *Database Standards*, for a discussion of data manipulation methods.

Data Combo Control

Purpose	Provides data-focused functionality similar to what is found in the Combo Box control.
Availability	Independent control
Hungarian Prefix	cbo
See Also	Combo Box Control, Image Combo Control

Use the Data Combo control as needed within your Visual Basic application. However, if you can perform the same functionality using the standard Combo Box control, then use the standard control instead.

The Data Combo control provides two methods for looking up list entries through the keyboard: Basic (single-key lookup) and Extended (multi-key lookup). You indicate the method to use through the MatchEntry property. Always use the Extended setting for this property unless you must maintain compatibility with other applications that use the Basic setting.

Several of the features of the Data Combo control access information that resides outside of the control of the Visual Basic application. Therefore, you must always use proper error handling in any procedure that uses these features. Make use of the On Error statement to capture any errors, and take the appropriate corrective action.

Many of the guidelines that apply to standard Combo Box controls also apply to the Data Combo control. See the entry for "Combo Box Control" elsewhere in this chapter for additional information

Data Grid Control

Purpose	Provides spreadsheet-style display and possible entry of user data in association with a data source.
Availability	Independent control
Hungarian Prefix	grd
See Also	Flex Grid Control, Hierarchical Flex Grid Control

Use the Data Grid control as needed within your Visual Basic application. The Flex Grid control has a slightly different visual presentation and feature set, which you may prefer in your application.

While the grid is useful for displaying record-based information, avoid using it for entry or update of records of data. When you consider the table view of data presented in Microsoft Access, it is a very useful tool for entering a lot of data in a small amount of screen real estate. However, it is often inadequate for the average user. That is why Microsoft Access has a form designer built in. If you need large amounts of data entered quickly by technical personnel, it is reasonable to use a grid entry form. In all other cases, create forms designed for the purpose of gathering record-based data, using distinct controls for each field of input.

Data List Control

Purpose	Provides data-focused functionality similar to what is found in the List Box control.
Availability	Independent control
Hungarian Prefix	lst
See Also	Data Combo Control, List Box Control

Use the Data List control as needed within your Visual Basic application. However, if you can perform the same functionality using the standard List Box control, then use the standard control instead.

The Data List control provides two methods for looking up list entries through the keyboard: Basic (single-key lookup) and Extended (multi-key lookup). You indicate the method to use through the MatchEntry property. Always use the Extended setting for this property unless you must maintain compatibility with other applications that use the Basic setting.

Several of the features of the Data List control access information that resides outside of the control of the Visual Basic application. Therefore, you must always use proper error handling in any procedure that uses these features. Make use of the On Error statement to capture any errors, and take the appropriate corrective action.

Many of the guidelines that apply to standard List Box controls also apply to the Data List control. See the entry for "List Box Control" elsewhere in this chapter for additional information

Data Repeater Control

Purpose	Repeats the display of a data bound control for entry or display of a series of data records.
Availability	Independent control
Hungarian Prefix	drp

Do not use the Data Repeater control within your Visual Basic application. In general, the user should not be required to simultaneously manipulate the details of multiple records of data. Use another method, such as separate summary and detail forms, to present data to or gather information from the user.

Date Time Picker Control

Purpose	Provides a data entry field specially designed for date or time input. Date input includes a drop-down calendar feature.
Availability	Windows Common Controls set 2
Hungarian Prefix	dtp
See Also	Calendar Control, Month View Control

Use the Date Time Picker control as needed within your Visual Basic application. If there are realistic minimum or maximum values for the range of dates processed with the control, always set the MinDate and MaxDate properties. Be aware that the format string supplied to the CustomFormat property is not the same as the format string used with the Visual Basic Format function.

    If you will be using a user-supplied value to initialize the Value property of the Date Time Picker control, verify that it is a valid date in the range you specify for the control. Visual Basic can represent dates as numeric values. If the user supplies a number that you pass to the Value property, unexpected displays may result. The following routine checks for a valid date, and also checks for a four-digit year.

```
Public Function CheckDate(sOrigDate As String) _
      As Boolean
   ' ----- Return True if the supplied value is a date
   '       with a four-digit year.
   CheckDate = False
   If (Not(IsDate(sOrigDate))) Then Exit Function
   If (InStr(sOrigDate, CStr(Year(sOrigDate))) <> 0) Then
      CheckDate = True
   End If
End Function
```

Dir List Box Control

Purpose	Provides a list of sub-directories in the indicated directory.
Availability	Core Visual Basic control
Hungarian Prefix	dir
See Also	Common Dialog Control, Drive List Box Control, File List Box Control, List View Control, Tree View Control

Avoid using the Dir List Box control in your Visual Basic applications. If possible, replace its functionality with the File Open or File Save dialog boxes (accessed through the Common Dialog control), with one of the other Windows provided dialog boxes (available through API calls), or with a third-party control. You can also design your own file and directory access controls using the Tree View control and the List View control.

Drive List Box Control

Purpose	Provides a list of local and mapped drives.
Availability	Core Visual Basic control
Hungarian Prefix	drv
See Also	Common Dialog Control, Dir List Box Control, File List Box Control, List View Control, Tree View Control

Avoid using the Drive List Box control in your Visual Basic applications. If possible, replace its functionality with the File Open or File Save dialog boxes (accessed through the Common Dialog control), with one of the other Windows provided dialog boxes (available through API calls), or with a third-party control. You can also design your own file and directory access controls using the Tree View control and the List View control.

File List Box Control

Purpose	Provides a list of files in the indicated directory.
Availability	Core Visual Basic control
Hungarian Prefix	fil
See Also	Common Dialog Control, Dir List Box Control, Drive List Box Control, List View Control, Tree View Control

Avoid using the File List Box control in your Visual Basic applications. If possible, replace its functionality with the File Open or File Save dialog boxes (accessed through the Common Dialog control), with one of the other Windows provided dialog boxes (available through API calls), or with a third-party control. You can also design your own file and directory access controls using the Tree View control and the List View control.

Flat Scroll Bar Control

Purpose	Provides a scroll bar, in both horizontal and vertical orientations, that appears in both a standard and a "flat" look.
Availability	Windows Common Controls set 2
Hungarian Prefix	hsb, vsb
See Also	Horizontal Scroll Bar Control, Slider Control, Vertical Scroll Bar Control

Use the Flat Scroll Bar control as needed within your Visual Basic application. If you do not need the special visual functionality provided by the Flat Scroll Bar control, consider the standard Horizontal or Vertical Scroll Bar controls instead. Note that, when using the Flat Scroll Bar control, the Hungarian prefix is either "hsb" or "vsb," depending on the orientation of the scroll bar.

Always set the SmallChange property to the smallest possible increment. When setting the LargeChange property, consider the functionality of the List Box control, which always overlaps the elements when the user performs a large change activity. In Figure 11–2, list element "5" remains in view after the user clicks in the scroll bar bucket.

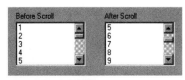

Figure 11–2   *A list box before and after a large change.*

The Flat Scroll Bar control provides two primary events for detecting changes to the thumb position: Change and Scroll. Use either or both events as needed. However, avoid complex or time-consuming processing within the Scroll event. Use the Scroll event to visibly inform the user that the data position is changing. Use the Change event to update all related screen elements and application values based on the Value property.

It is possible to size the Flat Scroll Bar control so small that the thumb between the two arrows of the control disappears. If you size a scroll bar based on the user sizing of a window, it is all right to let the scroll bar become this small. In other instances, do not use the Flat Scroll Bar without the thumb displayed. If you wish to use only the arrows of the control without the thumb, consider the Up Down control or other suitable replacement instead.

If the scroll bar is used only to obtain a value, and not to visibly scroll information in another control or screen area (as is done with the scroll bar of the List Box control), consider the Slider control instead.

Flex Grid Control

Purpose	Provides spreadsheet-style display and possible entry of user data.
Availability	Independent control
Hungarian Prefix	grd
See Also	Data Grid Control, Hierarchical Flex Grid Control

Use the Flex Grid control (MSFlexGrid) as needed within your Visual Basic application. The Data Grid control has a slightly different visual presentation and feature set, which you may prefer in your application.

When accessing the text within a cell, do not move to the cell by modifying the Col and Row properties. Instead, use the TextArray or TextMatrix property to access or modify the cell's contents. Only use the Text property if you have arrived at a cell due to user action or documented application behavior.

While the Flex Grid control is useful for displaying record-based or spreadsheet-style information, avoid using it for the entry of records of data. When you consider the table view of data presented in Microsoft Access, it is a very useful tool for entering a lot of data in a small amount of screen real estate. However, it is often inadequate for the average user. That is why Microsoft Access has a form designer built in. If you need large amounts of data entered quickly by technical personnel, it is reasonable to use a grid entry form. In all other cases, create forms designed for the purpose of gathering record-based data, using distinct controls for each field of input.

The Flex Grid control does not, by itself, have the proper visual interface for text entry, or any other type of data entry. The cells in the control are read only. While you can use the various keyboard events of the control to intercept user input, the control gives no visual indication as to which cell has the focus (such as the blinking line of the insertion point). To accept user input in the grid, "hover" a more applicable control, such as a text box, over the cell that would have the focus. The Flex Grid control has various properties, such as CellLeft, CellTop, CellWidth, and CellHeight, to assist you with the placement of the data entry control.

Frame Control

Purpose	Visually groups user interface controls.
Availability	Core Visual Basic control
Hungarian Prefix	fra
See Also	Picture Box Control

Use the Frame control as needed within your Visual Basic application. If your form contains only a Frame control with its constituent controls, and **OK** and **Cancel** buttons, remove the Frame control and place all other controls directly on the form.

Never hover a control over a Frame control. If a control is meant to appear visibly within the confines of a Frame control, draw the control directly on the Frame control, not on the form background.

If you set the Enabled property of a Frame control to False, all constituent controls are disabled as well. However, those subordinate controls do not give the appearance of being disabled. Therefore, always set the Enabled property of all constituent controls to False when disabling a Frame control.

Do not place permanently invisible controls or labels on a Frame control. Instead, place such informational controls directly on the form.

Hierarchical Flex Grid Control

Purpose	Provides spreadsheet-style display of data with expandable parent-child relationships.
Availability	Independent control
Hungarian Prefix	hgrd
See Also	Data Grid Control, Flex Grid Control

Use the Hierarchical Flex Grid control (MSHFlexGrid) with great restraint for displaying data within your Visual Basic application. In those cases where it is used, it should be limited to forms that only technical personnel will use. When designing interfaces for the end user, always use another method, such as multiple form views, to present data. Never use the Hierarchical Flex Grid control for direct input of user data, either through the events of the control, or by hovering other controls over the grid control.

If you must use the Hierarchical Flex Grid control to present data in your form, document the relationships between the different levels of the hierarchy in your source code comments.

Horizontal Scroll Bar Control

Purpose	Provides a scroll bar with a thumb that moves from left to right to left.
Availability	Core Visual Basic control
Hungarian Prefix	hsb
See Also	Flat Scroll Bar Control, Slider Control, Vertical Scroll Bar Control

Use the Horizontal Scroll Bar control (HScrollBar) as needed within your Visual Basic application. In some interfaces, you may also wish to consider use of the Flat Scroll Bar control, especially when your application responds to a scroll wheel available in some mouse input devices.

Always set the SmallChange property to the smallest possible increment. When setting the LargeChange property, consider the functionality of the List Box control, which always overlaps the elements when the user performs a large change activity. In Figure 11–3, list element "5" remains in view after the user clicks in the scroll bar bucket.

The Horizontal Scroll Bar control provides two primary events for detecting changes to the thumb position: Change and Scroll. Use either or both events as needed. However, avoid complex or time-consuming processing within the Scroll event. Use the Scroll event to visibly inform the user that the data position is changing. Use the Change event to update all related screen elements and application values based on the Value property.

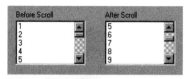

| Figure 11–3 | *A list box before and after a large change.* |

It is possible to size the Horizontal Scroll Bar control so small that the thumb between the two arrows of the control disappears. If you size a scroll bar based on the user sizing of a window, it is all right to let the scroll bar become this small. In other instances, do not use the Horizontal Scroll Bar control without the thumb displayed. If you wish to use only the arrows of the control without the thumb, consider the Up Down control or other suitable replacement instead.

If the scroll bar is used only to obtain a value, and not to visibly scroll information in another control or screen area (as is done with the scroll bar of the List Box control), consider the Slider control instead.

Image Control

Purpose	Displays images on a form or container control background.
Availability	Core Visual Basic control
Hungarian Prefix	pic
See Also	Image List Control, Picture Box Control, Picture Clip Control

Use the Image control as needed within your Visual Basic application. When including a picture in the control at design time, always store a separate copy of the graphic file within your set of technical documentation or source code directory tree. Note that the Hungarian prefix for this control is the same as that for the Picture Box control.

Image Combo Control

Purpose	Provides a drop-down list capable of displaying images as well as text.
Availability	Windows Common Controls set 1
Hungarian Prefix	icbo
See Also	Combo Box Control, Data Combo Control, Image List Control

Use the Image Combo control as needed within your Visual Basic application. Many of the guidelines that apply to standard Combo Box controls also apply to the Image Combo control. See the entry for "Combo Box Control" elsewhere in this chapter for additional information

Image List Control

Purpose	Provides a set of identically sized images for use with other controls or drawing commands.
Availability	Windows Common Controls set 1
Hungarian Prefix	img
See Also	Image Control, Picture Box Control, Picture Clip Control

Use the Image List control as needed within your Visual Basic application. When referencing images in your source code, either identify each image using its key value, or define a set of constants to use with the Index position of each image. Never identify an image by a literal numeric index.

When including a picture in the control at design time, always store a separate copy of the graphic file within your set of technical documentation or source code directory tree.

Internet Transfer Control

Purpose	Provides tools for accessing various Internet protocols, including FTP, HTTP, HTTPS, and Gopher.
Availability	Independent control
Hungarian Prefix	inet
See Also	Web Browser Control, Winsock Control

Use the Internet Transfer control as needed within your Visual Basic application. If the control will be used with a single protocol (such as FTP), always include the name of the protocol in the control name, as in "inetFtpRemote" for a remote FTP connection control.

Even if your application will always connect to a specific static address, do not hard code any network addresses or Uniform Resource Locators (URL) within your source code. Instead, store connection destinations in an INI-type file, in a proprietary format configuration file, or in the Windows registry.

Always formally close all open connections when they are no longer needed. Include in your technical documentation all connection usage information, indicating any special expectations for the remote system.

The Internet Transfer control accesses information that resides outside of the control of the Visual Basic application. Therefore, you must always use proper error handling in any procedure that deals with any functionality of the Internet Transfer control that can generate an error. In addition, you should expect that the remote server may become unavailable at any time. Handle all such connection changes gracefully.

Label Control

Purpose	Displays static text.
Availability	Core Visual Basic control

Hungarian Prefix   lbl
See Also   Line Drawing Object, Shape Drawing Object

Use the Label control as needed within your Visual Basic application. Only use labels to display static text, user data, or other messages. Never use a label as a data storage mechanism. If you need to share a piece of information between multiple forms, use a global variable, or pass the information from one form to another through public functions.

When using a Label control to display user-supplied or data source-supplied information, either set the UseMnemonic property to False, or convert all single ampersand characters ("&") to sets of two ampersand characters.

```
lblResult.Caption = Replace$(sResult, "&", "&&")
```

Always place labels in the proper tab order, along with the other controls on your form, even if you will not be using the label as a title for another control. When a label is a title for another control, it is essential that the Label control appear just before the related control in the tab order so that the shortcut key indicated in the label can properly transfer the focus to the related control.

Always set the AutoSize property to True for single-line, short labels. For multi-line labels, allow for some additional space in the size of the label to account for any font size differences between individual client workstations. Be aware that labels and other drawing objects exist in a different Z-order plane from other controls.

Line Drawing Object

Purpose   Displays a line on the form or control on which the object is placed.
Availability   Core Visual Basic control
Hungarian Prefix   lin
See Also   Shape Drawing Object

Use the Line drawing object as needed within your Visual Basic application. Unless you must have a line of a specific color, use system colors when assigning the color value of the line.

List Box Control

Purpose   Provides basic single and multiple selection from a list of items.
Availability   Core Visual Basic control
Hungarian Prefix   lst
See Also   Combo Box Control, Data List Control

Use the List Box control as needed within your Visual Basic application. If the user will only select one item from a relatively small list of items, it may be more efficient to use the Combo Box control.

When adding items to and referencing items in a List Box control, always identify an item by its associated ItemData value, never by its position. Even if you are adding a known number of items in a known order to the control, always supply and use the ItemData values. When adding new items, use the NewIndex property to correctly interact with the new item.

Incorrect

```
lstDiamond.Clear
lstDiamond.AddItem "First Base"
lstDiamond.ItemData(0) = FIRST_BASE
```

Correct

```
lstDiamond.Clear
lstDiamond.AddItem "First Base"
lstDiamond.ItemData(lstDiamond.NewIndex) = FIRST_BASE
```

Once you have added your items to the List Box control, you can access them by their ItemData value. The following function is useful for accessing the index of an item by its ItemData value. It returns -1 when no matching item is found.

```
Public Function ListByItem(ctrWhich As Control, _
        lItemData As Long) As Long
    ' ----- Locate an item in a List Box or Combo Box
    '        control.  Return the position, or -1 if
    '        the item is not found.
    Dim lCounter As Long

    On Error Resume Next
    ListByItem = -1

    ' ----- Compare each item in the list.
    For lCounter = 0 to ctrWhich.ListCount - 1
        If (ctrWhich.ItemData(lCounter) = lItemData) Then
            ' ----- Found a match.
            ListByItem = lCounter
            Exit For
        End If
    Next lCounter
End Function
```

In general, when adding a multiple selection List Box control to your form, use Extended selection (MultiSelect 2) instead of Simple selection (MultiSelect 1). If you do use a Simple multiple selection list, include both a **Select All** and a **Clear All** Command Button control next to the list box.

Do not use the Scroll event for major display or data processing. Use the Scroll event only to make minor display or data adjustments. Use the Click, DblClick, or ItemCheck event for complete display and data processing.

Never assume that a user selected a list item, especially when using a single selection List Box control. Always test the ListIndex property to verify that a list item was selected before you work with the control's ItemData, List, or Selected arrays.

By default, the List Box control moves to the next item that begins with the letter typed by the user when the control has the focus. For example, if you have a List Box control with a list of state names in the United States, pressing the letter "N" twice will first select "Nebraska" and then "Nevada." Another method of accessing list elements by name is to track the letters typed by the user and compare them to the first few letters of each list item until a match is found. The following code, found in the global code module, presents one method for implementing such a feature.

```
' ----- Constants used in the ListTyping routine
Public Const TYPING_GOTFOCUS = 1
Public Const TYPING_KEYDOWN = 2
Public Const TYPING_KEYPRESS = 3
Public Const CB_ERR = (-1)
Public Const CB_FINDSTRING = &H14C
Public Const LB_ERR = (-1)
Public Const LB_FINDSTRING = &H18F
Public Declare Function SendMessage Lib "user32" _
    Alias "SendMessageA" (ByVal hwnd As Long, _
    ByVal wMsg As Long, ByVal wParam As Long, _
    lParam As Any) As Long

Public Function ListTyping(ctrWhich As Control, _
    nMsgType As Integer, nMsgValue As Integer) As Integer
    ' ----- Allow the user to type the name of an item in
    '       a list box or combo box and have the list
    '       jump to that item in the list. This routine
    '       should be called during the GotFocus,
    '       KeyDown, and KeyPress events of the control.
    '       nMsgType is either TYPING_GOTFOCUS,
    '       TYPING_KEYDOWN, or TYPING_KEYPRESS.  If
    '       TYPING_KEYDOWN is used, nMsgValue is KeyCode.
    '       If TYPING_KEYPRESS is used, nMsgValue is
    '       KeyAscii.  WARNING: This function will alter
    '       the Tag property of the control.  The new
    '       KeyCode or KeyAscii is returned.
    Dim sSearch As String
    Dim lPos As Long

    ListTyping = nMsgValue
```

```
Select Case (nMsgType)
    Case TYPING_GOTFOCUS
        ' ----- Start all over
        ctrWhich.Tag = ""
    Case TYPING_KEYDOWN
        ' ----- If movement keys are used, start over
        Select Case (nMsgValue)
            Case vbKeyUp, vbKeyDown, vbKeyLeft, _
                    vbKeyRight, vbKeyHome, vbKeyEnd, _
                    vbKeyPageUp, vbKeyPageDown
                ctrWhich.Tag = ""
        End Select
    Case TYPING_KEYPRESS
        ' ----- Add this text to the on-going list of
        '       characters and search for a matching
        '       string.  We only care about characters
        '       in the range of printable letters.
        If (nMsgValue >= Asc(" ")) Then
            ctrWhich.Tag = ctrWhich.Tag & _
                UCase$(Chr$(nMsgValue))
            If (ctrWhich.ListIndex <> -1) Then
                If (Left$(UCase$(ctrWhich.List( _
                        ctrWhich.ListIndex)), _
                        Len(ctrWhich.Tag)) = _
                        ctrWhich.Tag) Then
                    ' ----- We're already on a
                    '           matching item
                    ListTyping = 0
                    Exit Function
                End If
            End If
            sSearch = ctrWhich.Tag & Chr$(0)
            If (TypeOf ctrWhich Is ComboBox) Then
                ' ----- Combo box
                lPos = SendMessage(ctrWhich.hwnd, _
                    CB_FINDSTRING, _
                    ctrWhich.ListIndex, ByVal sSearch)
            Else
                ' ----- List box
                lPos = SendMessage(ctrWhich.hwnd, _
                    LB_FINDSTRING, _
                    ctrWhich.ListIndex, ByVal sSearch)
            End If
            If (lPos = CB_ERR) Or (lPos = LB_ERR) Then
                ' ----- String not found
                ctrWhich.Tag = ""
            Else
                ' ----- Fount it.  Move there.
                ctrWhich.ListIndex = lPos
            End If
```

```
              ListTyping = 0
          End If
     End Select
End Function
```

To use this code, call it from the GotFocus, KeyDown, and KeyPress events of the List Box control.

```
Private Sub lstStates_GotFocus()
    ' ----- Handle the list-typing feature
    Call ListTyping(lstStates, TYPING_GOTFOCUS, 0)
End Sub

Private Sub lstStates_KeyDown(KeyCode As Integer, _
        Shift As Integer)
    ' ----- Handle the list-typing feature
    KeyCode = ListTyping(lstStates, TYPING_KEYDOWN, _
        KeyCode)
End Sub

Private Sub lstStates_KeyPress(KeyAscii As Integer)
    ' ----- Handle the list-typing feature
    KeyAscii = ListTyping(lstStates, TYPING_KEYPRESS, _
        KeyAscii)
End Sub
```

This code should not be used with lists that employ the Checkbox style (Style 1) or Simple multi-selection (MultiSelect 1). In both of these instances, the space character has a special meaning that would defeat the use of the "list typing" code.

List View Control

Purpose   Provides multiple views for a list of items, with optional subordinate data elements.

Availability   Windows Common Controls set 1

Hungarian Prefix   lvw

See Also   List Box Control, Tree View Control

Use the List View control as needed within your Visual Basic application. Always identify each node in the List View control by its key value, never by its absolute or relative position. Also, when referencing the columns in your source code, either identify each column using its key value, or define a set of constants to use with the position of each column. Never identify a column by a literal numeric index.

When accessing the sub-items of a list item, always use the ListSubItems property instead of the SubItems property. The SubItems property is used only for backward compatibility.

MAPI Message Control

Purpose	Manages the sending, receiving, and organization of mail messages.
Availability	Independent control
Hungarian Prefix	mpm
See Also	MAPI Session Control

Use the MAPI Message control as needed within your Visual Basic application. If you will be sending mail, deleting mail, or in any other way modifying the configuration of the user's mail transport, clearly inform the user, either through documentation or through application notification. Always document all connection expectations and resource requirements in your technical documentation.

Even if your application will always send mail to a specific user or destination, do not hard code any mail addresses within your source code. Instead, store address information in an INI-type file, in a proprietary format configuration file, or in the Windows registry. You may wish to prompt the user for address information.

Several of the features of the MAPI Message control access information that resides outside of the control of the Visual Basic application. Therefore, you must always use proper error handling in any procedure that uses these features. Make use of the On Error statement to capture any errors, and take the appropriate corrective action.

Once you establish a connection with a mail host through the MAPI Session control, there is no guarantee that the connection will remain until you no longer need it. Handle unexpected termination from the host gracefully. Alert the user to the situation, and either retry the connection, cleanly exit the application, or degrade performance where appropriate.

MAPI Session Control

Purpose	Establishes a connection to a mail host.
Availability	Independent control
Hungarian Prefix	mps
See Also	MAPI Message Control

Use the MAPI Session control as needed within your Visual Basic application. If you will be sending mail, deleting mail, or in any other way modifying the configuration of the user's mail transport, clearly inform the user, either through documentation or through application notification. Always document all connection expectations and resource requirements in your technical documentation.

Even if your application will always connect to a specific host, do not hard code any mail connection information within your source code. Instead, store connection information in an INI-type file, in a proprietary format configuration file, or in the Windows registry. You may wish to prompt the user for connection information.

Several of the features of the MAPI Session control access information that resides outside of the control of the Visual Basic application. Therefore, you must always use proper error handling in any procedure that uses these features. Make use of the On Error statement to capture any errors, and take the appropriate corrective action.

Once you establish a connection with a mail host, there is no guarantee that the connection will remain until you no longer need it. Handle unexpected termination from the host gracefully. Alert the user to the situation, and either retry the connection, cleanly exit the application, or degrade performance where appropriate.

Masked Edit Control

Purpose	Provides a text input field that limits user input to a specific data format.
Availability	Independent control
Hungarian Prefix	txt
See Also	Text Box Control

Use the Masked Edit control as needed within your Visual Basic application. However, if you can efficiently and correctly provide the same functionality using a simple Text Box control and data verification source code, use that method instead. Note that the Hungarian prefix for this control is the same as that for the Text Box control.

Menu Control

Purpose	Provides form-level and pop-up (shortcut) menu support.
Availability	Core Visual Basic control
Hungarian Prefix	mnu
See Also	Toolbar Control

Use menu controls as needed within your Visual Basic application. Menus are named using Hungarian naming conventions, but with some special differences. For details about naming guidelines for menus, see Chapter 9, *Declaration Standards*, and especially Table 9.9, which gives an example for naming menus.

Never create a top-level menu without a subordinate menu. If you are creating a dynamic list of items under a top-level menu, and there are currently no items available for display under the top-level menu item, either hide the menu altogether, or add a disabled subordinate menu item that says something like "Not Available." Figures 11–4 and 11–5 show correct and incorrect uses of a single-item menu.

It is often useful to include hidden menus on a form to be used as pop-up or shortcut menus. If you have such hidden menus, either document this

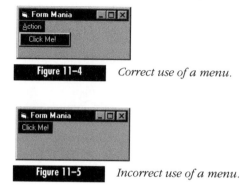

Figure 11-4   *Correct use of a menu.*

Figure 11-5   *Incorrect use of a menu.*

fact in the Declarations section of the form's source code, or include a label with its Visible property set to False that says something like "WARNING: Hidden menus on form."

Month View Control

Purpose	Provides a calendar for interactive date selection functionality.
Availability	Windows Common Controls set 2
Hungarian Prefix	mvw
See Also	Calendar Control, Date Time Picker Control

Use the Month View control as needed within your Visual Basic application. If there are realistic minimum or maximum values for the range of dates processed with the control, always set the MinDate and MaxDate properties.

If you will be using a user-supplied value to initialize the Value property of the Month View control, verify that it is a valid date in the range you specify for the control. Visual Basic can represent dates as numeric values. If the user supplies a number that you pass to the Value property, unexpected displays may result. The following routine checks for a valid date, and also checks for a four-digit year.

```
Public Function CheckDate(sOrigDate As String) _
     As Boolean
   ' ----- Return True if the supplied value is a date
   '        with a four-digit year.
   CheckDate = False
   If (Not(IsDate(sOrigDate))) Then Exit Function
   If (InStr(sOrigDate, CStr(Year(sOrigDate))) <> 0) Then
      CheckDate = True
   End If
End Function
```

Multimedia Control

Purpose	Provides access to multimedia (MCI) devices and data.
Availability	Independent control
Hungarian Prefix	mm
See Also	Animation Control

Use the Multimedia (MCI) control as needed within your Visual Basic application. Do not hard code any resource or device information within your source code. Instead, store such information in an INI-type file, in a proprietary format configuration file, or in the Windows registry. Document all resource expectations and interactions, and application-supplied file information, in your technical documentation.

The Multimedia control accesses information that resides outside of the control of the Visual Basic application. Therefore, you must always use proper error handling in any procedure that deals with any functionality of the Multimedia control that can generate an error. In addition, you should expect that communication with an MCI device may fail at any time. Handle all such failures gracefully.

OLE Control

Purpose	Allows a form to contain linked or embedded information from another application, data, or document source.
Availability	Core Visual Basic control
Hungarian Prefix	ole

Use the OLE (Container) control as needed within your Visual Basic application. Document all expectations and interactions for the contained OLE linked object, embedded object, data source, or document in your technical documentation. Also document the purpose and usage of the remote application or document.

The OLE control accesses information that resides outside of the control of the Visual Basic application. Therefore, you must always use proper error handling in any procedure that deals with any functionality of the OLE control that can generate an error. Make use of the On Error statement to capture any errors, and take the appropriate corrective action.

Option Button Control

Purpose	Provides selection from a small group of items.
Availability	Core Visual Basic control
Hungarian Prefix	opt
See Also	Check Box Control, Combo Box control, Frame Control

Use the Option Button control as needed within your Visual Basic application. Option Button controls must always appear as part of a control array. Always use more than one Option Button control together as a group of mutually exclusive choices. Never use the Option Button control as a stand-alone toggle control. Use a Check Box control to handle such Boolean functionality.

Always visually group related Option Button controls together on a form, either by surrounding the controls (for instance, with a Frame control), or through indentation under a parent control. If multiple groups of Option Button controls appear on a single form, make them visually distinct.

Include no more than six Option Button controls within a single selection group. If you have more than six choices, use a Combo Box control instead, populated with the selection choices.

Picture Box Control

Purpose	Displays images and contains other user interface controls.
Availability	Core Visual Basic control
Hungarian Prefix	pic
See Also	Image Control

Use the Picture Box control as needed within your Visual Basic application. If you will only use the Picture Box control to display an image, and the display functionality you need exists in the Image control, use the Image control instead. When including a picture in the control at design time, always store a separate copy of the graphic file within your set of technical documentation or source code directory tree.

If you do not need a Picture Box control to specifically receive the focus, set the TabStop property to False. If you are using a Picture Box control to contain other user interface controls, you should generally set the TabStop property to False.

Always set the ScaleMode property of the Picture Box control to the same setting as the ScaleMode property of the form on which the control is placed. If you need to have different ScaleMode settings between the form and the control, indicate the reason for this in the Declarations section's comments.

Do not place permanently invisible controls or labels on a Picture Box control. Instead, place such informational controls directly on the form.

Picture Clip Control

Purpose	Stores an image from which areas of the image can be conveniently accessed and used.
Availability	Independent control
Hungarian Prefix	clp
See Also	Image Control, ImageList Control, Picture Box Control

Use the Picture Clip control as needed within your Visual Basic application. When including a picture in the control at design time, always store a separate copy of the graphic file within your set of technical documentation or source code directory tree.

Progress Bar Control

Purpose	Provides a graphic gauge of the progress of an activity.
Availability	Windows Common Controls set 1
Hungarian Prefix	prg
See Also	Status Bar Control

Use the Progress Bar control as needed within your Visual Basic application. In general, place no more than one progress bar within a single window. If you need to provide status for multiple scales of information, use a single progress bar to indicate overall status, then use a Label control to provide additional information.

Remote Data Control

Purpose	Provides a VCR-style interface for scrolling through a set of remote data.
Availability	Independent control
Hungarian Prefix	dta
See Also	ADO Data Control, Data Control

Use the Remote Data control (MSRDC) within your Visual Basic application to connect one or more data bound controls to a database recordset. However, the Remote Data control itself should not be made visible to the user. Use more user-friendly data manipulation methods instead. See Chapter 12, *Database Standards*, for a discussion of data manipulation methods.

Rich Text Box Control

Purpose	Provides a text entry field with word processor-style features.
Availability	Independent control
Hungarian Prefix	rtf
See Also	Text Box Control

Use the Rich Text Box control as needed within your Visual Basic application. However, if you will use the control for standard text entry, and you have no need for formatting the text, use a standard Text Box control instead.

Even if your application will always use the same file as the text source for the control, do not hard code the name of the file either in the control's

FileName property, or in the source code of your application. Instead, prompt the user for the location of the file, or store the file name in an INI-type file, in a proprietary format configuration file, or in the Windows registry.

Shape Drawing Object

Purpose   Displays a shape on the form or control on which the
                       object is placed.
Availability   Core Visual Basic control
Hungarian Prefix   shp
See Also   Line Drawing Object

Use the Shape drawing object as needed within your Visual Basic application. Unless you must have a shape of a specific color, use system colors when assigning the color value of the shape.

Slider Control

Purpose   Provides a graphic method of selecting one of a range
                       of values from an overall range.
Availability   Windows Common Controls set 1
Hungarian Prefix   sld
See Also   Flat Scroll Bar, Horizontal Scroll Bar, Vertical Scroll Bar

Use the Slider control as needed within your Visual Basic application. Always set the SmallChange and LargeChange properties to reasonable values for your use of the control.

Status Bar Control

Purpose   Provides a display of grouped status values.
Availability   Windows Common Controls set 1
Hungarian Prefix   sts
See Also   Progress Bar Control, Tool Bar Control

Use the Status Bar control as needed within your Visual Basic application. The status bar should always be aligned along the bottom of the window in which it appears. Always display a minimal amount of status text within the control. At the very least, display generic text such as "Ready" or "Press F1 for help" in the first panel or in the Simple Text panel.

Sys Info Control

Purpose   Provides useful metrics and information about the
                       local system.
Availability   Independent control

| **Hungarian Prefix** | sys |
| **See Also** | Common Dialog Control |

Use the Sys Info control as needed within your Visual Basic application. Some information obtained through the Sys Info control can be accessed in other ways, especially through Windows API calls. For example, the ScrollBarSize property of the Sys Info control can be obtained through the GetSystemMetrics API call.

```
' ----- In the Declarations section
Private Const SM_CXVSCROLL = 2
Private Declare Function GetSystemMetrics Lib "user32" _
    (ByVal nIndex As Long) As Long

' ----- Later, in a routine
    nScrollBarSize = GetSystemMetrics(SM_CXVSCROLL) * _
        Screen.TwipsPerPixelX
```

Tab Strip Control

Purpose	Divides your form into distinct "tabbed" areas, to allow logical grouping of controls and functionality.
Availability	Windows Common Controls set 1
Hungarian Prefix	tab
See Also	Tabbed Dialog Control

Use the Tab Strip control as needed within your Visual Basic application. When referencing the tabs in your source code, either identify each tab using its key value, or define a set of constants to use with the position of each tab. Never identify a tab by a literal numeric index.

In general, you will include multiple Picture Box controls on your form as containers for your tabbed pages, one Picture Box control for each Tab in your Tab Strip control. When naming the Picture Box controls, give them names that are similar to the Key values assigned to the related tabs in the Tab Strip control. You may also wish to create the Picture Box controls in a control array. In this case, use the same Index value for both the tabs in your Tab Strip control and the associated Picture Box controls. Create a set of constants used to access both the tabs and the Picture Box controls.

When designing your form, you may find it useful to tile the Picture Box controls on top of each other, each slightly offset from the adjacent controls. Also, setting the BorderStyle property to Fixed Single (1) will make the Picture Box controls more distinct, as shown in Figure 11–6. Set the Visible properties of the Picture Box controls so that the default control is visible, but all other controls are invisible.

Use the Form_Load routine to arrange the elements of the form into their proper states.

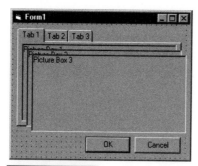

Figure 11-6   *Tab Strip and Picture Box controls.*

```
Private Sub Form_Load()
    ' ----- Prepare the form
    picTab2.Left = picTab1.Left
    picTab2.Top = picTab1.Top
    picTab3.Left = picTab1.Left
    picTab3.Top = picTab1.Top
    picTab1.BorderStyle = vbBSNone
    picTab2.BorderStyle = vbBSNone
    picTab3.BorderStyle = vbBSNone
End Sub
```

The Tab Strip control has many options for the placement and appearance of the tabs. In general, the tabs should always appear at the top of the control (Placement 0), and should look like tabs (Style 0), not buttons (Style 1) or "flat" buttons (Style 2). Also, the placement of non-selected tabs should be standard (TabStyle 0), not opposite (TabStyle 1).

The Tab Strip control does not automatically respond to the common key sequences used to cycle between tabs (CTRL+TAB and SHIFT+CTRL+TAB). To enable this feature, set the form's KeyPreview property to True, then add the following code to the form.

```
Private Sub Form_KeyDown(KeyCode As Integer, _
        Shift As Integer)
    ' ----- Handle Ctrl+Tab and Shift+Ctrl+Tab
    If (KeyCode = vbKeyTab) And _
            ((Shift And vbCtrlMask) = vbCtrlMask) Then
        ' ----- Check for forward or backward movement.
        '        The tab indexes are base 1.
        If ((Shift And vbShiftMask) = vbShiftMask) Then
            ' ----- Move backward
            If (tabActive.SelectedItem.Index = 1) Then
                tabActive.Tabs(tabActive.Tabs. _
                    Count).Selected = True
            Else
                tabActive.Tabs(tabActive.SelectedItem. _
```

```
                        Index - 1).Selected = True
            End If
        Else
            ' ----- Move forward
            If (tabActive.SelectedItem.Index = _
                    tabActive.Tabs.Count) Then
                tabActive.Tabs(1).Selected = True
            Else
                tabActive.Tabs(tabActive.SelectedItem. _
                    Index + 1).Selected = True
            End If
        End If
    End If
End Sub
```

When switching between the different tab pages, do not simply display one Picture Box control on another. Instead, use the Visible property to cause only one of the Picture Box controls to be visible at a time.

```
Private Sub tabActive_Click()
    ' ----- Update the screen based on the selected tab
    Select Case (tabActive.SelectedItem.Index)
        Case TAB_SET1
            picTab1.Visible = True
            picTab2.Visible = False
            picTab3.Visible = False
        Case TAB_SET2
            picTab1.Visible = False
            picTab2.Visible = True
            picTab3.Visible = False
        Case TAB_SET3
            picTab1.Visible = False
            picTab2.Visible = False
            picTab3.Visible = True
    End Select
End Sub
```

Tabbed Dialog Control

Purpose	Divides your form into distinct "tabbed" areas, to allow logical grouping of controls and functionality.
Availability	Independent control
Hungarian Prefix	tab
See Also	Tab Strip Control

Do not use the Tabbed Dialog control (SSTab) within your Visual Basic application. Use the Tab Strip control instead.

Text Box Control

Purpose	Displays and allows entry of simple text.
Availability	Core Visual Basic control
Hungarian Prefix	txt
See Also	Combo Box Control, Masked Edit Control, Rich Text Box Control

Use the Text Box control as needed within your Visual Basic application. Do not use a Text Box control when another control is more appropriate. For example, do not use a Text Box control to retrieve Yes or No values from the user. Use a Check Box control for Boolean input.

Set the MaxLength property when appropriate to limit the input length of the user's text, instead of testing the length of the text in a verification routine. Even if you use the KeyPress and KeyDown events to coerce the user's input into a correct format for the control, do not assume that the user has entered valid data. Always test user input (except for "free form" text entry fields) in a verification routine before use.

You should highlight the text in the text field when the control receives the focus. The following SelectText routine is useful for selecting text in both Text Box controls and Combo Box controls.

```
' ----- In the global Declarations section...
Public Declare Function GetKeyState Lib "user32" _
    (ByVal nVirtKey As Long) As Integer

Public Sub SelectText(ctrWhich As Control)
    ' ----- Highlight the text of a Text Box or
    '       Combo Box control, but not if the mouse
    '       was used to enter the control.
    If (GetKeyState(vbKeyLButton) >= 0) Then
        ctrWhich.SelStart = 0
        ctrWhich.SelLength = Len(ctrWhich.Text)
    End If
End Sub

' ----- And in the form's code view...
Private Sub txtAddress_GotFocus()
    ' ----- Highlight the entire text
    SelectText txtAddress
End Sub
```

The Text Box control has a Locked property that disables user input while keeping all other features of the control intact. While the Locked property is very useful, it does not give the control the appearance of being unavailable. If all of the text stored in the control will be visible at once in the control, and the user does not need to select or copy the text in the control, use the Enabled property instead of the Locked property to restrict access to the control.

When using a multi-line Text Box control, if there is any chance that all of the text will not be visible at once in the control, always include at least one scroll bar in the control.

Timer Control

Purpose	Provides a method for notifying the program of an event on a periodic basis.
Availability	Core Visual Basic control
Hungarian Prefix	tmr
See Also	Animation Control

Use the Timer control as needed within your Visual Basic application. Do not depend on the Timer control for precise timing of events; all events generated by the Timer control occur *approximately* at the requested interval.

Limit the number of active timers used within your application. If you are using more than three timers at once within your application, you should rethink your usage of timer functionality. Combine timers when applicable.

Toolbar Control

Purpose	Presents the user with a toolbar, a convenient set of graphic buttons for commonly used application features.
Availability	Windows Common Controls set 1
Hungarian Prefix	tlb
See Also	Cool Bar Control

Use the Toolbar control as needed within your Visual Basic application. For a more modern look, and the ability to add a variety of user interface controls, consider the Cool Bar control instead.

When including one or more pictures in the control at design time, always store separate copies of the graphic files within your set of technical documentation or source code directory tree. When referencing toolbar buttons in your source code, either identify each button using its key value, or define a set of constants to use with the position of each image. Never identify an image by a literal numeric index.

By setting the AllowCustomize property to True, the user can modify the organization of the toolbar at run time. Set the AllowCustomize property to True only if you will properly save and restore the user's settings, either using the SaveToolbar and RestoreToolbar methods, or through your own configuration code.

Tree View Control

Purpose   Provides an indented list of elements, with expand-
                       able and collapsible sections.
Availability   Windows Common Controls set 1
Hungarian Prefix   tvw
See Also   List View Control

Use the Tree View control as needed within your Visual Basic application. Always identify each node in the Tree View control by its key value, never by its absolute or relative position.

Up Down Control

Purpose   Provides a set of arrows to adjust a "buddy" value up
                       and down.
Availability   Windows Common Controls set 2
Hungarian Prefix   spn
See Also   Flat Scroll Bar Control, Vertical Scroll Bar Control

Use the Up Down control as needed within your Visual Basic application. If possible, limit the related "buddy" control to a valid input range. For example, if your buddy control is a text field that will hold a four-digit year, limit the text that can be entered in the field to four-digit years.

```
' ----- Set txtYear.MaxLength = 4.  Use this code too.
Private Sub txtYear_KeyPress(KeyAscii As Integer)
    ' ----- Limit the input to digits only
    If (KeyAscii = vbKeyBack) Then Exit Sub
    If Not (IsNumeric(Chr$(KeyAscii))) Then KeyAscii = 0
End Sub
```

If the buddy control is a text field, always validate the user's input before use.

Vertical Scroll Bar Control

Purpose   Provides a scroll bar with a thumb that moves from
                       top to bottom to top.
Availability   Core Visual Basic control
Hungarian Prefix   vsb
See Also   Flat Scroll Bar Control, Horizontal Scroll Bar Control,
                       Slider Control, Up Down Control

Use the Vertical Scroll Bar control (VScrollBar) as needed within your Visual Basic application. In some interfaces, you may also wish to consider use of the Flat Scroll Bar control, especially when your application responds to a scroll wheel available in some mouse input devices.

Always set the SmallChange property to the smallest possible increment. When setting the LargeChange property, consider the functionality of the List Box control, which always overlaps the elements when the user performs a large change activity. In Figure 11–7, list element "5" remains in view after the user clicks in the scroll bar bucket.

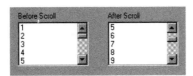

Figure 11–7   *A list box before and after a large change.*

The Vertical Scroll Bar control provides two primary events for detecting changes to the thumb position: Change and Scroll. Use either or both events as needed. However, avoid complex or time-consuming processing within the Scroll event. Use the Scroll event to visibly inform the user that the data position is changing. Use the Change event to update all related screen elements and application values based on the Value property.

It is possible to size the vertical scroll bar control so small that the thumb between the two arrows of the control disappears. If you size a scroll bar based on the user sizing of a window, it is all right to let the scroll bar become this small. In other instances, do not use the Vertical Scroll Bar control without the thumb displayed. If you wish to use only the arrows of the control without the thumb, consider the Up Down control or other suitable replacement instead.

If the scroll bar is used only to obtain a value, and not to visibly scroll information in another control or screen area (as is done with the scroll bar of the List Box control), consider the Slider control instead.

Web Browser Control

Purpose	Provides full World Wide Web browser functionality in a control.
Availability	Independent control
Hungarian Prefix	web
See Also	Internet Transfer Control, Winsock Control

Use the Web Browser control as needed within your Visual Basic application. Even if your application will always connect to a specific Uniform Resource Locator (URL) or Internet address, do not hard code any such addresses within your source code. Instead, store URLs in an INI-type file, in a proprietary format configuration file, or in the Windows registry. Document all relevant URL destinations and expectations in your technical documentation.

The Web Browser control accesses information that resides outside of the control of the Visual Basic application. Therefore, you must always use proper error handling in any procedure that deals with any functionality of the Web Browser control that can generate an error. In addition, you should expect that the remote server may become unavailable at any time. Handle all such service changes gracefully.

Winsock Control

Purpose	Provides access to the Windows sockets interface.
Availability	Independent control
Hungarian Prefix	skt
See Also	Internet Transfer Control, Web Browser Control

Use the Winsock control as needed within your Visual Basic application. Even if your application will always connect to a specific static address, do not hard code any TCP or UDP addresses within your source code. Instead, store connection destinations in an INI-type file, in a proprietary format configuration file, or in the Windows registry.

Always formally close all open connections when they are no longer needed. Include in your technical documentation all connection usage information, indicating any special expectations for the remote system.

The Winsock control accesses information that resides outside of the control of the Visual Basic application. Therefore, you must always use proper error handling in any procedure that deals with any functionality of the Winsock control that can generate an error. In addition, you should expect that the connection to a remote system may terminate at any time. Handle all such connection changes gracefully.

Summary

The user interface of your application exists solely to communicate with the user of your software. As with other forms of communication, you can "say" things that hinder the conversation, or you can "say" things that will enhance the dialog. The guidelines in this chapter seek to enhance the experience of the user in communicating with the essential data controlled by your application. Among the control guidelines listed in this chapter, the following key topics appeared as core issues.

- Design your forms so that the user recognizes the consistency found within your program. The features present on each of your screens should be similar in usage throughout the application, and where reasonable, they should be similar to the features found in popular off-the-shelf software packages. Consult the *Microsoft Windows User Experience* manual for a useful introduction to the "official Windows" way of thinking about the user interface.

- Never trust data supplied by the user. If there is any chance that the user could select or type in an invalid data entry (especially in Text Box controls), validate the data before its use. When presenting similar pieces of data (such as date fields), always use the same format so that the user has some expectation about how fields should be updated when needed. If possible, design your data entry fields so that the user cannot enter invalid data, either in individual fields, or in combinations of fields.

- If you place graphics within your forms or controls at design time, always store a separate copy of the graphic files outside of the application. Place these files in a single, known location, either within your technical documentation set, or as part of your source code directory tree.

- Several controls allow you to identify file and directory names, network addresses, Uniform Resource Locators (URLs), or other static destinations at either design time or run time. Never store such static locations directly in your controls or source code. Instead, store these destinations in an INI-type file, in a proprietary format configuration file, or in the Windows registry.

- Some features of the controls available within Visual Basic access information that resides outside of the control of the Visual Basic application. Therefore, you must always use proper error handling in any procedure that uses these features. Make use of the On Error statement to capture any errors, and take the appropriate corrective action. When communicating with a remote computer, never assume that the connection will remain valid throughout the lifetime of your application. Handle unexpected termination of such connections gracefully. Alert the user to the situation, and either retry the connection, cleanly exit the application, or degrade performance where appropriate.

- If you employ any advanced, obscure, or complex features of a control within your application, clarify the special expectations surrounding the control in your technical documentation. Also document custom resources or components used by your application, such as proprietary hardware devices.

- Above all, provide the user with an application that is efficient, convenient, and consistent in presentation and data handling. By establishing and using standards within your user interface, you bring the user one step closer to accurate communication with your software and the data it manages.

Database
Standards

· ·

Most Visual Basic applications manage important user data in one form or another. Generally, this data is stored in some sort of database system, either in relational database systems such as Oracle, multi-value database systems such as PICK, proprietary database formats such as Microsoft Exchange, or more simple data storage formats, such as text files and Microsoft Excel spreadsheets. Wherever the data is stored, the user demands that the data be accurate, stable, and presented in a meaningful way. Such is the craft of the professional Visual Basic developer.

In this final chapter, we discuss those standards that deal directly with data: the database, database communication tools, and data presentation from the user's point of view. When handling databases as a programmer, the key issue is "control." How much control do you have over the data? How much control are you allowed to have? How much control does the user have? Do you have any control over the design of the database? How about control over the software tools that allow you to communicate to the database? Identifying and managing these areas of control are essential to proper communication with the database, and with the user.

This chapter covers three primary areas of the database integration process: Design, Documentation, and Usage. Since most Visual Basic applications integrate with relational database systems, the examples in this chapter will focus on three key relational systems: Oracle, Microsoft SQL Server (and by extension MSDE), and Microsoft Access.

Database Design

The design of your database is as important as the design of your Visual Basic application. Unfortunately, while you as a developer will always play a key role in the construction of your application, there may be times when you have no say in the design or construction of the database with which you will communicate. Many Visual Basic applications present data stored in existing legacy or shared databases. In such cases, your design role may be limited to clearly documenting the components of the database that you will employ within your application.

For those times when the development of a database rests partially or fully on your shoulders, consistency and efficiency in the design of your database are essential. Some limitations in the design of your database may have to do with the tools available to you when you create your database and application. For instance, if the database driver (ODBC or other) that you are using does not support the use of stored procedures, you will either have to forgo their use within your application, or obtain a more advanced driver.

Database design is a broad topic. This chapter assumes that you already know how to create a database in your chosen database platform. For additional information on database design, consult the documentation supplied by your database vendor, and examine the sample databases supplied with the system. Also, most popular databases are fully equipped with shelves and shelves of books at your local mega-bookstore.

Nomenclature

Chapter 2, *Using Declaration*, underscored the importance of a consistent naming system within your source code. Consistent nomenclature usage is just as important in your database design. However, many other considerations affect the naming rules employed within your database.

- **Who designs it.** If you (as the Visual Basic programmer) are not the primary designer of the database, then you may have only limited input into the naming conventions used in its creation. On the other hand, self-designed databases give you full control over the content and structure of the database objects. If you have limited influence on the design of the database, compensate by including detailed documentation about the database in your technical documentation set.
- **Who uses it.** If your database will be used only by your application, then you are free to name elements as needed. However, if you will share the database with other non-Visual Basic systems and applications, you must take into consideration the needs of those other developers involved in the larger project. This may require you to give up VB-centric naming in deference to broader consistency with all involved parties.

- **Who sells it.** That is, the vendor and platform of the database is significant in your nomenclature. For example, Microsoft Access allows you a much wider variety in the naming of your database objects (such as including spaces in table names) then does Oracle. Each database vendor has stated its preference as well, either through explicit recommendations or through documented code samples. For instance, Oracle table names tend to be all upper case, with underscores separating key words, SQL Server table names tend to be all lower case with underscores between key words, and Access uses a mixed-case system, often with spaces between the name-words of the object. Although you are not bound to such a system when designing your objects and SQL queries, the database may override you. Oracle converts all object names to upper case, regardless of the capitalization style you employed when you created the objects.

While all of these considerations can affect the use of nomenclature in your database, the essential component that must be present in your database design is consistency. By using object names consistently and repeatedly throughout your database design (and from one database to another), you facilitate the programming experience for yourself, and for all others involved in the overall project.

If you will be designing your own database, use the following nomenclature recommendations.

- **Table and view names.** Name your tables and views (or queries) with mixed-case names, letters and digits only, with no punctuation or spaces. Always use singular names; avoid plurals. For example, a table of customer orders might be called "CustomerOrder." Never use the names "CUSTOMER_ORDER," "Orders," or "custorder." While it is true that some databases, such as Oracle, will ignore your capitalization, the use of mixed-case names should still appear anywhere you use the names: Visual Basic source code, stored procedures, documentation, and entity-relationship (ER) diagramming tools. Naturally, the name of the table or view should reflect the subject of the data contained within the table. For helper tables (such as lists of countries or credit card types), it may be useful to precede the table name with the prefix "Code," as in "CodeCountry." Such a system identifies those tables that exists only to supply field data to other tables.
- **Field names.** Use mixed-case field names, similar to the naming for tables. When selecting names for your fields (and all other objects), avoid all possible reserved words defined in your database, and in the database that may be the "next step" up on the ladder, in case you plan to scale your application to a larger database. For example, Microsoft Access allows you to name a field "Date" without error. But if you ever choose to convert the database to Oracle, you will need to rename the

field to something more specific, such as "WorkDate." Use common names for common fields throughout your tables. Consider "ShortName" or "FullName" as the name of any table's primary descriptive field, and "LongName" or "Description" for the longer version of the descriptive text.

- **Primary keys.** All tables in your database should have a primary key. If you need to create a table without a primary key, document the reason for this difference in your technical documentation. Make all primary keys of a common data type and name where applicable. Generally, I always name my primary keys "ID" with a data type of Number/Long Integer (Microsoft Access), int (SQL Server), or NUMBER(10) (Oracle). Each of these data types equate, more or less, to Visual Basic's Long data type, which is convenient for use in the ItemData array of List Box and Combo Box controls. Apply the proper Primary Key constraint to the appropriate field(s) when creating your table.

- **Indexes.** When creating custom indexes on one or more table fields, include the name of the table in the index name, prefixed with the token "idx." The remainder of the name should be one or two words that describe the fields or purpose of the index, as in "idxCustomerHome-Phone" for a customer's home phone number. If your database creates indexes automatically for you on special fields (such as primary or foreign keys), list these in your technical documentation as *unnamed*.

- **Sequences.** Sequences are database objects that generate sequential numeric values. (In Microsoft Access, sequences are contained within a table's definition through the AutoNumber field type.) If a sequence exists to supply values to a table's primary key (either through a trigger or through INSERT statements), give the sequence the same name as the table, prefixed with "seq." For a customer table named "Customer," the sequence name would be "seqCustomer."

- **Triggers.** If your database allows you to name triggers, include the table name in the name of the trigger, prefixed with "trg." To differentiate multiple triggers, append a one- or two-word purpose for the trigger on the end of the trigger name, as in "trgCustomerCleanDelete" to clean up various items on the removal of a customer.

- **Constraints.** Constraints allow you to have the database be a watchdog for you when you cannot be there to ensure the integrity of the data. If your database permits constraints to be named, always include the primary table name in the constraint name, prefixed by the token "cns." The remainder of the constraint name should be one or two words that identify the purpose of the constraint, as in "cnsOrderRefCustomer" for a constraint on the Order table that references the Customer table.

- **Stored procedures.** Provide meaningful, mixed-case names to each of your stored procedures, functions, and packages. Always keep separate copies of your stored procedures outside of the database, either in your technical documentation or in your source code directory tree.

- **Other objects.** For other types of objects found within your database, continue to employ the naming system found in these guidelines, using mixed-case names for primary objects.
- **SQL statements.** While SQL statements are not true objects within a database, they comprise the building blocks of most other objects, especially stored procedures and views. When writing SQL statements, continue to employ the mixed-case naming conventions of the database objects when referring to those objects in code. Keep all reserved words in upper case (such as the SELECT keyword). When referencing database-supplied objects, use the naming conventions of the database vendor. For example, in Oracle, use "USER_TABLES," not "user_tables," to reference the list of user-defined tables.

To summarize these guidelines, if an object is used in an independent fashion (such as a table, view, or stored procedure), give it a mixed-case name. If the object is used only in conjunction with an independent object (such as a trigger, sequence, index, or constraint), name it based on the object on which it depends, prefixed with a Hungarian-like token. All database objects must be documented within your technical documentation set.

Why are we being so picky about database naming when the database is just going to convert everything to upper or lower case before processing? The primary reason is to enhance the discipline of consistency within the world of the programmer. The more consistent you are in your use of database objects, the more your eye will quickly detect problems found within SQL code. Another reason to be consistent is that some database processing is done with the exact syntax you specify in your statements. For example, if you pass a SQL statement to Oracle, it first compares that statement to ones already found in its cache of recently issued statements. If it finds an exact match, it uses it, avoiding the need to recompile the statement before use. This comparison is case-sensitive. The following two statements will not match each other in the statement cache.

```
SELECT SYSDATE FROM DUAL;
select sysdate from dual;
```

Normalization

Normalization is the process of structuring the tables of your database so that the potential for data corruption is reduced. The process of normalization seeks to ensure that the logical structure of your database is efficient. However, you may find that the physical implementation of your normalized database is not always speedy and efficient, so you may need to make some compromises when you normalize your database. And, you should normalize your database.

Normalization occurs in multiple stages or "forms," starting with "First Normal Form," "Second Normal Form," and so on (although some of the forms have non-numerical names). Each stage adds an additional set of table structure rules. As an example of performing the process of normalization, consider the data found in Table 12.1.

Table 12.1	Baseball Teams and Players			
Team	**Player**	**Position**	**Sponsor1**	**Sponsor2**
Yankees	Smith, Sammy	Catcher	NY Deli	Sports Town
Yankees	Johnson, Johnny	Pitcher	NY Deli	Sports Town
Yankees	Marcus, Mark	Center Field	NY Deli	Sports Town
Dodgers	Albertson, Al	Pitcher	Video City	
Carps	Loux, Louis	First Base	Fish Market	Pet Village

This table suffers from several key problems.

- **Modification anomalies.** If you decide to change the name of a team or a sponsor for a team, you must update multiple rows of data. If for any reason only some of the required rows are updated, you are left with inconsistent data.
- **Insertion anomalies.** What do you do if you have a new player, but that player has not yet been assigned to a team? There is no place for this player to reside until a team is assigned or a new team is created.
- **Deletion anomalies.** Let us say that Al Albertson decides to quit the Dodgers. Do you delete the Dodgers' record? What about the team's relationship to Video City?
- **Repeating groups of similar data.** The two Sponsor columns are repeated for each team player entry. If a team does not have two sponsors (such as the "Dodgers"), some space is wasted, while a team with three or more sponsors will not have sufficient room.

While these problems may seem minor in this small table of data, it can wreak havoc on large databases. That is where normalization comes in.

First Normal Form (abbreviated as 1NF) requires that any repeating groups, also called "multi-value fields," be moved into separate tables. In this example, the Sponsor section of the table would be moved into a table of its own, as shown in Table 12.2. This form eliminates the repeating groups problem, and it also reduces some of the update anomalies.

Second Normal Form (2NF) says that fields not part of the primary key may not depend on only part of a primary key. Our baseball example does not show it, but if we had a table with two fields used together for the primary key, and another field could be uniquely identified by using only one of the primary key fields, that non-key field would have to be moved into a separate table. If the Team and Player columns in Table 12.1 were used together

Table 12.2		Sponsors for Each Team
ID	**Team**	**SponsorName**
1	Yankees	NY Deli
2	Yankees	Sports Town
3	Dodgers	Video City
4	Carps	Fish Market
5	Carps	Pet Village

as the primary key, the table would not be in 2NF because the Position column really only depends on the Player column, not the combination of the Team and Player columns. Note that if a table is in 1NF, and it only has a single field for the primary key, it is automatically in 2NF.

Third Normal Form (3NF) is similar to 2NF in that it attempts to remove columns not truly dependent on the primary key of the table. Consider an address table with city, state, and postal code fields. It is generally true that a city and state can be defined by the postal code value. If the postal code was not the primary key, then the table would not be in 3NF because a non-key field depends on another non-key field. However, it is not always in the best interest of your application to completely move a database into 3NF. 3NF attempts to reduce update anomalies. For example, if a city changed its name, you would have to update all records that use that city name. If you missed one or two, that would result in inconsistent data. Still, if this is a minor risk in your database, and adding a separate city-state-postal-code table would greatly reduce performance, it may be a wise decision to stick with 2NF.

Boyce-Codd Normal Form (BCNF) adds to the normalization requirements even more by requiring that a primary key field never depend on a non-key field. There are additional normal forms that extend beyond BCNF, including *Fourth Normal Form* (4NF), *Fifth Normal Form* (5NF), and *Domain Key Normal Form* (DK/NF). While these advanced forms are important aspects of relational database theory, they sometimes involve modifications to your database that would result in inefficiencies undesirable to your customer.

Database Documentation

Proper documentation of your database is the most important aspect of Visual Basic database application development. Even if you completely ignore all of the guidelines listed in the earlier "Database Design" section, adequate documentation will ease the burden of database integration. However, if you lack proper or complete database documentation, you are asking for headaches, especially when you need to modify your application years down the road.

There are several specialized tools to help you in the documentation of your database. The most common of these tools lets you craft *entity-relationship* diagrams. These diagrams look a little like the Relationships window within Microsoft Access, although they specify much more information about each entity (similar to tables). Some advanced entity-relationship modeling tools, such as Logic Works' *ERWin*, give you absolute control over every aspect of the logical and physical layout of your database. They can reverse-engineer existing databases, create databases or scripts for new databases based on a model you design, and can store platform-specific information, such as stored procedure source code. While these tools are very useful for database design and documentation, their features often come at a financial price that may be prohibitive for the individual developer.

Instead of an entity-relationship modeling tool (or as a complement to one), you can document all aspects of your database within your technical documentation, specifically the Resource Kit described in Chapter 5, *Documentation*. Include a section within the Resource Kit that presents all the tables and views of your database in alphabetical order, identifying each field, and all subordinate objects (such as triggers, indexes, and sequences). Create a separate Resource Kit section for those database objects that are not specifically dependent on a table or view (such as stored procedures).

Figure 12–1 shows sample Resource Kit documentation for a set of tables used to track baseball teams, players, and player positions.

CodePosition—The positions in which each team member plays. Used by Player.Position.

Field	Type	Description
ID	Long Integer	Primary key. Required.
FullName	Text(50)	The name of the position.

Other objects used by this table:
- **seqCodePosition**—Sequence for CodePosition.ID field values.
- **idxCodePositionID**—Primary key index: ID ASC.

Player—The list of all baseball players in the league.

Field	Type	Description
ID	Long Integer	Primary key. Required.
LastName	Text(30)	The last name of the player. Required.
FirstName	Text(30)	The first name of the player. Required.

Player—The list of all baseball players in the league *(Continued)*

Field	Type	Description
Team	Long Integer	To which team does this player belong? Foreign reference to Team.ID. Optional. If NULL, player is unassigned or in transition.
Position	Long Integer	What is the primary position played by this player? Foreign reference to CodePosition.ID. Required.

Other objects used by this table:
- **seqPlayer**—Sequence for Player.ID field values.
- **idxPlayerID**—Primary key index: ID ASC.

Team—The list of all baseball teams in the league. Used by Player.Team.

Field	Type	Description
ID	Long Integer	Primary key. Required.
FullName	Text(50)	The full name of the baseball team. Required.
GamesWon	Integer	Number of games won in the current season. Optional. Assumes 0 if NULL. Ranges from 0 to 20 (games played per season).
GamesLost	Integer	Number of games lost in the current season. Optional. Assumes 0 if NULL. Ranges from 0 to 20 (games played per season).
FeeDate	Date	OBSOLETE. The date on which the season fee was paid. Fees ceased to be collected on January 1, 2000, so this field is now obsolete.

Other objects used by this table:
- **seqTeam**—Sequence for Team.ID field values.
- **idxTeamID**—Primary key index: ID ASC.
- **idxTeamName**—Non-unique name index: FullName ASC.

Figure 12-1 *Sample database documentation.*

There are several things to note about this documentation.

- Each table identifies in its description the foreign references in which it appears.
- All fields are described in detail, providing names, data types, descriptions, valid data ranges (if any), required or optional status, and foreign-key relationships. Obsolete or unused fields are clearly marked.
- The data types indicated for each field are somewhat generic. For instance, the Team.FullName field might be created as Text(50) in Microsoft Access, as varchar(50) in Microsoft SQL Server, and as VARCHAR2(50) in Oracle.
- Subordinate objects are documented immediately following the table.

If you modify the structure of the database, the documentation must be immediately updated to reflect the current state of the database. If you are making changes to a test database for later inclusion in a production database, this section of the Resource Kit should reflect the latest changes to the test database. Include an additional section within the Resource Kit that indicates what database object changes must be made from one structural revision to the next.

The Resource Kit is an excellent place to discuss the formats of simple database types, such as text files or spreadsheets. If your application accepts or generates data in one of these or similar formats, include a section in your Resource Kit that describes the expected structure of the file in detail.

If your database depends on any vendor-specific or database-specific files, configuration information, or connection requirements, document them in the Resource Kit as well. What should not appear in your Resource Kit are the full source code listings for database stored procedures and triggers. Make note of these objects in the Resource Kit, then store text-file-based versions of these objects in your source code directory tree.

If your Visual Basic application will process data found in an existing and actively used database that is already fully documented, it is not necessary for you to replicate the existing documentation. Include in your Resource Kit enough documentation to redirect the reader to the location of the full database documentation. If you will be using only a subset of an existing database, at a minimum list the names of the database objects employed in your application, then direct the reader to the full documentation set.

Database Usage

Now that you have a database set up, and you have fully documented it, you are ready to use it. But how? Microsoft has recognized that most Visual Basic applications are data-centric, and has provided multiple object-based methods for accessing the data you need. Database vendors have chimed in as well, supplying their own object models for data management and database administration purposes. Data connection objects have become an alphabet soup of communication methods, including DAO (Data Access Objects), ADO (ActiveX Data Objects), RDO (Remote Data Objects), ODBC (Open Database Connectivity), Jet (Microsoft Access), SQL-DMO (SQL Server Distributed Management Objects), ISAM (Indexed Sequential Access Method), and OO4O (Oracle Objects for OLE), to name just a few. Which of the many methods do you pick?

To be honest, the data transport you select is not as important as the presentation of the data given to the user of your application. Microsoft recommends that you use ADO and OLE DB as your primary means of accessing all aspects of a database, especially for Internet-based development. While this is a good recommendation, you may still require the functionality or compatibility provided by another of the object collections. Use the database connectivity protocol that best meets your needs. Just be sure to document the features and expectations of the connectivity tool in your technical documentation set.

What is needed in presentation of data to the user is the element of control. In this case, "control" applies both to the use of Visual Basic user interface "controls," and to the amount of control you as the programmer exert over the user's experience with the application. In general, you should take the highest level of control onto yourself, and limit the control of the user as much as possible. This may seem strange, since it is often the user who is also the owner of the data, not you. However, if users really needed full control of the data, they would write the program themselves, and you would be out of a job.

There are several traditional methods by which Visual Basic programmers have presented data to the user. For simplicity of description, I call them "Spreadsheet," "Bound Field," and "Form Object" presentations. In each of the presentations, we will use the baseball-related tables shown in Figure 12-1.

Spreadsheet Presentation

The spreadsheet method of presenting and collecting data is one of the quickest to implement, assuming that you have the right tools. One tool that uses this interface as its default method of data presentation is Microsoft Access, and its Datasheet view. An Access view of the Team table appears in Figure 12-2.

ID	FullName	GamesWon	GamesLost	FeeDate
1	Yankees	0	0	
2	Dodgers	0	0	
3	Carps	0	0	
		0	0	

Figure 12-2   *Spreadsheet presentation of the Team table.*

The Spreadsheet presentation gives the user almost full and direct access to the data. In Visual Basic, you can employ a variation of this presentation using one of the available grid controls to allow the user to interact with the underlying table or view data.

While the Spreadsheet presentation is easy to achieve, it leaves much to be desired. Complex and fully normalized data relationships are not easily managed through such an interface. The method by which changes are canceled is not immediately obvious, if available at all. Also, the visual presentation of the Spreadsheet provides no indication of the relationships or priorities of the columns in the grid. These are some of the reasons why I recommended in Chapter 11 that grids be used in a limited fashion for data display, and seldom, if ever, for data entry. Avoid the Spreadsheet presentation of data within your Visual Basic application.

Bound Field Presentation

The Bound Field presentation of data is also popular in Microsoft Access, and it is often employed in standard Visual Basic applications as well. The Bound Field presentation has two primary traits. The first is an absolute dependence on the use of "data bound" controls. Most, if not all, of the controls displayed on each form take advantage of the data connection features available within many Visual Basic controls. The second trait of this mode of presentation is the active interaction between related tables. In Microsoft Access, such interactions are accomplished through the use of sub-forms, as shown in Figure 12–3.

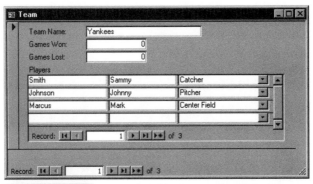

Figure 12–3   *Bound Field presentation of the Team and Player tables.*

The Bound Field presentation is much more advanced than the Spreadsheet presentation. Priorities and relationships between the different fields are much clearer on this form. The complex and normalized relationship between the Team and the Player tables is easily managed. Also, this presentation is not too difficult to implement in Visual Basic because of the tools supplied with the development environment. In the latest versions of Visual Basic, almost every control supplied with the system can be bound to a data source. Data sources themselves can be visually designed with drag-and-drop methods.

While there are many advantages to the Bound Field presentation, it still is not adequate for professional Visual Basic applications. It is still not obvious how data changes are canceled. Also, the transition from one instance of the major entity (in this case, the Team) to another gives no clear indication of the committal of the changes to the database. In this particular example, the two rows of VCR buttons can be confusing. While they could be replaced with more intuitive movement methods, that change alone would still leave the vagueness of the transition between two entities. Also, there is no clear way to move a Player from one team to another.

The biggest problem with the Bound Field presentation is that it removes control of the data from both the programmer and the user. The logic supplied through the data bound features of each control and connection object form the basis of data management. While this makes it easy to implement data solutions quickly and with little need for the actual writing of Visual Basic code, it also makes it easy to incorrectly handle legitimate errors that may occur in the communication and processing of the data. Avoid the use of the Bound Field presentation, and in general avoid all data bound control features.

Form Object Presentation

The third, and preferred, form of data presentation is the Form Object presentation, so named because a form contains an object's worth of data. The object may represent a single table entity, or it may be built up from complex database relationships. However, to the user each form is a single unit. The programmer controls the access to the elements and construction of the object, while the user has limited access to only those object elements made available by the programmer. Figures 12–4, 12–5, and 12–6 show the three primary forms involved in managing the Team and Player tables.

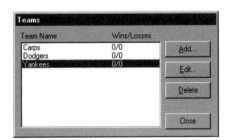

Figure 12–4   *The Team Management form.*

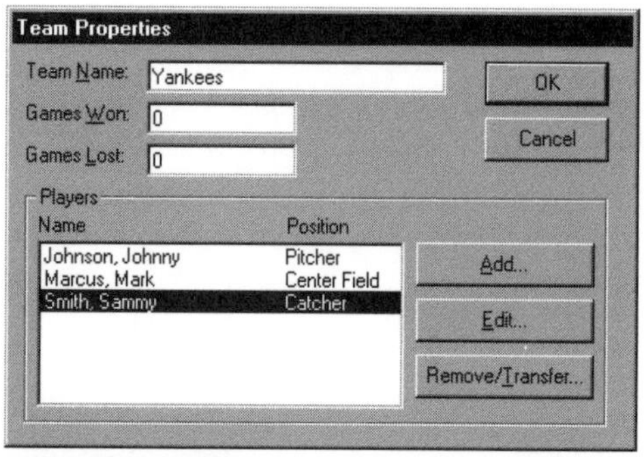

Figure 12–5   *The Team Properties form.*

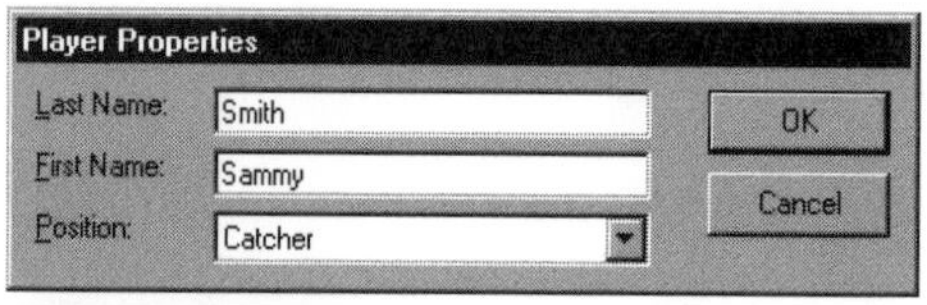

Figure 12–6   *The Player Properties form.*

In this presentation, the maintenance of each object (basically the table entities in this example) is now performed by separate forms. This divide-and-conquer method reduces the complexity of the data presented to the user, reserving to each form the management of a single thing, a data object. It is now clear from these forms how you cancel changes made to individual fields—simply click on the Cancel button. The relationships and priorities between the objects and fields are clear. Still, the number-one benefit of this method of presentation is that the user's control of the data is limited to just what the programmer desires, and the programmer's control of the data is maximized. This is true at the source code level as well. In fact, the only access to the fields on the Player Properties form from other forms is through a public function defined for the purpose of editing new and existing players. Consider the following DAO-based code associated with the Player Properties form.

```
' ----- Baseball Application
'       Written by Tim Patrick
'       Player.frm - Player Properties
Option Explicit

Private mnResult As Integer
Private mlPlayerID As Long

Public Function EditPlayer(lPlayerID As Long) As Long
     ' ----- Edit a new or existing player.  lPlayerID
     '       is the player's ID, or -1 to add a new
```

```
'           player.  Returns player ID on success,
'           or -1 on cancel.
        mlPlayerID = lPlayerID
        Me.Show vbModal
        If (mnResult = vbCancel) Then
            EditPlayer = -1
        Else
            EditPlayer = mlPlayerID
        End If
        Unload Me
End Function

Private Sub LoadData()
    ' ----- Load in the data for the existing
    '       player record
    Dim sSQL As String
    Dim rsInfo As Recordset

    On Error GoTo ErrorHandler

    ' ----- Retrieve the player's data
    sSQL = "SELECT * FROM Player WHERE ID = " & mlPlayerID
    Set rsInfo = gdbData.OpenRecordset(sSQL, _
        dbOpenSnapshot)
    txtLastName.Text = rsInfo!LastName & ""
    txtFirstName.Text = rsInfo!FirstName & ""
    cboPosition.ListIndex = ListByItem(cboPosition, _
        rsInfo!Position)
    rsInfo.Close
    Exit Sub

ErrorHandler:
    GeneralError "frmPlayer.LoadData", Err, Error$
    Resume Next
End Sub

Private Function SaveData() As Boolean
    ' ----- Save the user's data.  This routine
    '       assumes that the form data is valid.
    '       Return True on success and set mlPlayerID.
    Dim lNewID As Long

    On Error GoTo ErrorHandler
    SaveData = False

    If (mlPlayerID = -1) Then
        ' ----- Add a new player.  First get a
        '       new primary key.
        lNewID = GetTableID("Player")
        If (lNewID = -1) Then Exit Function
```

```
            ' ----- Now add the player's record
            sSQL = "INSERT INTO Player (ID, LastName, " & _
                "FirstName, Position) VALUES (" & lNewID & _
                ", " & CStrDB(Trim$(txtLastName.Text)) & _
                ", " & CStrDB(Trim$(txtFirstName.Text)) & _
                ", " & cboPosition.ItemData( _
                cboPosition.ListIndex) & ")"
            gdbData.Execute sSQL
            mlPositionID = lNewID
        Else
            ' ----- Update an existing player
            sSQL = "UPDATE Player SET LastName = " & _
                CStrDB(Trim$(txtLastName.Text)) & _
                ", FirstName = " & _
                CStrDB(Trim$(txtFirstName.Text)) & _
                ", Position = " & cboPosition.ItemData( _
                cboPosition.ListIndex) & " WHERE ID = " & _
                mlPositionID
            gdbData.Execute sSQL
        End If

        ' ----- Success!
        SaveData = True
        Exit Function

    ErrorHandler:
        GeneralError "frmPlayer.SaveData", Err, Error$
        Exit Function
    End Function

    Private Function VerifyData() As Boolean
        ' ----- Check the user's data entry.  Return
        '       True if all data is valid.
        VerifyData = False

        ' ----- Last name is required.
        If (Trim$(txtLastName.Text) = "") Then
            MsgBox "Last name is required.", _
                vbOKOnly + vbExclamation, PROGRAM_TITLE
            txtLastName.SetFocus
            Exit Function
        End If

        ' ----- First name is required.
        If (Trim$(txtFirstName.Text) = "") Then
            MsgBox "First name is required.", _
                vbOKOnly + vbExclamation, PROGRAM_TITLE
            txtFirstName.SetFocus
            Exit Function
        End If
```

```vbnet
    ' ----- Position is required.
    If (cboPosition.ListIndex = -1) Then
        MsgBox "Position is required.", _
            vbOKOnly + vbExclamation, PROGRAM_TITLE
        cboPosition.SetFocus
        Exit Function
    End If

    ' ----- Success!
    VerifyData = True
End Function

Private Sub cmdCancel_Click()
    ' ----- Cancel changes made to the player.
    mnResult = vbCancel
    Me.Hide
    ' ----- Continue with EditPlayer()
End Sub

Private Sub cmdOK_Click()
    ' ----- Save changes made to the player.
    If (VerifyData() = False) Then Exit Sub
    If (SaveData() = False) Then Exit Sub
    mnResult = vbOK
    Me.Hide
    ' ----- Continue with EditPlayer()
End Sub

Private Sub Form_Load()
    ' ----- Prepare the form.
    Dim sSQL As String
    Dim rsInfo As Recordset

    On Error GoTo ErrorHandler

    ' ----- Fill in the list of positions.
    sSQL = "SELECT ID, FullName FROM CodePosition " & _
        "ORDER BY FullName"
    Set rsInfo = gdbData.OpenRecordset(sSQL, _
        dbOpenSnapshot)
    Do While Not (rsInfo.EOF)
        ' ----- Add this position to the list.
        cboPosition.AddItem rsInfo!FullName
        cboPosition.ItemData(cboPosition.NewIndex) = _
            rsInfo!ID
        rsInfo.MoveNext
    Loop
    rsInfo.Close
```

```
      ' ----- If we will edit an existing player, load
      '       in that player's data now.
      If (mlPlayerID <> -1) Then LoadData
      Exit Sub

ErrorHandler:
      GeneralError "frmPlayer.Form_Load", Err, Error$
      Resume Next
End Sub

Private Sub txtFirstName_GotFocus()
      ' ----- Highlight the entire text.
      SelectText txtFirstName
End Sub

Private Sub txtLastName_GotFocus()
      ' ----- Highlight the entire text.
      SelectText txtLastName
End Sub
```

This code assumes the existence of some other functions defined else-where.

- **ListByItem.** This function is defined in Chapter 11, in the Combo Box Control entry.
- **SelectText.** This function is defined in Chapter 11, in the Text Box Control entry.
- **GeneralError.** This function is defined in Chapter 2, in the Order Of Code section.
- **GetTableID.** This function is not defined in this book, but it obtains the next primary key value for a table by using a database sequence or other similar platform-specific mechanism.
- **CStrDB.** This routine converts a string into a form suitable for insertion in an SQL statement.

```
Public Function CStrDB(sOrig As String) As String
      ' ----- Prepare a string for an SQL statement.
      If (Trim$(sOrig) = "") Then
          CStrDB = "NULL"
      Else
          CStrDB = "'" & Replace$(sOrig, "'", "''") & "'"
      End If
End Function
```

The Team Properties form initiates a call to the Player Properties form when the user clicks on either the **Add** or **Edit** button.

```
Private Sub cmdAdd_Click()
      ' ----- Add a new player
```

```
        If (frmPlayer.EditPlayer(-1) <> -1) Then
            RefreshPlayerList
        End If
    End Sub

    Private Sub cmdEdit_Click()
        ' ----- Add a new player
        Dim lPlayerID As Long

        If (lstPlayers.ListIndex = -1) Then Exit Sub
        lPlayerID = lstPlayers.ItemData(lstPlayers.ListIndex)
        If (frmPlayer.EditPlayer(lPlayerID) <> -1) Then
            RefreshPlayerList
        End If
    End Sub
```

I can promise you now, this method of data presentation will take longer to program, you will have more forms in your finished application, and your user documentation needs will expand. When you consider the code to populate the data fields, verify all data supplied by the user, save the user's changes, and transition between the different forms, the amount of coding goes from basically no lines to several hundred lines. However, professional programming is not about meeting the needs of the programmer, but about meeting the needs of the user. And I can guarantee you, if you generate professional-quality applications for your users, you will receive the accolades and rewards that you deserve.

Summary

When developing database applications, keep in mind the guidelines presented in this chapter, summarized as follows:

- When naming database objects, use mixed-case names with no spaces or punctuation. For dependent objects, include the name of the supporting object, prefixed with a Hungarian-like token.
- Use the normalization process to develop more structured and efficient relational databases.
- All database objects must be documented in your technical documentation set, specifically in the Resource Kit. Keep the documentation up to date as you make changes in structure or usage.
- In addition to database structures, describe the structures of simpler files (such as text files and spreadsheets) in your Resource Kit.
- Select the appropriate object model to meet your database connectivity needs. If the object model requires any special configuration or connectivity needs, document them in the Resource Kit.

- The primary goal in data presentation is to reduce the control of the user, and to increase the control of the programmer. To this end, avoid Spreadsheet and Bound Field presentations in your application. Instead, use the Form Object presentation to maximize control over the data.

INDEX